# ETHICAL ISSUES IN INTERPERSONAL COMMUNICATION

*Friends, Intimates, Sexuality, Marriage, and Family*

# ETHICAL ISSUES IN INTERPERSONAL COMMUNICATION

## Friends, Intimates, Sexuality, Marriage, and Family

ELAINE E. ENGLEHARDT, EDITOR

Under the general editorship of

ROBERT C. SOLOMON
*University of Texas at Austin*

HARCOURT COLLEGE PUBLISHERS

*Fort Worth   Philadelphia   San Diego   New York   Orlando   Austin
San Antonio   Toronto   Montreal   London   Sydney   Tokyo*

*To my daughter Kellie Englehardt and the memory of Sarah Carter*

| | |
|---|---|
| Publisher | Earl McPeek |
| Executive Editor | David Tatom |
| Market Strategist | Adrienne Krysiuk |
| Project Manager | Andrea Archer |

Cover Image: Digital Imagery® copyright 1999 PhotoDisc, Inc.

ISBN: 0-15-508257-4
Library of Congress Catalog Card Number: 00-033538

*Address for Domestic Orders*
Harcourt College Publishers, 6277 Sea Harbor Drive, Orlando, Florida 32887-6777
800-782-4479

*Address for International Orders*
International Customer Service
Harcourt College Publishers, 6277 Sea Harbor Drive, Orlando, FL 32887-6777
407-345-3800
(fax) 407-345-4060
(e-mail) hbintl@harcourtbrace.com

*Address for Editorial Correspondence*
Harcourt College Publishers, 301 Commerce Street, Suite 3700,
Fort Worth, TX 76102

*Web Site Address*
http://www.harcourtcollege.com

Printed in the United States of America

0 1 2 3 4 5 6 7 8 9 066 9 8 7 6 5 4 3 2 1

Harcourt College Publishers

# PREFACE

## DEFINING INTERPERSONAL COMMUNICATION ETHICS

We spend an astonishing amount of time communicating with friends, acquaintances, lovers, spouses, parents, and family members. Every time we communicate with someone, the communication is based on a multitude of choices we have made—either consciously or unconsciously. Often these communications are ineffective or just don't turn out the way we had hoped. Studying our interpersonal communication habits and beliefs helps create better understanding between each other. Awareness of the communication choices we make is paramount to "doing the right thing," to communicating based on our ethical beliefs. The power that comes from understanding our own beliefs and practicing these beliefs brings clarity, satisfaction, and an ethical approach to interpersonal communication.

This text encourages the readers to broaden and challenge their understanding of ethical complexities in interpersonal communication. The ethical complexities of interpersonal communication stem from a variety of sources including self-concept, friendships, the development of relationships, notions of sexuality and marriage, family structure, and lifestyle choices, harm and beneficence.

Interpersonal ethics are systemic in nature in that they exist within larger systems and smaller subsystems. For the purpose of this text, ethics is used in interpersonal communication in defining harm and beneficence in both the content of a communication exchange as well as the interpersonal and relational and dynamic. Ethics is also involved in the rational justifications for actions toward one another and within a society.

By studying the writings of various scholars, past and present, in ethics and interpersonal communication, we focus on the study of morality and moral behavior and how ethics sheds light on complex interpersonal relationships and moral behavior within these relationships. Morality is the system of behavior that each of us is born into. Ethics is the study of morality and moral behavior. Perhaps you were born into a system in which only white men were executives, and that was seen as moral at the time. But strong rational discussions in ethics have helped bring about changes in society and law. This process is called ethics.

Communicating with someone is an act, a process that may or may not be ethically justified and may be ethically wrong in a variety of ways. What we communicate is also subject to ethical analysis. We can communicate the wrong thing even if our timing is right, and yet again what we say can be criticized. We can also court disaster by communicating the wrong thing at the wrong time.

This text examines how interpersonal relationships are important in ethics:

- They help the individual with self-understanding;
- They help the individual think critically about the multifaceted environment; and
- They demonstrate how self-understanding encourages an approach to ethics that begins with avoiding harm and focuses on doing good for and with others.

We can think about interpersonal communication by assuming that all of us communicate with others in a variety of ways. We could also assume that most of the things we try to define are human constructions. As we experience the phenomenal world, each of us tries to make sense of it by creating mental representations of it. Because we each have different experiences, histories, and cultures, our individual understandings often vary.

Interpersonal communication is sometimes described as merely a vehicle for people to advance their own self-interest through interactions with others. However, this text emphasizes that self-interest is only one element of personal communication and should be mixed with a dose of ethics for fair or just interactions with others.

It is important to study morality and examine moral behavior in friendships, intimate connections, and marital and committed relationships. Defining family and permanent relationships is an important element in the study of interpersonal communication ethics. When only select individuals are defined as part of a group, those left out of the definition may be harmed. Other harms in society come through discrimination based on gender, race, sexual preference, or other factors are focal topics for this study of ethics and interpersonal communication.

This ethics text is designed to challenge students to read and think critically about issues that confront our nation, our society, and each of us. Such issues go beyond simple politics and group mentalities and transcend the temporal nature of current practice and acceptability. Studying interpersonal communication ethics will help us examine problems we may confront in life. The readings in this text include classic and contemporary articles by authors who range in discipline from philosophy to psychology, to communication. The readings are designed to enhance readers' critical thinking skills and to provide practice engaging in serious reflections on varying world views. With these skills, readers develop their own set of ethical approaches to interpersonal communication.

# CONTENT

Chapter 1, "Introduction to Ethics in Interpersonal Communication," provides foundational material to help students use this text to the fullest advantage. The first section, What is Ethics? introduces the importance of studying interpersonal communication ethics as a system of guidance that assists each of us in living within a society. It covers the importance of ethics as a social enterprise, rational justification as a component of ethics, and that ethics is based on concrete actions.

Practicing Ethics in Interpersonal Communication asserts the importance of "doing ethics." To help students define their own ethical beliefs, this section presents five systems of ethics: duty, rights, utility, virtues, and relationships. The discussion of each of these systems of ethics is a resource for students to refer back to as they work with the ethical implications in the articles that follow. The discussion piece also helps students comprehend the complexities of systems of ethics and how these systems can and do conflict with one another.

Guidelines for analyzing and writing cases, as well as a sample analysis of a case, are also included. These guidelines are intended as a reference for students as they analyze the contemporary case at the end of each chapter and as they write cases, as suggested, after each selection. The sample analysis of a case provides a model for students as they analyze each chapter's contemporary case.

Chapter 1 concludes with a section that highlights specific questions for students to consider as they discover their personal ethical beliefs and a list of key concepts that defines terms used throughout the text.

Chapter 2, "Self and the Nature of Ethics in Interpersonal Communication," focuses on ethical analyses of the "self" and the self in interpersonal relationships. This includes knowing the self in numerous cultural and historical contexts. It could also include understanding the basic components of self-love. Selected authors in this section address arguments on the importance of developing a sense of trust for oneself and others. Other authors stress the need for kindness, selflessness, and charity. Postmodern authors challenge the position of the traditional concept of the individual as an essential unit that exhibits autonomy. In its place it offers a self appearing in some self/other relationship as the acting agent.

The first article, a classic from Eric Fromm, "Selfishness, Self-Love and Self-Interest," examines the importance of self-love and how this differs from selfishness and self-interest. Fromm believes that the self must be the object of the individual's love as much as any love the self would have for someone else. Jim Anderson examines postmodern approach to identity in "Identity and the Self." Anderson states that the self is a composite of society, family, history, organizations, and other elements of the individual's interaction. Kenneth J. Gergen looks into the historical and cultural implications defining the individual in the postmodern piece, "Moral Action from a Constructionist Standpoint." Gergen cannot conclude that moral language is both essential and desirable for agreeable forms of social life.

Concluding the chapter is a classic expression on the importance of individual liberties by John Stuart Mill. Many believe that Mill only advocates "the greatest good for the greatest number of people." However, in "Of Individuality as One of the Elements of Well-Being," Mill extols the virtues of the individual understanding and claiming appropriate liberty.

Chapter 3, "Importance of Friendship," emphasizes interpersonal relationships involving two or more individuals, such as dyadic relationships (in particular friendships), and other important aspects of close interaction and socialization with another human. The writers explain the importance of understanding the nature of friendships and valuing other individuals with whom we share the important elements of friendship. The concept of interpersonal harm is an important discussion in the fields of ethics and communication. Considerable harm is caused to individuals in friendship relationships through selfish or uncaring acts, neglect, indifference, and discontinuation of relationships.

In "Friendship," Aristotle defines the types of friendships one is most likely to encounter, and he discusses which are temporary and which are long lasting. Epicurus also defines friendship as one of the most important elements of life. In "Of Friendship" the Greek sage explains that one's life is enhanced through intellectual conversations with those one admires. He believes that the limits of friendships also keep a life from unnecessary disturbances. Laura Tracy examines "Intimacy and Judgment Among Friends and Sisters," an excerpt from *The Secret Between Us: Competition Among Women*. She believes that complications arise in relationships between sisters and friends because of competition, a major problem in relationships among women. "Adult Friendships" by William K. Rawlins explains that adult friendships change, mature, or decline depending on one's choices in life. Friendship between races is explored in the short story "Mama and the Dentist." Maya Angelou relates how friendship between a white dentist and her grandmother, a black woman, was acceptable when the dentist needed a favor. However, when Angelou's grandmother needed a favor from the dentist, his discrimination was both excruciatingly painful and demoralizing for the young black granddaughter.

Chapter 4, "Development and Stability in Interpersonal Relationships," explores communication processes. Communication is an important factor in fostering close relationships. As communication processes are better understood, those in the relationship better understand needs, wants, desires, and problems. Sometimes cultural and historical barriers limit the boundaries of relationships; however, many of the writers concentrate on understanding elements of relationships that may have been ignored, unstudied, misunderstood or denied such as trust, networking in personal relationships, variations in communication style, and the morality of care. Many of this chapter's readings are part of a broader feminist movement in ethics that rejects the traditional approach to philosophy such as that of Hobbes, Rawls, and Kant. The excerpt from *In a Different Voice* by Carol Gilligan explains how men have traditionally defined women and placed them within the life cycle of men. Gilligan points out the importance of making ethical, interpersonal decisions based on relationship and care. "An Ethics of Care" is an excerpt from a book by Nel Noddings in which she explains concepts of interpersonal relationships, ethics, and a sense of love and duty. Using the analogy of a crying infant, Nodding explains that one does not pick up the infant out of a sense or ethics duty, but rather of caring. Interpersonal relationship scholars Marcia Dixson and Steve Duck write about shared meanings between others in "Understanding the Relationship Process: Uncovering the Human Search for Meaning." Dixson and Duck examine ways that partners can experience a commonality of meaning and symbolism between themselves on a variety of topics and concerns.

In "The Practice of Moral Judgment," Barbara Herman outlines the importance of relationships, intimacy, and connections in being human. She also examines the relationship motives behind decisions made for children, friends, or intimates. In an excerpt from "Myth and Reality," Simone de Beauvoir examines the myth of the unchanging nature of women throughout history. de Beauvoir explains some myths may be built on the female form while others are built simply on the constructions the male would like the female to be.

Approaching interpersonal ethics from a basis of trust is an excerpt from "Trust and Antitrust" by Annette Baier. Because human beings are not self-sufficient, Baier believes that trust relationships are basic to our existence. Baier further questions why past philosophers haven't understood or written about the important factors involved in trust relationships. Martin Luther King, Jr., explains the need for trust and love in his essay "On Being a Good Neighbor." King believes that considering one another as neighbors and trusting one another regardless of race are fundamental aspects of civility, respect, and acceptance.

Chapter 5, "Intimate Communication," defines an intimate relationship as different from other interpersonal relationships because of the sexuality manifest in intimate communication, which is not a defining issue when interacting with friends and others. Most individuals desire intimacy and seek someone to love intimately who will also return the intimacy. What ethical rules and duties are expected and communicated in an intimate relationship? Profound harms can be incurred when committed, intimate relationships disintegrate. This chapter contains readings that highlight the importance of empathy, sensitivity, receptivity, and tenderness in the intimate relationship. The readings also point out that actions such as duplicity, deception, and fraud are particularly unethical in the intimate relationship. Defining the intimate relationship is not only an issue for these authors but also is an issue that students will be eager to explore.

Opening this topic is "The Virtue of Love" by philosopher Robert C. Solomon. Within this selection Solomon explains that love or eros often is not considered a virtue by philosophers because it deals with sexuality, emotions, and the self-indulgence of desire. Solomon defends all three as virtuous and substantial to a meaningful life.

Scholar Michel Foucault explains notions of sexuality in a postmodern perspective. In "Aphrodisia," he argues that individuals in the past have had narrow notions of sexuality and have created moral difficulties through what became circumscribed definitions. Foucault is perplexed with the absence of sexual detail within the ancients' writings.

Also taking issue with narrow definitions of sexuality is philosopher Catharine MacKinnon. In the excerpt, "Sex and Violence," MacKinnon notes that women historically have been seen as the property of men and that violence was part of a patriarchal prerogative.

Intimate communication between homosexuals brings about violence in some sectors of society. The effects of this violence are addressed in "Can You Outlaw Hate?" an article by Sean McCollum. He develops the notion of harm to others because of sexual preference differences. McCollum argues for an understanding for, rather than condemnation of, intimate relationships between gays in an effort to overcome hate crimes against homosexuals.

Chapter 6, "Sexual Morality and Marriage," advances views on marriage and committed relationships, including traditional marriage, communal structures of relationships, sexual fidelity, and patriarchy. The readings in the second half of this chapter advocate a life free from marriage and a traditional sexual morality. Throughout history, most societies have adopted rules, traditions, customs, and rites relating to marriage and permanent partnership. When religion is a factor, sexual rules and mores take on different meanings, often with spiritual dimensions to partnership and procreation. With the advent of reliable and multiple forms of birth control, sexuality in marriage has also changed, with intercourse no longer necessarily linked to reproduction. Feminist philosophies have produced strong arguments for equal or separate partnerships rather than a patriarchal family setting. A host of specialists have taken on the study of the committed relationship in society, including politicians, religious leaders, philosophers, communication scholars, historians, anthropologists, sociologists, psychologists, and linguists.

Fidelity and sexual morality are themes in "Love's Constancy" by Mike W. Martin. Martin recognizes that committed relationships are often flawed; however, he believes it is a virtue to remain faithful to support the good of the imperfect partners.

Adultery and divorce have often been the topic of moralists. Bertrand Russell is opposed to divorce but understands the need for occasional adultery. In "Marriage and Morals" Russell defends the societal need for a stable family relationship, but he believes that monogamy need not be part of the marriage contract. Presenting a historical and cultural perspective on marriage and adultery is Helen E. Fisher in "Anatomy of Love." As a social scientist, Fisher explains that depending on the culture, many forms of human sexual coupling are accepted. Fisher's research examines the sexual variety found within different times, cultures, and societies.

Fredrich Engels is not convinced of the social importance of patriarchy or of the monogamous marriage in the excerpt "The Origin of the Family: Private Property and the State." Engels examines inequalities in gender from his book *The Origin of the Family*. He believes that once man took command of the home, the woman was degraded and reduced to servitude, slavery, and procreation responsibilities. In

"The Sexual Revolution," Kate Millett commends Engels for his far-sighted understanding of inequalities in marriage. She believes that Engels' work has been essential to understanding female equality and sexuality in society. Claudia Card also agrees with Engels and believes that the state should not define intimate unions. She believes society would be improved if the rearing of children were the concern of an appropriate community. In "Against Marriage and Motherhood," Card explores a society that often harms gays and lesbians who would like a partnership structure and children.

Chapter 7 revolves around the theme "Ethics and Concepts of Family in Interpersonal Relationships." The most common and persistent form of society is the family. Throughout history the family has been defined in generalities including parents, children, grandparents, aunts, uncles, cousins, and so on. The extended family is no longer the focus of most family structures. Rather, as several authors point out, family is very difficult to define and sometimes is defined in injurious ways. Within current society the need for a "nuclear" family is strongly presented by some religious authorities, politicians, academics, and other advocates. Other writers disagree with the definitions of family entirely, offering a variety of parings for the term "family." Some authors present arguments for enduring family values while others explain how notions of the family have been injurious for women and children.

This chapter begins with the Greek philosophers Plato and Aristotle. In an excerpt from *The Republic*, Book V, "A Proposal to Abolish the Private Family," Plato explains the need for all things being held in common, including women and children. Plato believes the greatest unity for a community is for all men to be able to claim the community of women and children as their own. Aristotle counters Plato in "On Plato's Proposal." He states that those things that are common often have the least care bestowed on them, and he argues that men will take care of something that belongs to them but leave to others the care of common property, including women and children. John Simmons explains John Locke's notions of family as a moral, not a legal relationship in "Rights and the Family." However, Simmons also points out Locke's need to give the husband "priority" over his wife, as well as Locke's contractual stand for a husband to have the final say in an argument.

A look at recent family compositions is outlined by Alan Donagan in "First Order Precepts." Donagan examines the "contracts" between adults and children and defines the family as relations working with parenthood. Susan Moller Okin explains the unequal partnerships between men and women, particularly after a marriage ends, in "Marriage and the Unjust Treatment of Women." Okin argues that the family needs to be a just institution and that current theories of justice neglect women and ignore gender. In the conclusion from "The Ultimate Revolution," Shulamith Firestone sees a household as a concept preferable to that of family. Her concept of household is short term, in that it would last perhaps 10 years and encourage the end of family chauvinism and prejudice while fostering equality.

## FEATURES

In addition to providing a broad range of historical and current articles on ethics by an interdisciplinary group of authors, this text incorporates features that enhance the desire to think critically about ethical issues.

- **Chapter 1** includes foundational material on five systems of ethics, plus an analysis of a case and guidelines for writing cases. Writing and analyzing cases urges students to work with complex ethical issues and encourages the application of ethics to contemporary situations.
- **Biographic and introductory information** is presented at the opening of each article. This material orients the reader to the historical perspective of the article as well as relevant ethics and communication perspectives.
- **Critical Thinking questions** are included with each selection to check comprehension of the material. These critical thinking questions aid the process of developing one's ethical beliefs and allow the reader to work through dilemmas presented in the article.
- **A Contemporary Case with questions** concludes each chapter, with a case study presenting a contemporary ethical situation. These cases are intended to provoke in-depth classroom discussion. The questions that follow each case guide students to pertinent issues.
- **Key Concepts,** provided at the end of Chapter 1, define ethics terminology used throughout the text.

## ACKNOWLEDGMENTS

For their help with this anthology, I would like to thank colleagues and scholars Bob Solomon, David Keller, Wade Robinson, and James Anderson. Appreciation also extended to assistants Harriet Eliason, Kellie Englehardt, Chad Wright, Steven Carter, Jennifer Howard, Melanie Hubbard, and Kathryn Henrie. Kudos to Harcourt Brace Developmental Editor Ann Greenberger for a careful job and to Harcourt Brace Acquisitions Editor David Tatom. Thanks to Michael McConnell, Graphic World Publishing Services, and his team of astute editors. My husband, Kirk Englehardt, and son, Rich, support me in everything.

Special thanks to reviewers Aarne Vesilind, Duke University; Cathy Ayers, Lewis University; James P. Sterba, University of Notre Dame; and Jennifer Parks, Loyola University.

Thanks to Utah Valley State College Ethics Across the Curriculum faculty for assistance in the case studies. Without the support of UVSC President Kerry Romesburg, Lucille Stoddard, and Scott Abbott, this book would not have been possible.

# TABLE OF CONTENTS

# 1

## INTRODUCTION TO ETHICS IN INTERPERSONAL COMMUNICATION

### WHAT IS ETHICS?

Throughout the text ethics is defined through two fundamental, distinguishing characteristics, **harm** and **mutual aid.** Most individuals have a basic and universal aversion to harm, both physical and psychological. Nobody wants to be harmed in a physical or interpersonal arena or submits to harm without his or her consent. In interpersonal ethics we need to make the claim that individuals do not want to be harmed (without their consent), as well as the claim that most, if not all humans, are inclined to inflict harm on others without their consent. These coexisting realities—the universal human aversion to harm and the universal tendency to inflict harm—are the conditions that make the study of interpersonal communication ethics necessary.

The study of interpersonal communication ethics is important for a variety of reasons. Communication satisfies practical needs such as contributing to health, identity, and social relationships. Interpersonal relationships are often defined as intrinsically rewarding, interdependent and unique. However, some interpersonal relationships are merely superficial and mechanical. Ethics must always be a part of the interpersonal relationship, whether it be a relationship with friends, an intimate, family members, business colleagues, or social groupings.

Let's look at some of the important aspects of ethics within interpersonal relationships.

### A SYSTEM OF GUIDANCE

Ethics is a system of guidance designed to assist in living within a society. A primary goal of ethics is to establish appropriate constraints on ourselves.

Because of a diversity of relations and relationships, we are asked to curb our inclination to do anything that pleases us. These constraints are necessary because we have conflicting interests and selfish desires that can inflict harm on ourselves and others.[1] We are a social animal, and our species would not survive if each of us lived in isolation. That we must live together installs the positive requirement of doing good for one another. We would not need ethical guidelines if people lived together peaceably and in mutual support without harming one another. The fact that we do not so live is the major condition requiring ethics.

We do not get to "invent" our own system of ethics. Further ethics are not created by each generation. We find that justified ethical systems survive the test of public scrutiny and debate. William K. Frankena observes, "like one's language, state or church, [ethics] exists before the individual, who is inducted into it and becomes more or less of a participant in it, and it goes on existing after him [or her]."[2]

Morality is a system of guidance. Ethics is the study of morality and moral behavior. Ethics continually represents the tension between the person and others. Ethics is not *just* a coda for individual behavior. It is a social enterprise that consists of a system of rules, ideals, and sanctions that facilitate the basic social functions of accord and cooperation. We expect each of the social organizations in which we have membership to function in ethically appropriate ways. We expect ethical standards among and between the interpersonal relationships within those organizations. Most individuals would feel uncomfortable and awkward if asked by a superior to perform an unethical function.

## REASON AS A GUIDE TO TRUTH

An important component in the definition of ethics concerns the concept of rational justification. Ethics is located within the discipline of philosophy; as such, work in the field of ethics rests ultimately on reason and its power to justify beliefs and actions. Ethicists generally hold that while reason is not the only guide the truth, it provides the best direction. Ethics involves our analysis of and reflection on moral choices and judgments. Other guides to truth may involve religion, intuition, or advice from trusted others. However, within the study of ethics and interpersonal ethics, each of us

---

[1] Schmeltekopf, D. (1992). Morality. In E. Englehardt & D. Schmeltekopf (Eds.), *Ethics and Life.* Dubuque, IA: Wm. C. Brown.

[2] Frankena, N. K. (1963). *Ethics* (p. 98). Englewood Cliffs, NJ: Prentice-Hall.

must accept the difficult challenge of rationally defending our choices and actions. We often need to explain our decisions, and "because it feels right" is not an appropriate response. It is hard work to understand ourselves and examine how our decisions and actions interact with others. It is important to understand the Socratic dictum that an unconsidered life is not worth living. We must consider carefully our lives and the effects our interactions have on others.

## TAKING ACTION

Finally, ethics is concerned with what we actually do. Experiences of harm and mutual aid occur because concrete actions are, or are not, committed. Motivation, intention, and character are certainly of interest in the field of ethics, but in the end what we actually do, or don't do, is what we must justify ethically.

Ethics, then, concerns judgments about the quality of our actions in terms of their capacity to do harm or provide benefit. Ethics provides the means to manage obligation and desire and requires us to explicitly evaluate our choices from the principle of harm and benefit. Interpersonal communication ethics helps us understand that there is no single ideal way to communicate and no single way of providing ethical guidance. Interpersonal ethics must involve using rational justification, flexibility, self-control, and self-monitoring in our communications and interactions with others.

A more detailed discussion on foundations in ethics is found in the first reading in Chapter 1. This essay can be referenced for guidance and interpretation as differing ethical problems are discussed in the readings that follow.

ELAINE E. ENGLEHARDT

# PRACTICING ETHICS IN
# INTERPERSONAL COMMUNICATION

It is important to understand what we are doing when we "do" ethics. Thinkers for centuries have tried to define the best way to live a moral life. Their practice typically begins with an act of questioning. Socrates, whose questioning greatly disturbed an Athens at war and ultimately cost him his life (ethics is not a bloodless exercise), justified his approach with the phrase, "the unexamined life is not worth living." But contemplation is not enough; the contemplation must form a platform for action. John Finnis (1983) helps define the practice of ethics through the following:

> One does ethics properly, adequately, reasonably, if and only if one is questioning and reflecting in order to be able to act, i.e., in order to conduct one's life rightly, reasonably, in the fullest sense well. (p. 1)

The "doing of ethics," then, involves reflection, analysis, and the reasoned application of the means of ethical practice. The "doing of ethics" cannot be without consequence. It is not a set of propositions to be posted on the wall. Rather it is implicative knowledge (Harrison, 1991). It is knowledge that changes the knower. To demonstrate the effect of implicative knowledge, we offer an analysis of a story.

# A FABLE

Maxwell thinks it is fun to dress the human body in beautiful fashions, particularly the female human body. However, as an accountant for SRYX, Maxwell's opinion on dressing the female human body is not part of his job description. For years Maxwell has been complimenting female coworkers on their choice of fashions along with color selection and fabric. Many of these coworkers are friends of Maxwell. On occasion they have even invited Maxwell on shopping excursions on weekends or after work hours. Some new coworkers do not appreciate Maxwell's comments on their clothing. They find him creepy and a bit weird. On a few occasions, Janie has told Maxwell that she doesn't appreciate his comments on her clothing and would like him to stop. Maxwell just can't seem to contain himself. Generally when he sees a style or fabric which particularly suits a coworker, he has been able to express his opinion in a kind, friendly manner. He is puzzled as to why Janie is so against his comments. He continues to comment on Janie's clothing styles and fit.

Janie is offended personally by his continued comments on her apparel and believes she has no other choice but to file a sexual harassment grievance against Maxwell. She has asked him to cease his comments, but he won't. She knows she could offend Maxwell and many other coworkers in the office if she does file the grievance. But, she also knows other female employees who do not want Maxwell's opinions on their clothing styles and fit. Janie files the grievance through a confidential process in the human resource's office.

## ANALYSIS

Maxwell thinks what he is doing is kind and innocent. Janie thinks she is right in what she is doing. She has asked Maxwell on a few occasions to cease his comments on her apparel. He didn't stop. Janie believes she must now move to the next step and file a confidential, formal grievance against Maxwell. The formal grievance invokes more than an interpersonal or professional office relationship. The process now brings the company Personnel Department and the law into Janie's and Maxwell's relationship.

Where is Maxwell making unethical decisions regarding his personal comments to Janie? From what set of beliefs has he allocated his ethical duties? How has he determined harm? How has he established that Janie would want his comments on her fashions? Maxwell has developed an analysis that serves only his interests. He could have taken the view of Janie and asked, "How would I react if someone commented on my clothing who I didn't particularly know or care for?" "How would I react if I asked the person a few times to stop the comments, yet she wouldn't?" "Would I go so far as to use company policy and law to enforce the person to cease her behavior, or would I just suffer through her fumbling comments?"

Maxwell believes he is a superior employee. He rarely misses work, always turns assignments in on time, gets along with others and attends all meetings sponsored by the human resource department. He has been to the training sessions on sexual harassment. He believes the lewd individuals who sexually harass others should be warned then fired.

Maxwell can't believe that a sexual harassment grievance has been filed against him. He doesn't understand how Janie could think he harassed her. In his standpoint he is innocent. He just kindly complimented Janie on her choice of clothing and the way it fit her. He hasn't moved to the view of the other or the rule of law. He now has to use both views to balance his self-interests, and stop his unwanted comments to Janie. Maxwell's action has unintentionally caused harm in another person's life. After a few warnings to stop, Maxwell still didn't understand that he had an obligation to Janie to cease his unwanted comments. It is an obligation he failed to discharge.

Our situation between Maxwell and Janie has gone beyond ethics to the law. Within the rubric of ethics, we are expected to understand when we are harming another individual. Individuals who are harmed through interpersonal ways, such as Janie, have an obligation to let their coworker know of the discomfort in the unwanted comments. The coworker then has the responsibility to recognize the harm and cease from causing this harm again to the individual. If the harm does not cease, it is appropriate to move from using ethics to solve the problem to the next step, the law. It is unfortunate when interpersonal communications are ineffective in analyzing an ethical problem and bringing it to a conclusion.

## INTERPERSONAL ETHICS: BEST SCENARIO

Let's look at a best case scenario for interpersonal communication ethics. Janie files the confidential grievance against Maxwell. She and Maxwell tell no one of the grievance. Maxwell is embarrassed and horrified that he has been so insensitive, and promises Janie he will never make personal comments about her clothing to her again. He understands her standpoint, and knows that she is correct. Janie says she understands Maxwell's standpoint, and that he probably didn't intend to cause harm. However, he did harm her. Janie accepts Maxwell's apology. Now life in office is better for Janie and hopefully Maxwell and others.

There could also be the slippery slope of several other unpleasant interpersonal actions. Maxwell could inform all his friends of the grievance and they could cause Janie problems. Janie could inform all her friends of the grievance and they could cause Maxwell problems. The office environment could deteriorate with warlike tactics being played by and against each side. From an interpersonal communication ethics standpoint, this would be the worst standpoint of harm. It escalates a small problem between two individuals into an ethical problem for the entire office. Janie and Maxwell's problem can be solved easily in one, two, or three steps. By failing to understand the other, and rallying forces against the other, the problem could continue for years. This doesn't happen at SRYX. Idealistic interpersonal communication ethics in this fable involves understanding the position of the other, the harm caused the other, the process of solving the harm in a confidential manner, the ability to offer an apology and the ability to accept an apology and move on.

## ETHICS AS SYSTEMATIC REFLECTION

Ethics, then, can be considered as a systematic reflection on the practical accomplishment of obligation that, in turn provides the means of performing, analyzing, and evaluating those accomplishments. The following section discusses selected ethical traditions. Many decisions within ethics can be based on five systems or constructs of ethical analysis, duties, rights, utility, virtues, and relationships.

These theories each seek to define what it means to act morally. These theories are not flawless, and sometimes a theory does not perform well when used in a professional or practical ethical situation. Further, through analysis of these theories, we will find that these systems of ethics can and do conflict with one another. It is important to understand the similarities and differences with each of these systems.

## DUTY ETHICS

Duty is concerned with the obligation of the individual to the collective. The duties one has are usually seen as natural, revealed, rationally self-evident or in some other way universalized. One of the first examples of a duty ethics is found in divine command theory in which the participant makes an ethical decision because it is based on a law of God. Consider the Judeo-Christian text, The Ten Commandments. In this text, a God tells followers they have a duty to obey these commands. The followers are to obey these rules because their God said they have a duty to obey these rules. As part of these moral guidelines, there are punishments and rewards given by a God for performance or nonperformance of these morally defined behaviors. Other ethical systems rely on rational justification, consequences, or individual moral knowledge.

Another approach to duty ethics is to refer to them as *moral rules,* meaning that one performs a particular action because there is a moral rule that says it is so. Not all duty theories, however, trust universal rules to portray the moral truth accurately. For some thinkers, ethical truth also depends on the details of individual situations.

### DUTY ETHICS AND KANT

The ethicist most known for duty theory is Immanuel Kant (1785/1988). Kant, a German philosopher (1724–1804), is best known for defining duty ethics through a system of thought known as deontology. Deontology bases its argument of right and wrong on the intrinsic character of the act rather than on its consequences. To understand his concept of duty consider this scenario:

A panhandler approaches you, and you give the individual $5. What made you give that individual the money? Was it to impress the individuals who were watching you? Was it because you didn't want the fellow to starve? Was it because you feared this individual would attack you if you didn't hand over the money? Was it because you considered it was the right thing to do? For Kant, only the last reason meets the standard of duty. He believes we should make moral choices based on what one ought to do from a non-consequentialist perspective; we have a duty to humanity to do so. Kant states that we do something because it is the right thing to do, not because it appears the consequences will be favorable. One makes a choice and follows through with an action out of a moral sense of duty.

In order to specify the universal character of duty, Kant states his theory in terms of the Categorical Imperative. This principle states that you should always act so that your personal principle of behavior would stand as a universal for all rational beings. Kant wants us to move from a self-centered way of making decisions to decision making that could be universalized. This formula includes that anyone could make the same decision and it would be right or desirable for all humanity.

## A Case

Melanie and Steve have been dating for a year. Currently they are enrolled together in a physics class. They generally study together. Melanie's sister Karen is taking the class from the same instructor in an earlier time slot. Melanie, Steve, and Karen study for the midterm examination together. After Karen takes the midterm, she tracks down Melanie and Steve and asks if they would like to know which questions are on the examination. Melanie says no, and Steve says yes. Steve walks down the hall with Karen as Melanie watches in astonishment. Who is closer to understanding the duty ethics prescribed by Immanuel Kant, Melanie or Steve and Karen?

## Analysis

Kant's Categorical Imperative wouldn't allow for cheating, unless we are willing that everyone else could act in a similar manner. Basically, Karen shouldn't give the questions to anyone because in an education system, this type of unfair advantage in unacceptable; it is cheating. Giving questions or answers to persons who have not yet taken the test is not a behavior we can universalize. Could you allow that several members of your class have the midterm questions in advance, but you are not given access to them? We cannot universalize the practice of cheating.

You may counter, "But this isn't realistic. Melanie's sister could give her the questions, so that Melanie could get a better grade on the test." Kant's philosophy isn't concerned with the consequences. His philosophy is concerned with duty. Melanie has a moral duty to humankind not to cheat on the test. As a deontological theorist, Kant would ask if Karen's behavior is the right thing to do in all cases. Since the answer is "no," we are guided by Kantian theory that we have a duty not to cheat on examinations because we "ought" not act in this manner.

Kant gives three tests of lawfulness for his Categorical Imperative. They are similar and even repetitive in some respects. (Kant is sometimes called a dense theorist and takes small steps as he moves us forward in this theory.) In *Fundamental Principles of the Metaphysics of Morals,* he defends in detail these tests of lawfulness. Succinctly they are:

◆ Act always that you can will your maxim (personal principle of action) to be a universal for all humankind.
◆ Never treat an individual merely as a means to an end but always as an end in and of themselves. (Don't use anyone.)
◆ Act as if you were a legislating member of the universal kingdom of ends. (p. 7)

If one were living in a perfect world, how would one act, and how would one legislate all actions? These questions reflect Kant's views on a universal kingdom of ends.

Kant sought to find universal laws in morality by insisting that if an action were right for one, it had to be right for all. One of the most clear but seemingly most difficult actions to actually achieve was that of always telling the truth. Kant held that it was never acceptable to lie. His proof of this maxim came by trying to prove the counterfactual maxim, "It is permissible for everyone to lie when it is in their best interests to do so." His proof showed, at least to his satisfaction, that the whole institution of truth would collapse if the maxim of permissible lying were universalized.

Kant concluded that we have a duty to tell the truth to others in all cases. Through this principle, Kant believed that we could develop a perfect civilization where other moral problems would disappear as well.

Kant's ethical theory has many strengths, but weaknesses are also apparent. Critics accuse Kant of rigid absolutism. His critics question, for example, whether we have an absolute duty to tell the truth. "If by lying to a mob hit squad, one could save the life of an innocent co-worker, should that person do so?" Kant's answer is simply and profoundly, "No." Kant believed the duty to tell the truth always prevails since lying cannot be universalized. This stance, however, seems to violate moral common sense. Perhaps one answer to this paradox is that in Kant's perfect world, there would be no mob hit squads seeking the life of innocents.

## U~~TILITARIANISM~~

The ethics of utility concerns the outcomes of a moral proposition. It is a consequentialist theory. Consequentialist theories attach value on an act's ultimate consequences. This is the opposite of Kant's deontological view, which is a nonconsequentialist theory. Deontologists generally make decisions for actions, intentions, and so on, that are quite independent of their consequences.

Consequentialist theories declare that an action, intention, or principle of social organization should be judged by its consequences. Something is good if and only if it has, or tends to have, good effects. Although what is defined as good can be universalized, consequentialism does seem to open the door to actual situations of enactment, something not readily apparent in Kant's categorical imperative.

Not all consequentialists are utilitarians, because consequentialists can seek to find the greatest good for the individual or for the collective. Consequentialism itself does not resolve the issue of the primacy of the self or the collective. Utilitarianism, however, does resolve this issue by taking the collective as primary.

## J~~EREMY~~ B~~ENTHAM~~ AND J~~OHN~~ S~~TUART~~ M~~ILL~~

Jeremy Bentham and John Stuart Mill were both utilitarians. They held the utilitarian view that we should always maximize good, or that the more moral action is one that produces the greater good for the greater number of individuals. As in many other consequentialists theories, utilitarianism rests on an independent characterization of good results. It can also be termed a strong collectivist theory because it concerns only the total amount of good; it makes no difference who enjoys this good or where the good is found.

Mill refined utilitarian philosophy to take on the concept that the moral action would be that which brings about the greatest good for the greatest number of people. In stating this principle he stressed that the good of an individual may be sacrificed for the good of many.

## UTILITARIANISM: CASE

Matt's parents Brenda and Kim learned they are carriers of a genetic attribute that causes glaucoma. They learned of the attribute after Matt's birth and then determined they would adopt to complete their notion of family. As they researched and analyzed adoption procedures, they determined that even though they were Caucasian, that they would prefer to adopt children who might have a hard time being placed for adoption. Matt's parents adopted two minority children, and both had disabilities. Matt and his family were deeply devoted to each other. Matt spent hours with his siblings in play time and educational experiences. He was also proud of his brothers even though they were racially different from other classmates at his elementary, junior high and high school. Matt occasionally had to defend his brothers against racial slurs or jeers about disability status.

One day while in a high school literature class, one of Matt's classmates uttered a horrible racial slur. The teacher and other classmates seemed to agree. Matt couldn't believe his ears. He wanted to say something, but as he looked around the room, he decided he would just keep quiet. There were too many popular students in the class, and Matt didn't want to appear foolish. Matt now feels horrible that he did not confront the student and the class at the time the racial slur was made.

## ANALYSIS

Within this case study what action will bring about the greatest amount of pleasure and the least amount of pain? At the time Matt believed that silence would bring about the least amount of pain. But now Matt is suffering deeply. He believes he has betrayed his family by not pointing out the egregious and prejudicial comments made by his classmate. Matt now believes that the greater pleasure would be in rectifying the harm by asking the teacher if he could make a class presentation on discrimination and diversity.

Matt also understands the racial damage that has occurred in the classroom when the slur was left unchallenged. Often when persons are in the position of the majority, they don't take time to understand the problems of those not within their group. However, in this case we understand the great harm that has occurred not only to Matt, and members of the disparaged race, but also to other classmates because the unkind remark was allowed without dispute.

An additional utilitarian issue in the case is the decision by Matt's parents to have genetic testing. Once they learned of the abnormality, they then made the decision of adoption rather than further reproduction. This is a decision which involves looking at the long-term consequences of a genetic condition and making a determination to no longer reproduce those genetic lines. Issues of pleasure and pain are also part of this important issue, including pleasure and pain for individuals who have been born with a predilection toward glaucoma. The issue of adopting children who are difficult to place in homes is also an issue of pleasure and pain. For Matt's family it appears pleasure has far outweighed the pain that could be incurred in raising disabled children.

## Useless Self Sacrifice

Mill also discusses the view of useless self sacrifice. In this he explains that one must always survey the long-term consequences of an action before pursuing that action. It is important to understand that critically thinking through reactions to emergency situations before they actually happen could save lives—even one's own. If you see a vehicle completely consumed in flames, with an individual inside, should you attempt a rescue? The answer is not easy. If it does not appear that you can save the life of the individual without also putting your life in great danger, Mill would contend there is no obligation to make the heroic rescue. Mill's theory of useless self sacrifice asks you to examine if two lives would most likely be lost, not one. Mill is not stating that risks are objectionable, but that the risks need to be appropriate to the good to be gained and the likelihood of success. Mill's philosophy would have you do any moral action, which will bring about good or desirable long-term consequences. You would avoid those actions that produce the opposite.

## Rights

One of the first examples of rights based ethics could be Babylonian's Code of Hammurabi (also spelled Hammurapi) which was drafted sometime between 1792 and 1750 B.C., when King Hammurabi ruled Babylon. He combined codes from ancient Summerian and Akkadian laws to codify accepted behavior in Near Eastern countries. The code covered legal matters such as false accusation, land and business regulations, family laws, wages, trade, loans and debts. The massive document also detailed some acceptable practices in medicine. The moral and political justification for the Code of Hammurabi was, "The strong shall not injure the weak." It advocated a social order based on individual rights backed by the authority of the Babylonian gods and the state (Snyner).

In more modern times, the theory of rights looks at the obligation between self and other from the standpoint of the duty of the collective toward the individual—what every individual is owed. Again, one's rights are usually universalized by declaring them natural, divinely conferred or rationally self-evident. For example, in 1776, Thomas Jefferson wrote in the Declaration of Independence, "We hold these truths to be self-evident; that all men are created equal; that they are endowed by their creator with certain unalienable rights; that among these are life, liberty, and the pursuit of happiness." There is no doubt that Jefferson had an understanding of the writings of Thomas Hobbes, John Locke, and others who had previously written theories that all humans had the same basic nature and as such were to be treated as equals.

## THOMAS HOBBES

Thomas Hobbes believed that humans should be able to establish a social compact in which members of a society could covenant to keep certain agreed-upon practices. Hobbes based his theory on egoism, meaning that individuals would keep their covenants out of a sense of self-preservation. More important, however, Hobbes established through theory that individuals should have rights in a society. These rights can be determined by the members of a society and then sustained by the society. Hobbes believed that humans are capable of rational thought, and as such, the laws of society would be derived from natural laws.

Natural law is knowable by human reason, applies to all human beings, and is grounded in human nature. The natural law grounds the moral law because moral law must fit the necessary consequences of whom we humans are. What we ought to do according to natural law theory is determined by considering some aspects of our nature as human beings and then seeking that action that best fits that nature.

Not everyone agrees on what rights are encompassed in natural law. The 1948 United Nations' "Universal Declaration of Human Rights" listed rights to food, clothing, shelter, and basic security. These are known as basic "welfare" rights. Other philosophers argue for rights well beyond these. There are liberty rights such as the right not to be interfered with in our daily life, rights of self-expression as in freedom of speech, and rights to political action as in the right to vote.

## JOHN RAWLS

The contemporary philosopher John Rawls helps envision rights by placing moral agents behind a veil of ignorance or in "the original position." In the original position, individuals have no concept of their past history, their present circumstances, or future worth. Behind this veil, then, they cannot personally benefit to any extent greater than anyone else. From this position, moral agents are to determine what basic rights all should have to maintain a minimum level of dignity. Through this concept of rights, Rawls believes that fairness can be attained. For Rawls, in working out the conception of justice as fairness, one main task clearly is to determine which principles of justice would be chosen in the original position. His effort at the task generated two principles:

> *First:* each person is to have an equal right to the most extensive scheme of equal basic liberties compatible with a similar scheme of liberties for others.

> *Second:* social and economic inequalities are to be arranged so that they are both (a) reasonably expected to be to everyone's advantage, and (b) attached to positions and offices open to all (p 53).

Rawls believes that society organized on such principles will accord the right to each individual to maximize happiness and to achieve the greatest good that each individual can justly attain. One's fullness of happiness may not happen, of course, but it will be chance or personal failure and not the action of society that will be the cause.

## VIRTUES

### ARISTOTLE

The writings of Aristotle encapsulate some of the thinking on ethics and virtues. Aristotle makes the point that virtues should be connected to the good of human kind. This means that all human activities should aim for the ultimate good of happiness. Happiness, he points out, can be defined in many ways, such as wealth, health, pleasure or honor. He believes that the ultimate human happiness must come through reason. The best life for a human is the life of reason. Aristotle defines virtue as, "a rational activity in accordance with a rational principle."

For Aristotle right action does not result from knowing and following the "right" principle. Rather, right action results from living a harmonious life. Living that balances all aspects of life is the state of happiness. Aristotle explains we can achieve this by living virtuously. Happiness, for Aristotle, is the state when our actions accomplish their goals. We need all of our characteristics together to help us accomplish our goal. So happiness is in the harmony of all these characteristics that allow us to act in accord with our human character, and happiness includes living a successful moral life, among other things.

How did Aristotle think we get all the activities of our lives working together in harmony? First, he looked at the different activities of the mind or soul, since they are the most important for happiness. The activity of the soul is rational, and in two parts, moral and intellectual. Aristotle describes intellectual and moral virtues as those that help us perform the activities of the soul well, so there are moral virtues and intellectual virtues.

A moral virtue is generally seen as the characteristic of avoiding both excess and deficiency in moral action. Activity that is neither excessive nor deficient, but seeks "the mean," is virtuous action. For example, courage could be selected as the mean between foolhardiness (an excess) and cowardice (a deficit). When Aristotle advises we seek the "Golden Mean," he is advising we seek that which is reasonable, not the mediocre. And Aristotle thinks we must choose the mean relative to us. By "relative to us" Aristotle means according to the particular situation we are in, and who we are. If I am extremely generous by nature, then giving away ten percent of my income may not be virtuous. The mean relative to me may require I give thirty-five percent for virtue's sake. Giving any more might be excessive, but giving any less would be miserly. The mean depends on the concrete circumstances and the person.

Another important feature of moral virtues, according to Aristotle, is that they cannot be taught as prepositional rules. Aristotle said we learn moral virtue only by performance. Learning moral virtues, the characteristics that let us perform the moral function well, depends on training, upbringing, and practice. Our need for training is why Aristotle thought it so important that nations (city-states) develop good laws, because good laws habituate good practices in its citizens. Without good laws, without a good city, Aristotle held that people cannot live the moral life well (if at all). In the same vein, Aristotle declared that the primary duty of a friend is to help the other achieve a moral life.

## CASE AND ANALYSIS

As an example a married couple, Jose and Maria, are taking a course entitled "Achieving Happiness in Marriage." Both partners get A's on all of the examinations. They are mastering the intellectual virtues of the course. However, at home they still argue and find little application for the principles they have read in class. In not being able to practice or achieve the subject matter, Jose and Maria have not achieved the moral virtues they are seeking. They are unable to form habits to bring about a happy marriage. Intellectual virtues are important, but moral virtues indicate that the knowledge is applied as a habit.

## RELATIONSHIPS

An emerging theory of ethics is currently in the spotlight. It is a theory based on caring, sharing and relationships. Much of the work on this moral theory has been done in the field of psychology through the research and writing of moral psychologist Carol Gilligan. Gilligan believes that through psychologists such as Freud, Erikson and particularly Lawrence Kohlberg, moral research has focused on male patterns of decision making as the only or superior pattern of making decisions. According to Gilligan, Kohlberg's six stages of moral development were based on male models of maturity such as autonomy, which excluded moral development based on the strengths of relationships and the caring and sharing that can take place among others.

According to Gilligan our culture and our values create a discrepancy between "womanhood" and "adulthood." Gilligan laments that maturity is equated with personal autonomy, and concern with relationships appears as a weakness, rather than a human strength. "In the different voice of women lies the truth of an ethic of care, the tie between relationship and responsibility, and the origins of aggression in the failure of connection" (1982).

Gilligan explains researchers' notion of the primary caretaker as female with interpersonal dynamics different for boys and girls. Girls identify with their mothers while boys are expected to separate themselves from their mothers around the age of five. Gilligan's research finds that in the process the boys curtail primary love and a sense of empathy. She further explains that since masculinity is defined through separation, and femininity is defined through attachment, the male gender is threatened by intimacy while the female gender identity is threatened by separation (1982).

Gilligan's primary work is titled *In a Different Voice*. The title is meant to indicate that men have had the primary voice in society. The conversation becomes different as women's voices are added to the conversation (1999). The silencing of women in society is also a primary research area for Gilligan. Perhaps in an effort to please men, women silence strengths such as intellect, strength, abilities, potency, power, aggression and even anger. She believes women's strengths must be part of society's voice, and not silenced as in the past (1982).

For scholar Nel Noddings, we make moral choices based on an ethic of care. One of her primary examples focuses on a mother picking up a crying baby. She does not pick up the child because of a sense of duty or because she is worried about the consequences of not picking up the child. Noddings theorizes the mother picks up her baby out of a sense of care based on their relationship (82, 83).

"Caring requires me to respond to the initial impulse with an act of commitment: I commit myself either to overt action on behalf of the cared-for (I pick up my crying infant) or I commit myself to thinking about what I might do . . . But the test of my caring is not wholly in how things turn out; the primary test lies in an examination of what I considered, how fully I received the other, and whether the free pursuit of his projects is partly a result of the completion of my caring in him" (83).

Noddings believes that genuine moral sentiment arises from an evaluation of the caring relation as good as, better than, and superior to other forms of relatedness. However, she also analyzes the effects of caring for someone who does not appreciate or want the care. The person may have a different ethic of care than that of the care giver. Noddings believes that the future may permit young boys to develop a strong ethics of care for others and appreciate the care given them by various care givers (102).

Relationship theorists reinforce that this is not a gender-based ethics or an ethics system to be used in exclusion of other systems of analysis. They believe it is an important way of thinking that should be included within an overall analysis of an ethical dilemma.

## SUMMARY OF THE FIVE SYSTEMS

The five moral systems of duties, rights, utility, virtues, and relationships can be compared across the terms of their obligation, the basis for their standard of moral action, and the criteria for what moral action is. The following table provides that comparison.

**Moral System**

|  | DUTIES | RIGHTS | UTILITY | VIRTUES | RELATIONSHIPS |
|---|---|---|---|---|---|
| *Terms* | Obligation of individual to moral rules | Obligation of community to individual | Obligation to maximize happiness | Obligation to self and community | Obligation to the relationship |
| *Basis* | Based on universal, self-evident requirements | Universal, self-evident prerogatives of the individual | Based on consequences of action | Based on integrity of character | Based on the social practices of care |
| *Action* | Moral action discharges duty | Moral action preserves individual rights | Moral action produces favorable consequences | Moral action improves the individual & state | Moral action produces caring relationships |

(SOURCE: Anderson J.A., 2001)

*My thanks to Jim Anderson who created this table and greatly assisted with this article.*

## BIBLIOGRAPHY

Anderson, J. A. (1996). *Communication theory: Epistemological foundations.* New York: Guilford.

Anderson, J. A., & Englehardt, E. (2001). *The organizational self and ethical conduct: Sunlit virtue and shadowed resistance.* Fort Worth, TX: Harcourt.

Bellah, R. N., Madsen, R., Sullivan, W. M., Swindler, A., & Tipton, S. M. (1996). *Habits of the heart: Individualism and commitment in American life.* Berkeley: University of California Press.

Caputo, J. D. (1993). *Against ethics.* Bloomington, IN: Indiana University Press.

Finnis, J. (1983). *Fundamentals of ethics.* Oxford, UK: Clarendon Press.

Gilligan, C. (1982). *In a different voice.* Cambridge, MA: Harvard University Press, 1982.

Gilligan, C. "In a different voice: sixteen years later." Address at Utah Valley State College, Orem, UT, November 18, 1999.

Hobbes, T. (1921/1651). *Leviathan Part 1.* New York: Hafner.

Kant, I. (1959) *Foundations of the metaphysics of morals.* (L. W. Beck, Trans.). New York: Liberal Arts Press, p. 7.

MacIntyre, A. (1988). *Whose justice? Which rationality?* Notre Dame, IN: University of Notre Dame Press.

Mill, J. S. (1897). *Utilitarianism.* London: Longmans Green.

More, T. (1516/1964). *Utopia.* New Haven, CT: Yale University Press.

Noddings, N. (1984). *Caring: A feminine approach to ethics and moral education.* Berkeley: University of California Press, pp. 82, 83.

Rawls, J. (1971/1999). *A theory of justice,* second edition. Cambridge, MA: Harvard University Press, p. 53.

Romesburg, K. (1999). Class Discussion. Orem, Ut.

Snyner, J. W. (1989). "Hammurabi," *The World Book Encyclopedia.* Chicago: The World Book Encyclopedia.

Wilson, J. Q. (1993). *The moral sense.* New York: Free Press.

Wong, D. (1984). *Moral relativity.* Berkeley: University of California Press.

## DEVELOPING YOUR ETHICAL BELIEFS

### QUESTIONS TO CONSIDER

1. Define Rawls's veil of ignorance. Is this a realistic metaphor?
2. Find the definitions of *consequentialist, nonconsequentialist,* and *utilitarian* in this article. Do you consider yourself to be a consequentialist or a nonconsequentialist? Explain.
3. Aristotle believed that "right action does not result from knowing and following the 'right' principle. Rather, right action results from living a harmonious life. Living that balances all aspects of life is the state of happiness. . . . we can achieve this by living virtuously." Give an example of how you live a harmonious life. Do you believe that "right" actions come from living a harmonious life? Support your point of view.
4. Kant says it's unacceptable to lie. Do you agree with Kant, or can you think of a time when it might be necessary to lie? Support your point of view.

5. What are some of the ways that we intentionally harm others? What are ways that we unintentionally cause harm? How does rational justification help us gain a better understanding of the harms we can and do cause?

## GUIDELINES FOR ANALYZING A CASE STUDY

At the end of each chapter is a contemporary case that is related to the readings in that chapter. As you analyze each case, you can apply the ideas and information you learned about in the various articles. This is your chance to actually use some new ideas and ways of thinking about a problem. As you actively take part in resolving the problems in the case, you are involved in developing your own ethical beliefs. Follow these step-by-step guidelines to analyze each case study.

1. **Read the case and identify the problems.** As you read the case, write down any problems that you can identify in the case. Are any of the problems moral problems or are they merely tough decisions? A tough decision can be as simple as the choice to have your car repaired by Bob rather than Ted. A moral or ethical problem is the decision to sell your car with various mechanical problems to Ted without disclosing the car's problems.

2. **Brainstorm possible responses to the moral problems in this case.** What argument could you defend? What would Kant say? What would Mill or Aristotle argue is the best solution? Would Hobbes have a different response? Select one of these philosophers to help you make your argument.

3. **Write a rough draft.** This is your opportunity to write down everything you are thinking about the case. Remember to reread your draft and take out any information that doesn't strongly support your argument. You might want to add some additional information to make sure your analysis is clearly and logically written. It is important to refine your writing. You will learn something new about the subject, your thinking, or your writing each time you refine the case. As you write, think of the consequences and obligations that are tied into the case.

4. **Write an introduction with a thesis statement.** The introduction is a general statement about the case, perhaps even a short restatement of the case. The thesis specifically states the position you will

follow on the case. Example: "I am in favor of passive euthanasia."
or "I don't believe capital punishment is a moral penance in our society." The thesis is usually the last sentence of the first paragraph.

5. **Identify the moral or ethical problems.** Write about each moral or
   ethical problem that you feel is substantial and central to this case.
   You will probably want to limit yourself to no more than three
   problems. Argue why each of these is a moral problem.

6. **Explain what one or more major philosophers would say about
   this case.** Discussing major philosophers provides support for your
   point of view. You are letting your reader know that it's not only
   you that holds this opinion, but also some well-respected philosophers would agree with you. Remember to make a list of all the
   sources from which you got your information about these philosophers. Keep in mind that one of the main purposes of a case analysis is to be self-confrontive. This means that merely reporting find-
   ings from newspaper articles or other sources or just giving your
   own opinion is not enough. You must include the views of one or
   more credible philosophers that will support your argument. At
   least two sources should be cited in each case, but limit the number
   of times you refer to these sources in your case analysis. You want
   to maintain your personal viewpoint, which is required in a case
   analysis. You don't want your reader to be overwhelmed by the
   thinking of other philosophers or the case analysis won't have
   enough of your voice and your opinion shining through. Use your
   sources to help argue and support your point of view.

7. **Explain what you think should be done.** Explain why you agree (or
   disagree) with the philosopher(s) you selected. In particular, this is
   when you should discuss consequences and obligations that are involved in any of the solutions you present.

8. **Write a conclusion.** Tie together the problems, the ethical points of
   view you discussed, and the actions you suggest. You may even have
   ideas for preventing this type of moral problem in the future.
   Consider explaining how interpersonal communication offers an
   opportunity for preventing the specific problems that are in the case.

## GUIDELINES FOR WRITING A CASE STUDY

After each article in this text, there is a suggestion for writing a case study.
This provides an opportunity to take an active role in arguing the ethical

dilemmas raised in the article. Write a case study based on something you know about that involves either your personal experience; interpersonal experience; or your involvement with work, school, or community.

1.  **Brainstorm.** Take a few minutes to brainstorm about the following question: What was your toughest ethical problem? What did you do? Looking back did you make the right choice?

2.  **Make a list of the ethical problems.** In a confidential journal or file begin writing about tough ethical problems that are personal, interpersonal, work related, or societal.

3.  **Select one ethical problem.** Select one of the ethical problems and begin filling in details about individuals involved, the setting, the time sequence, politics and group dynamics, and other pertinent information.

4.  **Define the situation that led up to the ethical problem.** Help the reader understand why at least two choices were possible, with neither being pleasant from an ethics standpoint.

5.  **Explain the interpersonal decisions that were made.** Explain in detail how others' decisions brought about the ethical problem. Help the reader understand the interpersonal complications.

6.  **Discuss technical or professional complications.** Help the reader understand as best as possible the technical or professional complications.

7.  **Write and refine your case until it reads like a short story.** Ask a friend to review the case and comment on it. Does it provoke interest? Is there really an ethical problem or is it merely a difficult problem? A difficult problem may be the decision to accept a scholarship at University of Snow or at the College of Sunshine. A moral or ethical problem is the decision of whether or not to lie on your application about volunteer work that you haven't done but is necessary for the scholarship.

8.  **Answer the last two questions in question #1.** What did you do? Looking back did you make the right choice?

## SAMPLE ANALYSIS OF STUDENT CASE STUDY

*Case Study* (written by a student group)

In the movie *A Few Good Men*, a secret group of soldiers in the military have killed a fellow soldier who they believe is not fit to be a Marine. Jack

Nicholson plays the character in charge of this group of soldiers. The group believes that it is in the best interest of the country and the military to kill this soldier. *Our group believes it is never acceptable to kill another human being in cold blood.*

## Analysis of the Case

### [Summary of case]

In the movie *A Few Good Men*, Jack Nicholson is a military officer who has covered up a murder. When he is in court on the witness stand, Nicholson yells, "You want to know the truth? You want to know the truth? Well, you can't handle the truth." Nicholson gives testimony that some military crimes must be covert for national security purposes. He implies that it is acceptable to murder one cadet who isn't going along with the rest of the company. He further states it is acceptable for him to lie about the death under oath to protect the company involved as well as the military overall.

### [Identify ethical problem(s)]

This case presents an ethical dilemma for three reasons: (1) A murder has been committed. It is not acceptable to take a human life because this individual doesn't get along with the rest of the company. (2) The investigation of the murder is hindered. It is not acceptable to murder then to lie about the cause of death in an effort to preserve public relations or personal esteem. (3) Cadets and officers lie about the murder under oath in court. It is unacceptable to lie in court. The military has determined that it is essential this case be investigated and prosecuted to the full extent of the law. A subgroup in the military can't make its own rules of military morality.

### [Opinion of the students writing this case analysis]

Murder is wrong. This murder was committed with careful planning, and in cold blood. It is immoral, and those causing the murder should be punished to the fullest extent of the law. It is unacceptable to cover-up the murder. The character of Jack Nicholson defends the practice of lying under an area of lying covered by Plato.

### [Explanation of what major philosophers might say about this case]

Plato gave support for some lies when he said: "It is the business of the rulers of the city, if it is anybody's, to tell lies, deceiving both its enemies and its own citizens for the benefit of the city; and no one else must touch this privilege."[1] It is preferable to only use one major philosopher in a short paper. However, this case demonstrates the systems of three philosophers by giving brief examples of common arguments posed by them.

If using the Plato type justification for the cover-up, Nicholson and those around him have a deluded sense of their place in national security. Their actions are not for the preservation of the military. Their actions and lies are for preservation of their own positions. . . . *(More information should be given here if your paper is written from a virtue point of view.)*

Duty is often represented by Kant and his deontological views on lying. Kant tells us that it is never acceptable to lie and places this on the level of a moral law, or a categorical imperative. He contends that lies always harm others—the individual or society. "To be truthful (honest) in all declarations, therefore, is a sacred and absolutely commanding decree of reason, limited by no expediency."[5]

Kant declares: "A lie is a lie . . . whether it be told with good or bad intent. . . . But if a lie does no harm to anyone and no one's interests are affected by it, is it a lie? Certainly."[2] Kant believes truthfulness is a duty, an "unconditional duty which holds in all circumstances."[3] According to the categorical imperative, if there is even one case in which it is acceptable to lie and honesty can be overridden, then the "perfect" status of the duty not to lie is compromised. Kant is strident in not allowing for even a seemingly innocent lie. He merely asserts that if something terrible happens it is not your fault. The terrible act is something wholly unjustified in the first place.[4] . . . *(More information should be given here if your paper is written from a Kantian point of view.)*

Utilitarian Jeremy Bentham also would not allow for the Nicholson defense of the coverup. Bentham delivered a frothy lecture to England's judges who were using their power and lying to the people. Bentham sees nothing more abhorrent than using lies and power to further one's position.[6] . . . *(More information should be given here if your paper is written from a utilitarian point of view.)*

*[Conclusion]*

This incident in *A Few Good Men* is an example of a series of unethical behaviors, with murder the most severe. The justification for the behaviors is weak, with hundreds of years of morality, ethics, and laws written in opposition to Nicholson's rationale.

## LIST OF SOURCES

1.  Popper, K.R. (1980). *The open society and its enemies,* vol. 1 (p. 138). London: Routledge and Kegan Paul.

2.  Kant, I. (1930, 1963). *Lectures on Ethics.* (L. Infield, Trans.) (p. 228). New York: Harper & Row.

3.  Kant, I. (1949) "On a supposed right to lie from benevolent motives." In L.W. Beck (Ed.), *The critique of practical reason and other writings in moral philosophy* (pp. 92–96). Chicago: University of Chicago Press.

4.  Ibid.

5.  Kant, I. (1949). *Critique of practical reason and other writings in moral philosophy* (p. 348). L.W. Beck, Ed., Trans. Chicago: University of Chicago Press.

6.  Bentham, J. (1838–43) "Pension for Justice." In Bowring J. Sir, Ed., *The Works of Jeremy Bentham,* pp. 205, 206.

# KEY CONCEPTS

**Categorical Imperative**   This concept refers to a command or law that is unconditional. It instructs us to do something regardless of the consequences. According to Kant, we should act always that our behavior could be a universal for all humankind.

**Consequentialist**   Consequentialist theories declare that an action, intention, or principle of social organization should be judged by its consequences.

**Collectivist theory**   Collectivist theory concerns the total amount of good.

**Deontology**   The ethical theory invoking duty as the basis of morality. In Kant's writings it is interpreted as some acts are morally obligatory regardless of their consequences.

**Divine command theory**   A belief that an action is morally right because God commands or wills it.

**Duty**   Duty is concerned with the obligation of the individual to the collective, or community.

**Egoism**   Hobbes based his theory on egoism, meaning that individuals would keep their covenants out of a sense of self-preservation.

**Ethics**   The study of morality and moral behavior.

**Morality**   Morality is the system of behavior that we are born into.

**Nonconsequentialist**   Kant's moral guideline, which is nonconsequentialist, would have you do an action because you "ought" to do it—because it is your duty.

**Relationship ethics**   Relationship ethics involves the notion of making moral decisions based on caring, sharing and other relationship concerns.

**Rights**   The theory of rights looks at the obligation between self and other from the standpoint of what every individual in the community is owed.

**Teleology**   The word comes from the Greek *telos* (goal, purpose, or end) and *logos* (word, reason, study), hence, literally, "the study of ends or goals." It refers to theories that stress that the consequences or outcomes of actions are what determines their moral value.

**Utilitarianism**    A moral theory centered on the value of an action resides in its utility for the production of pleasure or happiness.

**Virtue ethics**    Virtue ethics are often based on the writings of the ancient Greeks. They concentrate on daily actions that would bring an overall good to the individual and the entire community.

# 2

## SELF AND THE NATURE OF ETHICS IN INTERPERSONAL COMMUNICATION

ERIC FROMM

### SELFISHNESS, SELF-LOVE AND SELF-INTEREST

*Eric Fromm (1900–1980) was a practicing psychoanalyst who published extensively in the fields of contemporary philosophy and psychology. Published in 1947, this excerpt from* Man for Himself: An Inquiry into the Psychology of Ethics *explains the need for individual self-interest and how self-interest differs from selfishness.*

> *Thou shalt love thy neighbour as thyself.*
> —*Bible*

Modern culture is prevaded by a tabu on selfishness. We are taught that to be selfish is sinful and that to love others is virtuous. To be sure, this doctrine is in flagrant contradiction to the practice of modern society, which holds the doctrine that the most powerful and legitimate drive in man is selfishness and that by following this imperative drive the individual makes his best contribution to the common good. But the doctrine which declares

---

[1]Cf. Erich Fromm, "Selfishness and Self-Love," *Psychiatry* (November, 1939). The following discussion of selfishness and self-love is a partial repetition of the earlier paper.

selfishness to be the arch evil and love for others to be the greatest virtue is still powerful. Selfishness is used here almost synonymously with self-love. The alternative is to love others, which is a virtue, or to love oneself, which is a sin.

This principle has found its classic expression in Calvin's theology, according to which man is essentially evil and powerless. Man can achieve absolutely nothing that is good on the basis of his own strength or merit. "We are not our own," says Calvin. "Therefore neither our reason nor our will should predominate in our deliberations and actions. We are not our own; therefore let us not propose it as our end to seek what may be expedient for us according to the flesh. We are not our own; therefore, let us, as far as possible, forget ourselves and all things that are ours. On the contrary, we are God's; for Him, therefore, let us live and die. For, as it is the most devastating pestilence which ruins people if they obey themselves, it is the only haven of salvation not to know or to want anything by oneself but to be guided by God Who walks before us."[2] Man should have not only the conviction of his absolute nothingness but he should do everything to humiliate himself. "For I not call it humility if you suppose that we have anything left . . . . we cannot think of ourselves as we ought to think without utterly despising everything that may be supposed an excellence in us. This humility is unfeigned submission of a mind overwhelmed with a weighty sense of its own misery and poverty; for such is the uniform description of it in the word of God."[3]

This emphasis on the nothingness and wickedness of the individual implies that there is nothing he should like and respect about himself. The doctrine is rooted in self-contempt and self-hatred. Calvin makes this point very clear: he speaks of self-love as "a pest."[4] If the individual finds something "on the strength of which he finds pleasure in himself," he betrays this sinful self-love. This fondness for himself will make him sit in judgment over others and despise them. Therefore, to be fond of oneself or to like

---

[2]Johannes Calvin, *Institutes of the Christian Religion,* trans. by John Allen (Philadelphia: Presbyterian Board of Christian Education, 1928), in particular Book III, Chap. 7, p. 619. From "For, as it is . . ." the translation is mine from the Latin original (Johannes Calvini. *Institutio Christianae Religionis. Editionem curavit,* A. Tholuk, Berolini, 1935, par. 1, p. 445).

[3]*Ibid.,* Chap. 12, par. 6, p. 681.

[4]*Ibid.,* Chap 7, par. 4, p. 622.

anything in oneself is one of the greatest sins. It is supposed to exclude love for others[5] and to be identical with selfishness.[6]

The view of man held by Calvin and Luther has been of tremendous influence on the development of modern Western society. They laid the foundations for an attitude in which man's own happiness was not considered to be the aim of life but where he became a means, an adjunct, to ends beyond him, of an all-powerful God, or of the not less powerful secularized authorities and norms, the state, business, success. Kant, who, with regard to the idea that man should be an end in himself and never a means only, was perhaps the most influential ethical thinker of the Enlightenment period, nevertheless had the same condemnation for self-love. According to him, it is a virtue to want happiness for others, but to want one's own happiness is ethically indifferent, since it is something for which the nature of man is striving, and since a natural striving cannot have a positive ethical value.[7] Kant admits that one must not give up one's claims to happiness; under certain circumstances it may even be a duty to be concerned with it, partly because health, wealth, and the like may be means necessary for the fulfillment of one's duty, partly because the lack of happiness—poverty—can prevent one from fulfilling his duty.[8] But love for oneself, striving for one's own happiness, can never be a *virtue*. As an ethical principle, the striving for one's own happiness "is the most objectionable one, not merely because it is false . . . . but because the springs it provides for morality are such as rather to undermine it and destroy its sublimity . . . ."[9]

Kant differentiates egotism, self-love, *philautia*—a benevolence for oneself—and arrogance, the pleasure in oneself. But even "rational self-love"

---

[5]It should be noted, however, that even love for one's neighbor, while it is one of the fundamental doctrines of the New Testament, has not been given a corresponding weight by Calvin. In blatant contradiction to the New Testament, Calvin says: "For what the schoolmen advance concerning the priority of charity to faith and hope, is a mere reverie of a distempered imagination.. . ."—Chap. 24, par. 1, p. 531.

[6]Despite Luther's emphasis on the spiritual freedom of the individual, his theology, different as it is in many ways from Calvin's, is pervaded by the same conviction of man's basic powerlessness and nothingness.

[7]Compare Immanual Kant, *Kant's Critique of Practical Reason and Other Works on the Theory of Ethics,* trans. by Thomas Kingsmill Abbott (New York: Longmans, Green & Co., 1909), Part I, Book I, Chap. I, par. VIII, Remark II, p. 126.

[8]*Ibid.,* in particular Part I, Book I, Chap. III, p. 186.

[9]*Loc. cit., Fundamental Principles of the Metaphysics of Morals;* second section, p. 61.

must be restricted by ethical principles, the pleasure in oneself must be battered down, and the individual must come to feel humiliated in comparing himself with the sanctity of moral laws.[10] The individual should find supreme happiness in the fulfillment of his duty. The realization of the moral principle—and, therefore, of the individual's happiness—is only possible in the general whole, the nation, the state. But "the welfare of the state"—and *salus rei publicae suprema lex est*—is not identical with the welfare of the citizens and their happiness.[11]. . .

. . . Nietzsche too denounces love and altruism as expressions of weakness and self-negation. For Nietzsche, the quest for love is typical of slaves unable to fight for what they want and who therefore try to get it through love. Altruism and love for mankind thus have become a sign of degeneration.[17] For Nietzsche it is the essence of a good and healthy aristocracy that it is ready to sacrifice countless people for its interests without having a guilty conscience. Society should be a "foundation and scaffolding by means of which a select class of beings may be able to elevate themselves to their higher duties, and in general to a higher existence."[18] Many quotations could be added to document this spirit of contempt and egotism. These ideas have often been understood as *the* philosophy of Nietzsche. However, they do not represent the true core of his philosophy.[19]

There are various reasons why Nietzsche expressed himself in the sense noted above. . . . The "love" which he attacks is rooted not in one's own strength, but in one's own weakness. "Your neighbor-love is your bad love of yourselves. Ye flee unto your neighbor from yourselves and would fain make a virtue thereof! But I fathom your 'unselfishness.'" He states explicitly, "You cannot stand yourselves and you do not love yourselves sufficiently."[20] For Nietzsche the individual has "an enormously great significance."[21] The "strong" individual is the one who has "true kindness, nobility, greatness of

[10]*Loc. cit.*, Part I, Book I, Ch. III, p. 165.

[11]Immanual Kant, *Immanual Kant's Werke* (Berlin: Cassierer), in particular "Der Rechtslehre Zweiter Teil" I. Abschnitt, par. 49, p. 124. I translate from the German text, since this part is omitted in the English translation of *The Metaphysics of Ethics* by I. W. Semple (Edinburgh: 1871).

[17]Friedrich Nietzsche, *The Will to Power*, trans. by Anthony M. Ludovici (Edinburgh and London: T. N. Foulis, 1910), stanzas 246, 326, 369, 373, and 728.

[18]Friedrich Nietzsche, *Beyond Good and Evil*, trans. by Helen Zimmer (New York: The Macmillan Company, 1907), stanza 258.

[19]Cf. G. A. Morgan, *What Nietzsche Means* (Cambridge: Harvard University Press, 1943).

soul, which does not give in order to take, which does not want to excel by being kind;—'waste' as type of true kindness, wealth of the person as a premise."[22] He expresses the same thought also in *Thus Spake Zarathustra:* "The one goeth to his neighbor because he seeketh himself, and the other because he would fain lose himself."[23]

The essence of this view is this: Love is a phenomenon of abundance; its premise is the strength of the individual who can give. Love is affirmation and productiveness, "It seeketh to create what is loved!"[24] To love another person is only a virtue if it springs from this inner strength, but it is a vice if it is the expression of the basic inability to be oneself.[25] However, the fact remains that Nietzsche left the problem of the relationship between self-love and love for others as an unsolved antinomy.

The doctrine that selfishness is the arch-evil and that to love oneself excludes loving others is by no means restricted to theology and philosophy, but it became one of the stock ideas promulgated in home, school, motion pictures, books; indeed in all instruments of social suggestion as well. "Don't be selfish" is a sentence which has been impressed upon millions of children, generation after generation. Its meaning is somewhat vague. Most people would say that it means not to be egotistical, inconsiderate, without any concern for others. Actually, it generally means more than that. Not to be selfish implies not to do what one wishes, to give up one's own wishes for the sake of those in authority. "Don't be selfish," in the last analysis, has the same ambiguity that it has in Calvinism. Aside from its obvious implication, it means, "don't love yourself," "don't be yourself," but submit yourself to something more important than yourself, to an outside power or its internalization, "duty." "Don't be selfish" becomes one of the most powerful ideological tools in suppressing spontaneity and the free development of personality. Under the pressure of this slogan one is

---

[20]Friedrich Nietzsche, *Thus Spake Zarathustra*, trans. by Thomas Common (New York: Modern Library), p. 75.

[21]*The Will to Power*, stanza 785.

[22]*Ibid.*, stanza 935.

[23]*Thus Spake Zarathustra*, p. 76.

[24]*Ibid.*, p. 102.

[25]See Friedrich Nietzsche, *The Twilight of Idols*, trans. by A. M. Ludovici (Edinburgh: T. N. Foulis, 1911), stanza 35; *Ecce Homo*, trans. by A. M. Ludovici (New York: The Macmillan Company, 1911), stanza 2; *Nachlass, Neitzsches Werke* (Leipzig: A. Kroener), pp. 63-64.

asked for every sacrifice and for complete submission: only those acts are "unselfish" which do not serve the individual but somebody or something outside himself.

This picture, we must repeat, is in a certain sense one-sided. For besides the doctrine that one should not be selfish, the opposite is also propagandized in modern society: keep your own advantage in mind, act according to what is best for you; by so doing you will also be acting for the greatest advantage of all others. As a matter of fact, the idea that egotism is the basis of the general welfare is the principle on which competitive society has been built. It is puzzling that two such seemingly contradictory principles could be taught side by side in one culture; of the fact, however, there is no doubt. One result of this contradiction is confusion in the individual. Torn between the two doctrines, he is seriously blocked in the process of integrating his personality. This confusion is one of the most significant sources of the bewilderment and helplessness of modern man.[26]

The doctrine that love for oneself is identical with "selfishness" and an alternative to love for others has pervaded theology, philosophy, and popular thought; the same doctrine has been rationalized in scientific language in *Freud's* theory of narcissim. Freud's concept presupposes a fixed amount of libido. In the infant, all of the libido has the child's own person as its objective, the stage of "primary narcissism," as Freud calls it. During the individual's development, the libido is shifting from one's own person toward other objects. If a person is blocked in his "object-relationships," the libido is withdrawn from the objects and returned to his own person; this is called "secondary narcissim." According to Freud, the more love I turn toward the outside world the less love is left for myself, and vice versa. He thus describes the phenomenon of love as an impoverishment of one's self-love because all libido is turned to an object outside oneself. . . .

To love is an expression of one's power to love, and to love somebody is the actualization and concentration of this power with regard to one person. It is not true, as the idea of romantic love would have it, that there is only *the* one person in the world whom one could love and that it is the great chance of one's life to find that one person. Nor is it true, if that person be found that love for him (or her) results in a withdrawal of love from others. Love which

---

[26]This point has been emphasized by Karen Horney, *The Neurotic Personality of Our Time* (New York: W. W. Norton & Company, 1937), and by Robert S. Lynd, *Knowledge for What?* (Princeton: Princeton University Press, 1939).

can only be experienced with regard to one person demonstrates by this very fact that it is not love, but a symbiotic attachment. The basic affirmation contained in love is directed toward the beloved person as an incarnation of essentially human qualities. Love of one person implies love of man as such. The kind of "division of labor," as William James calls it, by which one loves one's family but is without feeling for the "stranger," is a sign of a basic inability to love. Love of man is not, as is frequently supposed, an abstraction coming after the love for a specific person, but it is its premise, although, genetically, it is acquired in loving specific individuals.

From this it follows that my own self, in principle, must be as much an object of my love as another person. *The affirmation of one's own life, happiness, growth, freedom, is rooted in one's capacity to love,* i.e., in care, respect, responsibility, and knowledge. If an individual is able to love productively, he loves himself too; if he can love *only* others, he can not love at all.

Granted that love for oneself and for others in principle is conjunctive, how do we explain selfishness, which obviously excludes any genuine concern for others? The *selfish* person is interested only in himself, wants everything for himself, feels no pleasure in giving, but only in taking. The world outside is looked at only from the standpoint of what he can get out of it; he lacks interest in the needs of others, and respect for their dignity and integrity. He can see nothing but himself; he judges everyone and everything from its usefulness to him; he is basically unable to love. Does not this prove that concern for others and concern for oneself are unavoidable alternatives? This would be so if selfishness and self-love were identical. But that assumption is the very fallacy which has led to so many mistaken conclusions concerning our problem. *Selfishness and self-love, far from being identical, are actually opposites.* The selfish person does not love himself too much but too little; in fact he hates himself. This lack of fondness and care for himself, which is only one expression of his lack of productiveness, leaves him empty and frustrated. He is necessarily unhappy and anxiously concerned to snatch from life the satisfactions which he blocks himself from attaining. He seems to care too much for himself but actually he only makes an unsuccessful attempt to cover up and compensate for his failure to care for his real self. Freud holds that the selfish person is narcissistic, as if he had withdrawn his love from others and turned it toward his own person. *It is true that selfish persons are incapable of loving others, but they are not capable of loving themselves either.*

### CRITICAL THINKING QUESTIONS

1. According to Fromm, what is the nature of self-interest and selfishness?
2. Is it ethical to show self-interest or selfishness?
3. Give examples of self-interest that is selfish and self-interest that is not selfish. In other words, give examples of acts of self-interest that are also acts of doing good for someone else, and acts of self-interest that are *not* doing good for someone else.
4. Write a case and analyze it using examples of self-love.

JAMES ANDERSON

## IDENTITY AND SELF

*James Anderson is a professor of communication at the University of Utah. He has published numerous books and articles in the field, particularly in mediated communication. This article published in 2001 explains postmodern perspectives in regard to the self, society, and culture.*

Ethics concerns the quality or value that is attached to or is inherent in the action of some agent-who-could-do-otherwise. One place to start an analysis of ethical action is to consider the constitution of the acting agent.

In traditional forms, most ethical arguments are founded on a vision of the acting agent as a fully-realized, rational intellect who can accurately read the world around it. This vision made use of an ideal Cartesian mind that was ultimately capable of right reason and a material reality that would ultimately yield its secrets to empirical methods. It was the good man thinking well after careful study of the world he was in. And, indeed, it was a man, good by Western cultural values, thinking well in the lines of Aristotelean logic as only a man could, according to prevailing thought, whose careful study was in the mold of European masculinist science. For example Rachels (1993) writes:

> The conscientious moral agent is someone who is concerned impartially with the interests of everyone affected by what he or she does; who

carefully sifts facts and examines their implications; who accepts principles of conduct only after scrutinizing them to make sure they are sound;
who is willing to "listen to reason" even when it means that his or her earlier convictions may have to be revised; and finally, is willing to act on the
results of his deliberation. (p. 14)

## CHALLENGING THE TRADITION

This traditional vision is still very much with us, but it is no longer unchallenged. The first of these challenges has been directed toward the Cartesian
mind—that unitary intellect that if sufficiently trained and disciplined
could reliably reach truth. The work of Freud and Jung and more recently
Lacan have thoroughly destabilized the concept of a single, rational faculty.
We are left instead with an often squabbling multiplicity of mental faculties
thoroughly inhabited by desire. Further, the training and discipline by
which the mind would work have been shown to be a particular cultural in-
vention rather than a gift from God or nature. There is, consequently, no
*right* reason, no Archimedean standpoint of impartiality, but rather a dis-
puted set of conventions by which reasoning is done and contested territo-
ries from which we can state our claim.

The second set of challenges has been directed toward the idea of "a good
man" as an internally secure and persisting identity. This identity has been considered to be some essential character that uniquely carries the mark of the
person. That mark has been called the *soul* or the *enduring* or *essentialist self.*
The challenges to the essentialist self have come in two major forms: The first
has been from work in psychology that has atomized the soul into attributes,
aptitudes, attitudes, and personality traits. There is no unitary force of action,
only a kaleidoscopic composite of probabilities. The second challenge has
come from sociological work that has shown that much of identity—much of
who we are—is the product of social action not internal character. It is social
action that creates the identifying marks of gender, ethnicity, age, caste. These
socially derived identities are more than just a descriptive badge.

## THE SELF AS IDENTITY AND SUBJECTIVITY

With some 350 years to rehearse the idea, it would not be unusual for us to
persist in believing that we are not only the same material object but also
somehow the same person whether in interpersonal relationships or as an
employee at our workplace, the president of a volunteer group, a parent in

one home, and a child in another. In the Enlightenment notion, those roles are simply things we take on; the center of our self remains unchanged. In more contemporary terms, there is no center: We are a living organism always involved in varying rates of change that must manage its self-expression within a socially produced framework of performance requirements. The parent-self appears within a framework of understanding of what is true and, therefore, right that is different from framework in which the working-self appears. It may be appropriate to tell a child that a package will arrive "soon," but wholly inappropriate to tell that to a customer standing at the counter even though the time may be the same. The value and character of time is not the same in those two cases. And, therefore the value and character of statements about time are not the same.

Answers to questions of right and wrong, consequently, depend on the answer to the question of who we are. The answer to who we are, in turn, depends upon the particular circumstances in which the self appears. We will define the self as the acting agent—the entity we would point to in answer to the question, "Who did this?" When we talk about an agent, as we have noted, we use the term simultaneously in two ways. First, the agent is a particular and identifiable *agent of* action, providing some impetus, some momentum, some resource of the action. This is the identity agent. Second the agent is an *agent for* some recognizable intersection of cultural signs. This intersection is also called a subject position. It denotes a recognizable model of action or Weberian ideal type—such as parent, child, adult, worker, manager, customer, tourist, teacher, student, friend, and on and on. This is the subjective agent. Identity and subjectivity appear together as the self. It is the self that acts; not identity alone; not subjectivity alone.

The self acts within some domain of agency. Agency has been defined as the ability to do otherwise. Agency requires some degree of freedom. Freedom involves the availability and recognizeability of alternatives of action and some degree of autonomy—one's self-governance.[1] The absence of choices or of the ability to choose negates agency.

---

[1]The relationship between freedom and autonomy is sometimes difficult to see. Try this example: A parent has received consistent medical advice from competent and reputable practitioners that her child undergo a difficult, risky, but potentially life-saving procedure. There is freedom, here, in that there are alternatives of action, but there is little autonomy because the parent is wholly dependent upon outside advice. She is not in a condition of self-governance, having surrendered that governance to a culture of experts. She still has to make the decision, but there is little room for choice. Her agency is nearly absent. On the other hand, that same parent living under conditions without medical support may be entirely self-governed in her choice but without recognizable alternatives. She has autonomy but no freedom and, therefore, once again little agency.

Intellectually we hold a conflicted position about agency. Traditional human sciences resist the idea of agency and any other form of a self-caused cause in their bias toward determinism. Some traditional studies in morality, however, are founded on the principle of free will—that Cartesian intellect we saw earlier. We will take a position somewhere in between these extremes. We will hold that people make choices that in the end make a difference and that also have no other explanation than the choice itself. Those choices, however, will be in an agency domain that will define the limits of freedom and autonomy for the acting agent. As living entities, we must act. There is no condition of non-acting. As semiotic entities, our acting must make sense in action. It is the meaningfulness of our self in action that sets the domain of agency.

There are, then, three elements to consider when evaluating the acting agent. First, there are the particular and persistent characteristics of *identity* that provide us with the particular agent—this individual rather than that. Second, there are the cultural meanings by which we enact our *subjectivity* in the paradigmatic values of ethnicity, gender, age, caste, as well as relational and member roles. Identity and subjectivity provide for the *self*. The self is the sign of the person, the answer to who we are. And third, there is agency. *Agency* puts the self in action as the acting agent—a *one-who-makes-a-difference*.

Who we are comes into its fullness in our action, action typically made meaningful within frames of organizing. These ideas write against any notion of a central principle of the individual that carries itself mostly unchanged through life and whose rights, privileges, obligations, and responsibilities are in ready view. These ideas promote the concept of a situated, enacted self that will necessarily change across time and occasion and whose rights, privileges, obligations, and responsibilities will change also.

One's identity therefore is in no small part dependent upon relationships and memberships to provide the resources for being this or that person. Those relationships and memberships do more than just give us a title; they also provide a basis for evaluating the moral character of our action. Taking risks on a rock face may be appropriate for a single person, but if a fall leaves two small children bereft of a parent, the terms of what is appropriate risk taking change. The activity has not changed, but the consequences have because of the identity of the person involved.

## BIBLIOGRAPHY

Lacan, J. (1977). *Ecrits: A selection.* (A. Sheridan, Trans.). New York: Norton.
Rachels, J. (1993). *The elements of moral philosophy* (2nd Ed.). New York: McGraw-Hill, Inc.

## CRITICAL THINKING QUESTIONS

1. Postmodernism challenges the traditional concept of the individual as autonomous. In its place it offers a *self* appearing in some self/other relationship as the acting agent. Explain the concept of the acting agent.
2. The organizational settings, in which we act and are an agent in and of, are often described as frames of meaning. Analyze how the agent makes ethical decisions within different frames of meaning.
3. Write a case and analyze how the acting agent might make a moral decision in the context of an organization.

KENNETH J. GERGEN

# MORAL ACTION FROM A CONSTRUCTIONIST STANDPOINT

*Kenneth J. Gergen is a professor of psychology at Swathmore College. This article from the 1994 publication,* Realities and Relationships: Soundings in Social Construction, *details the importance of communication in the cultivation of reason.*

To open consideration on a social constructionist alternative, it is useful to consider a line of argument developed by Alisdair MacIntyre (1984) in *After Virtue.* MacIntyre lends strong voice to those who find both romanticist and modernist attempts to generate universal moral precepts to be failed enterprises. Contemporary moral debate for MacIntyre is both "interminable and unsettlable" (p. 210). It suffers in particular in its attempt to establish principles or values that transcend the contexts of their usage. Without a context of usage, these abstractions lose practical consequence and susceptibility to assessment. MacIntyre traces moral action to communal tradition. It is when individuals are embedded in communal life, and develop self-identifying narratives that render them intelligible to others and to themselves, that moral action is possible. It is because of the self-identifying narratives and their embeddedness in communal life that the individual can be held morally responsible. "To be the subject of a narrative that runs from one's birth to one's death is . . . to be accountable for the actions and experiences which compose a narratable life" (p. 202). On this view, what we take to be virtues are inseparable from the tissue of social relations: "The virtues find their point and purpose not only in sustaining those relationships necessary if the variety of goods internal to practices are to be achieved . . . but also in sustaining those traditions which provide both practices and individual lives with their necessary historical context" (p. 207).

With these arguments MacIntyre succeeds in moving the fulcrum of moral action from the individual mind to relations among persons. It is only persons within relationship who can sustain (and be sustained by) a view of moral action. In my view, however, MacIntyre does not extend the case to its full potential. When its implications are pressed further, the individual is removed as the central concern of moral deliberation. More explicitly, if the narratives in which we are embedded are products of ongoing interaction, then problems of moral action may be separated from issues of mental state. Moral action is not a byproduct of a mental condition, a private act within the psyche, but a public act inseparable from the relationships in which one is (or has been) participating. According to this account, morality is not something one possesses *within,* it is an action that possesses its moral meaning only within a particular arena of cultural intelligibility. One participates in the cultural forms of action as in a dance or a game; questions of why one is moral or immoral do not require a specifically psychological answer any more than questions of why one moves in three-quarter time when dancing a waltz or plays tennis with balls rather than shuttlecocks. Such actions can be fully understood as sequences of coordinated action within particular communities. A moral life, then, is not an issue of individual sentiment or rationality but a form of communal participation.[9]

From the constructionist vantage point, how are we then to understand individual moral sentiment, moral reasoning, personal values, intentions, and the like? Are we wholly to abandon concern with such states? Although this question is complex, let me propose for now that for the constructionist these various terms are not abandoned so much as reconstituted. This reconstitution requires both an ontological deconstruction and a discursive reconstruction. Again to extend MacIntyre's thesis, if the narratives by which we understand ourselves and our relationships are forms of social accounting, then so is their content. This content would include what we take to be states of mind—matters of "intention," "moral feelings," "values," and "reason." To speak about one's mental life is thus to join in a form of cultural story telling; to claim an "intention" or to possess a "value" is to relate intelligibly to other participants in Western culture. . . . When psychologists and philosophers speak of the necessary psychological ingredients for a moral life, they are participating in a form of cultural narration. The psychological ingredients—the major locus of concern for romanticists and modernists—are thus de-ontologized. The language of moral sentiments and moral deliberation does not then refer to mental events located within the minds of single individuals and directing their actions. Rather, we can reconstitute them as linguistic (poetic, rhetorical) forms of communal practice.

If mental language does not acquire its meaning and significance from mental states, how does it function? What is its bearing on issues of moral action? From a constructionist perspective, accounts such as "I feel this is right," "such an action would violate my principles," or "I think this is immoral" are in their very saying constitutive features of everyday life. Such sentences are used by people in carrying out various social rituals, patterns of interchange, or cultural projects. They operate within relationships to prevent, admonish, praise, and invite various forms of action; they can also establish one's identity, furnish others with guides to one's future conduct, and achieve unity within a group. In effect, moral and ethical languages are among the resources available for playing the games and participating in the dances of cultural life. They are moves or positionings that enable persons to construct the culture in what we take to be a moral or ethical way.

In certain respects these arguments are congenial with the thesis developed in Taylor's (1989) *Sources of the Self.* Taylor attempts to resuscitate the assumptions underlying the Western conception of self, assumptions which, from his perspective, serve as the implicit basis for moral action. These implicit "frameworks provide the background ... for our moral judgments, intuitions or reactions ... To articulate a framework is to explicate what makes sense of our moral responses" (p. 26). It is not simply that this attempt to lay out the "moral topography" of Western culture may "counteract the layers of suppression of modern moral consciousness" (p. 90). Rather, as Taylor sees it, the languages of self-understanding—and thus of moral action—serve as "moral sources." They are "constitutive of human agency," such that "stepping outside these limits would be tantamount to stepping outside what we would recognize as integral, that is, undamaged human personhood" (p. 27).

In proposing that moral language is essentially a resource for generating and sustaining actions that we hold to be moral within the culture, Taylor's position is congenial to the constructionist thesis developed here. However, in its valorization of the language of individual morality, and the underlying supposition that this language is uniquely suited for generating the moral society, the constructionist might raise substantial questions. With Taylor, the constructionist would join the enterprise of tracing moral discourse through history; however, the constructionist would not necessarily champion such languages, but try to account for the conditions and circumstances in which such linguistic conventions came to play a functional role in social (and intellectual) life.[10] For the constructionist the languages of individual morality would be resuscitated, not because they are essential to a moral life, but because they may open up or remind us of potentially useful modes of speaking (and acting) that might otherwise be lost or destroyed in the hurly-burly of contemporary life. At the same time, the constructionist would be alerted to the possible dangers inherent in these same languages and actions. It is to this prospect that we now turn.

### MORAL DISCOURSE: NECESSARY AND DESIRABLE?

Although the language of individual morality plays a significant role in the organization and coherence of social life, and the revitalizing of traditional moral languages enriches the range and potential of our interchanges, we cannot thereby conclude that moral language is both essential and desirable for agreeable forms of social life. Such discourse may figure prominently in our daily actions, enabling us to intercede, give significant pause, and consider the broad consequence of our actions. However, as we have seen, this is not to say that the terms of morality (ethics, values, rights) are essential to the formation of a "good society." Rather, we must ask whether—and which—communal interests are best served by these sorts of performatives. Does talk of "the good" and "the moral" necessarily improve the likelihood of valued actions?

In the first instance, are the languages of "ought," "duty," "rights," "principles," and the like essential to agreeable forms of social life? It seems doubtful. For example, a smooth and unproblematic parent-infant relationship may be achieved without the benefit of specifically moral discourse. In the same way, most friendships, collegial relationships and business proceedings take place with little recourse to a vocabulary of moral approbation. There is little reason to believe, then, that without moral language, society would deteriorate or regress to savagery. People are fully capable of coordinating their actions without moral performatives.

More speculatively, I propose that such languages owe their development primarily to breaches in the acceptable patterns of interchange. Should an individual or group violate common customs, moral language can be employed as a means of correcting or rechanneling the offending action. In effect, moral language functions largely as a means of sustaining patterns of social interchange in danger of erosion. Such languages are not so much responsible for the generation of agreeable forms of society as they are rhetorical means for reinforcing lines of action already embraced. Satisfactory relationships require neither persons with moral states within their heads nor social institutions with moral credos.

This is not to say that moral languages are of small consequence in sustaining the existing order. However, if moral language chiefly serves performative functions—and particularly those of sustaining particular traditions—we must question whether such language is the most useful or effective vehicle for enhancing the quality of cultural life. If moral language is not essential, how does it function in comparison to other possible means of achieving the same ends? Here it is useful to consider Felson's (1984) research on convicted criminals. Individuals convicted for crimes of aggressive assault were asked to describe the incidents leading up to their assaultive actions. As these narratives revealed, the majority traced their actions to incidents in which someone (often the victim) was seen as acting immorally (breaking a proper rule), there was often a verbal admonishment (typically made by the offender), and the putative rule breaker often attempted to save face through a hostile reaction. Such hostility would then trigger the aggressive assault. In effect, when principles of the good were introduced into the situation, the human condition was not enhanced but rapidly deteriorated.

In my view this deterioration is often intensified by that very tradition fostering the search for moral foundations for society—from early theology and romanticist intuitionism to modernist attempts at rational foundations. And here I am speaking of traditions attempting to establish universal standards of the good—principles of right and wrong, codes of ethics, constitutional principles, bills of universal rights, and so on that aspire to speak beyond time and place. The problematic repercussions of such approaches are revealed in Gewirth's (1987) attempt to secure a rational basis for moral action. In his preface, Gewirth first attacks conventionalist forms of morality, that is, principles or rules that simply capture or express one's cultural tradition. As he points out,

> This approach . . . incurs a severe difficulty. For so long as the rightness or correctness of the principle itself . . . it not established, such a procedure still leaves the system without any warrant of its rightness or correctness.

> Partisans of *opposed* cultures, traditions, or social systems may each claim self-evidence for their own moral principles, and they hold their respective rules and judgments are the morally right ones. Hence a moral principle's success in justifying . . . any one culture, ideology, or tradition does nothing, of itself, to *prove [its] superiority* over the moral rules or judgments of *opposed* cultures or traditions. (p. x)

Gewirth then goes on to point out that "this fact has supplied one of the strongest intellectual motivations for the various ancient and modern thinkers who have tried to provide a firm, nonrelativist foundation for ethics. By giving a rational justification of one or another supreme moral principle, they have hoped to *disprove or establish the wrongness of rival principles*" (p. x). And Gewirth then notes, no attempt to establish a superior system has been successful; in each case critics have located serious flaws. His challenge, then, is to "present a new version of rational justification" that will give precedence to one moral system over all others.[11]

I have italicized several key words and phrases in these passages in order to reveal a central metaphor underlying much work within the universalist tradition. In effect, it is a metaphor of conflict—of opposition, of rivalry, and the ultimate quest for one system or culture that will achieve superiority over all. Or, to put it in the extreme, it is a quest for universal dominion.

Such hegemonic tendencies often act to disrupt otherwise satisfactory forms of cultural life—forms that often have long histories and operate with a finely balanced sophistication. As the precepts of any group strive toward universality, they operate to discredit ways of life on other groups and to champion as their replacement home customs and folk mores. Thus, as Christian missionaries carry the gospel to other lands, their moral injunctions serve to discredit local customs and justify actions that are disruptive, thus damaging patterns of long-standing utility within the local setting. As Westerners concerned with the liberation of women, we may decry the veiling of the female race in the Islamic world; are the veils not oppressive to women and thus both unjust and inhumane? Yet within traditional Islamic culture the veil plays an important role in constituting and sustaining a large number of interrelated customs and rituals. To remove it on Western ideological grounds would be to threaten Islamic cultural identity itself. (To estimate the effects of removing the veil, consider the results on an expansionary Muslim movement that sought, in the name of a superior morality, to place such veils on the faces of contemporary Western women.) It is not ultimately a matter of ideology or morality that is at stake here, for there is nothing about desiring gender equality that necessarily, and without considerable interpretive work, speaks to matters of facial veiling. Rather, valuational precepts become the justification for undermining congenial and satisfying ways of life in other worlds.[12]

More extreme than the deterioration of cultural traditions are the corrosive hostilities invited by the language of moral superiority. When preferred ways of life are labled as universally good and deviations as immoral, evil, and inferior, the stage is set for brutalizing conflict. The major problem of arrogating local preferences to the status of universal principles is that the latter brook no compromise, and deviants take on an inhuman demeanor. The number of deaths resulting from claims to superior values is, I suspect, beyond calculation.

## CRITICAL THINKING QUESTIONS

1. According to Gergen, Western culture has traditionally celebrated the individual mind as the locus of reason, and thus, of knowledge. How does Gergen believe that communication is the most important factor in this process?
2. As a social constructionist, Gergen believes the relationship, not the individual is the locus of knowledge. Explain this concept.
3. How can dialogue enhance the ethical character of a relationship.
4. Write and analyze a case involving the concept of communication within relationships.

## NOTES

9. See also supportive work by Shweder and Much (1987) and Packer (1987) on the development of moral discourse.
10. In his subsequent work, *The Ethics of Authenticity* (1991), Taylor argues more forthrightly for the moral potential of an individualized discourse. As he avers, "I think that authenticity should be taken seriously as a moral ideal" (p. 22), where authenticity is taken to be "a certain way of being human that is *my* way. I am called upon to live my life in this way, and not in imitation of anyone else's . . . If I am not, I miss the point of my life, I miss what being human is for *me*" (p. 29).
11. Gewirth's own theory is based on what he takes as a transparent truth of human action: that it is voluntary, purposive, and under the individual agent's conscious control. Thus, at its core it is committed to a particular ontology of the person and a particular ideology of individualism—neither of which is shared across cultures and history.
12. See also Said's (1993) critique.

JOHN STUART MILL

# OF INDIVIDUALITY AS ONE OF THE ELEMENTS OF WELL-BEING

*John Stuart Mill (1806–1873), an English philosopher and economist, is best known as an ethicist for his work in* On Liberty *and* Utilitarianism. *This excerpt from* On Liberty, *printed in 1859, explains the ethics of understanding individual liberties within a society.*

Such being the reasons which make it imperative that human beings should be free to form opinions, and to express their opinions without reserve; and such the baneful consequences to the intellectual, and through that to the moral nature of man, unless this liberty is either conceded, or asserted in spite of prohibition; let us next examine whether the same reasons do not require that men should be free to act upon their opinions—to carry these out in their lives, without hindrance, either physical or moral, from their fellow-men, so long as it is at their own risk and peril. This last proviso is of course indispensable. No one pretends that actions should be as free as opinions. On the contrary, even opinions lose their immunity, when the circumstances in which they are expressed are such as to constitute their expression a positive instigation to some mischievous act. An opinion that corn-dealers are starvers of the poor, or that private property is robbery, ought to be unmolested when simply circulated through the press, but may justly incur punishment when delivered orally to an excited mob assembled before the house of a corn-dealer, or when handed about among the same mob in the form of a placard. Acts of whatever kind, which, without justifiable cause, do harm to others, may be, and in the more important cases absolutely require to be, controlled by the unfavorable sentiments, and, when needful, by the active interference of mankind. The liberty of the individual must be thus far limited; he must not make himself a nuisance to other people. But if he refrains from molesting others in what concerns them, and merely acts according to his own inclination and judgment in things which concern himself, the same reasons which show that opinion should be free, prove also that he should be allowed, without molestation, to carry his opinions into practice at his own cost. That mankind are not infallible; that their truths, for the most part, are only half-truths; that unity of opinion, unless resulting from the fullest and freest comparison of opposite opinions, is not desirable, and diversity not an evil, but a good, until mankind are much more capable than at present of recognizing all sides of the truth, are principles applicable to men's modes of action, not less than to their opinions. As it is useful that while mankind are imperfect there should be different opinions, so is it that there should be different experiments of living; that free scope should be given to varieties of character, short of injury to others; and that the worth of different modes of life should be proved practically, when any one thinks fit to try them. It is desirable, in short, that in things which do not primarily concern others, individuality should assert itself. Where, not the person's own character, but the traditions of customs of other people are the rule of conduct, there is wanting one of the principal ingredients of human happiness, and quite the chief ingredient of individual and social progress.

In maintaining this principle, the greatest difficulty to be encountered does not lie in the appreciation of means towards an acknowledged end, but in the indifference of persons in general to the end itself. If it were felt that the free development of individuality is one of the leading essentials of well-being; that it is not only a coordinate element with all that is designated by the terms civilization, instruction, education, culture, but is itself a necessary part and condition of all those things; there would be no danger that liberty should be undervalued, and the adjustment of the boundaries between it and social control would present no extraordinary difficulty. But the evil is, that individual spontaneity is hardly recognized by the common modes of thinking as having any intrinsic worth, or deserving any regard on its own account. The majority, being satisfied with the ways of mankind as they now are (for it is they who make them what they are), cannot comprehend why those ways should not be good enough for everybody; and what is more, spontaneity forms no part of the ideal of the majority of moral and social reformers, but is rather looked on with jealousy, as a troublesome and perhaps rebellious obstruction to the general acceptance of what these reformers, in their own judgment, think would be best for mankind. Few persons, out of Germany, even comprehend the meaning of the doctrine which Wilhelm von Humboldt, so eminent both as a *savant* and as a politician, made the text of a treatise—that "the end of man, or that which is prescribed by the eternal or immutable dictates of reason, and not suggested by vague and transient desires, is the highest and most harmonious development of his powers to a complete and consistent whole;" that, therefore, the object "towards which every human being must ceaselessly direct his efforts, and on which especially those who design to influence their fellow-men must ever keep their eyes, is the individuality of power and development;" that for this there are two requisites, "freedom, and a variety of situations;" and that from the union of these arise "individual vigor and manifold diversity," which combine themselves in "originality."[1]

Little, however, as people are accustomed to a doctrine like that of Von Humboldt, and surprising as it may be to them to find so high a value attached to individuality, the question, one must nevertheless think, can only be one of degree. No one's idea of excellence in conduct is that people should do absolutely nothing but copy one another. No one would assert that people ought not to put into their mode of life, and into the conduct of their concerns, any impress whatever of their own judgment, or of their own individual character. On the other hand, it would be absurd to pretend that people ought to live as if nothing whatever had been known in the world before they came into it; as if experience had as yet done nothing towards showing that one mode of existence, or of conduct, is preferable to another. Nobody denies that people should be so taught and trained in youth, as to know and benefit by the ascertained results of human experience. But it is the privilege and proper condition of a human being, arrived at the maturity of his faculties, to use and interpret experience in his own way. It is for him to find out what part of recorded experience is properly applicable to his own circumstances and character. The traditions and customs of other people are, to a certain extent, evidence of what their experience has taught *them;* presumptive evidence, and as such, have a claim to this deference: but, in the first place, their experience may be too narrow; or they may not have interpreted it rightly. Secondly, their interpretation of experience may be correct but unsuitable to him. Customs are made for customary circumstances, and customary characters: and his circumstances or his character may be uncustomary. Thirdly, though the customs be both good as customs, and suitable to him, yet to conform to custom, merely *as* custom, does not educate or develop in him any of the qualities which are the distinctive endowment of a human being. The human faculties of perception, judgment, discriminative feeling, mental activity, and even moral preference, are exercised only in making a choice. He who does anything

---

[1] *The Sphere and Duties of Government,* from the German of Baron Wilhelm von Humboldt, pp. 11-13.

because it is the custom, makes no choice. He gains no practice either in discerning or in desiring what is best. The mental and moral, like the muscular powers, are improved only by being used. The faculties are called into no exercise by doing a thing merely because others do it, no more than by believing a thing only because others believe it. If the grounds of an opinion are not conclusive to the person's own reason, his reason cannot be strengthened, but is likely to be weakened by his adopting it: and if the inducements to an act are not such as are consentaneous to his own feelings and character (where affection, or the rights of others are not concerned), it is so much done towards rendering his feelings and character inert and torpid, instead of active and energetic.

He who lets the world, or his own portion of it, choose his plan of life for him, has no need of any other faculty than the ape-like one of imitation. He who chooses his plan for himself, employs all his faculties. He must use observation to see, reasoning and judgment to foresee, activity to gather materials for decision, discrimination to decide, and when he has decided, firmness and self-control to hold to his deliberate decision. And these qualities he requires and exercises exactly in proportion as the part of his conduct which he determines according to his own judgment and feelings is a large one. It is possible that he might be guided in some good path, and kept out of harm's way, without any of these things. But what will be his comparative worth as a human being? It really is of importance, not only what men do, but also what manner of men they are that do it. Among the works of man, which human life is rightly employed in perfecting and beautifying, the first in importance surely is man himself. Supposing it were possible to get houses built, corn grown, battles fought, causes tried, and even churches erected and prayers said, by machinery—by automatons in human form—it would be a considerable loss to exchange for these automatons even the men and women who at present inhabit the more civilized parts of the world, and who assuredly are but starved specimens of what nature can and will produce. Human nature is not a machine to be built after a model, and set to do exactly the work prescribed for it, but a tree, which requires to grow and develop itself on all sides, according to the tendency of the inward forces which make it a living thing.

It will probably be conceded that it is desirable people should exercise their understandings, and that an intelligent following of custom or even occasionally an intelligent deviation from custom, is better than a blind and simply mechanical adhesion to it. To a certain extent it is admitted, that our understanding should be our own: but there is not the same willingness to admit that our desires and impulses should be our own likewise; or that to possess impulses of our own, and of any strength, is anything but a peril and a snare. Yet desires and impulses are as much a part of a perfect human being, as beliefs and restraints: and strong impulses are only perilous when not properly balanced; when one set of aims and inclinations is developed into strength, while others, which ought to coexist with them, remain weak and inactive. It is not because men's desires are strong that they act ill; it is because their consciences are weak. There is no natural connection between strong impulses and a weak conscience. The natural connection is the other way. To say that one person's desires and feelings are stronger and more various than those of another, is merely to say that he has more of the raw material of human nature, and is therefore capable, perhaps of more evil, but certainly of more good. Strong impulses are but another name for energy. Energy may be turned to bad uses; but more good may always be made of an energetic nature, than of an indolent and impassive one. Those who have most natural feeling, are always those whose cultivated feelings may be made the strongest. The same strong susceptibilities which make the personal impulses vivid and powerful, are also the source from whence are generated the most passionate love of virtue, and the sternest self-control. It is through the cultivation of these, that society both does its duty and protects its interests: not by rejecting the stuff of which heroes are made, because it knows not how to make them. A person whose desires and impulses are his own—are the expression of his own nature, as it has been developed and modified by his own culture—is said to have a character. One whose desires and impulses are not his own, has no character, no more than a steam-engine has a character. If, in addition to being his own, his impulses are strong, and are under the government of a strong will, he has an energetic character. Whoever thinks that individuality of desires and impulses should not be encouraged to unfold itself, must maintain that society has no need of strong natures—is not the better for containing many persons who have much character—and that a high general average of energy is not desirable. . . .

In our times, from the highest class of society down to the lowest every one lives as under the eye of a hostile and dreaded censorship. Not only in what concerns others, but in what concerns only themselves, the individual, or the family, do not ask themselves—what do I prefer? or, what would suit my character and disposition? or, what would allow the best and highest in me to have fair play, and enable it to grow and thrive? They ask themselves, what is suitable to my position? what is usually done by persons of my station and pecuniary circumstances? or (worse still) what is usually done by persons of a station and circumstances superior to mine? I do not mean that they choose what is customary, in preference to what suits their own inclination. It does not occur to them to have any inclination, except for what is customary. Thus the mind itself is bowed to the yoke: even in what people do for pleasure, conformity is the first thing thought of; they like in crowds; they exercise choice only among things commonly done: peculiarity of taste, eccentricity of conduct, are shunned equally with crimes: until by dint of not following their own nature, they have no nature to follow: their human capacities are withered and starved: they become incapable of any strong wishes or native pleasures, and are generally without either opinions or feelings of home growth, or properly their own. Now is this, or is it not, the desirable condition of human nature?

## CRITICAL THINKING QUESTIONS

1. Examine Mill's concepts of the individual and liberty.
2. How does Mill suggest that one make ethical decisions within the concept of liberty?
3. Give an example from your own experience that involved losing an individual freedom that benefited the whole group.
4. Write and analyze a case involving a loss of individual liberty. Examine the moral complications between the self and society when loss of liberty occurs.

# CONTEMPORARY CASE

## *Self Versus Society: A Case of Date Rape*

Deb, a 37-year-old woman, was date raped by a man she had been out with twice. The morning after the rape, Deb called her general practitioner (GP), told the receptionist/nurse what had happened, and requested emergency contraception. The receptionist replied, "We don't do that kind of medicine; you'll have to go to your OB-GYN." The receptionist/nurse at the OB-GYN office told Deb that they didn't give out "morning after pills," and if she were raped, she would have to go to the emergency room (ER) at the local hospital for help. Deb then called the ER, and the receptionist there told her that they did have such medication, but in order for them to give it to her, Deb would have to file a criminal complaint and go through a police investigation. Deb had experienced the misogyny inherent in our legal system and did not choose to go on trial for having been raped. So Deb called the Women's Health Center, where she was told that they only functioned as a reference and support system, and didn't actually administer medication, but if she wanted to talk about it, they would be glad to listen. Finally Deb called Planned Parenthood and was immediately admitted. After instructing Deb about the emergency contraception, the person who treated her then suggested Deb take a wide-spectrum antibiotic, which would cover venereal diseases caused by bacteria.

The next week Deb was at her GP's office for her son's school physical (preventive medicine) and asked to speak privately with the doctor. Deb told him of her experience and how frustrated and disappointed she was with the "disgraceful" manner in which his office had handled the situation. He replied, "We have to be very careful; what we're really talking about here is a moral issue." To which Deb thought, "Of course it's a moral issue—I was raped and no one would help me!" But before she could say anything, he went on, "If I had seen you, I would have counseled you differently. We, at this office, don't believe in giving abortion pills." Deb then explained to the doctor that the medication she took was not an "abortion pill." The medication she took alters the lining of the uterus so that if an egg is fertilized, it cannot implant; consequently, calling it an abortion pill is a misnomer because there is never anything to abort. To that the doctor replied that he wasn't going to argue and essentially dismissed Deb from the office.

Deb had been divorced 12 years, and had two graduate degrees, which is to say that she had a certain amount of experience and knowledge. She knew the medical treatment that she needed and was determined to do what was necessary to see that she received such treatment. But being refused at four different medical services was very intimidating, especially when Deb was so vulnerable, suffering from great pain, shame, and confusion. It is likely that if she were in her teens, or even in her early twenties, she would have been so intimidated by the response she received from the medical offices that she wouldn't have continued her search for help.

1. How does an understanding of self-interest help in this type of dilemma? Would a less mature individual have had problems pursuing their desired course of action?

2. What social constructions made it difficult for Deb to take emergency precautions following the rape? How are these social constructions replaced? Should they be?

3. Why is this case a question of individual liberty for Deb? How would Mill support the request made by Deb?

4. What nonverbal communication is present in this case? How is it important?

# 3

## IMPORTANCE OF FRIENDSHIP

### ARISTOTLE

### FRIENDSHIP

*Born in northern Greece, Aristotle (384–322 B.C.E.) studied with Plato for 18 years then set up his own school in Athens. The bulk of his numerous writings consists of either his lecture notes or other treatises used by his students. In this selection, Aristotle emphasizes three types of friendships, with the true friend being the most rare and important.*

### BOOK VIII

#### FRIENDSHIP OR LOVE

AFTER the foregoing, a discussion of friendship will naturally follow, as it is a sort of virtue, or at least implies virtue, and is, moreover, most necessary to our life. For no one would care to live without friends, though he had all other good things. Indeed, it is when a man is rich, and has got power and authority, that he seems most of all to stand in need of friends; for what is the use of all this prosperity if he have not opportunity for benevolence, which is most frequently and most commendably displayed towards friends ? or how could his position be maintained and preserved without friends ? for the greater it is, the more is it exposed to danger. In poverty and all other misfortunes, again, we regard our friends as our only refuge. We need friends when we are young to keep us from error, when we get old to tend upon us and to carry out those plans which we have not strength to execute ourselves, and in the prime of life to help us in noble deeds—"two together" [as Homer says]; for thus we are more efficient both in thought and in action. . . .

Again, it seems that friendship is the bond that holds states together, and that lawgivers are even more eager to secure it than justice. For concord bears a certain resemblance to friendship, and it is concord that they especially wish to retain, and dissension that they especially wish to banish as an enemy. If citizens be friends, they have no need of justice, but though they be just, they need friendship or love also; indeed, the completest realization of justice* seems to be the realization of friendship or love also.

Moreover, friendship is not only an indispensable, but also a beautiful or noble thing: for we commend those who love their friends, and to have many friends is thought to be a noble thing; and some even think that a good man is the same as a friend.† . . .

The kinds of friendship accordingly are three, being equal in number to the motives of love; for any one of these may be the basis of a mutual affection of which each is aware.

Now, those who love one another wish each other's good in respect of that which is the motive of their love. Those, therefore, whose love for one another is based on the useful, do not love each other for what they are, but only in so far as each gets some good from the other.

It is the same also with those whose affection is based on pleasure; people care for a wit, for instance, not for what he is, but as the source of pleasure to themselves.

Those, then, whose love is based on the useful care for each other on the ground of their own good, and those whose love is based on pleasure care for each other on the ground of what is pleasant to themselves, each loving the other, not as being what he is, but as useful or pleasant.

These friendships, then, are "accidental;" for the object of affection is loved, not as being the person or character that he is, but as the source of some good or some pleasure. Friendships of this kind, therefore, are easily dissolved, as the persons do not continue unchanged; for if they cease to be pleasant or useful to one another, their love ceases. But the useful is nothing permanent, but varies from time to time. On the disappearance, therefore,

---

*τῶν δικαίων τὸ μάλιστα, sc. τὸ ἐπιεικές : cf. V. 10, and VI. 11, 2.

† Cf. Plato, Rep., 334.

of that which was the motive of their friendship, the friendship itself is dissolved, since it existed solely with a view to that.

Friendship of this kind seems especially to be found among elderly men (for at that time of life men pursue the useful rather than the pleasant) and those middle-aged and young men who have a keen eye to what is profitable. But friends of this kind do not generally even live together; for sometimes they are by no means pleasant (nor indeed do they want such constant intercourse with others, unless they are useful); for they make themselves pleasant only just so far as they have hopes of getting something good thereby.

With these friendships is generally classed the kind of friendship that exists between host and guest.*

The friendship of young men is thought to be based on pleasure; for young men live by impulse, and, for the most part, pursue what is pleasant to themselves and what is immediately present. But the things in which they take pleasure change as they advance in years. They are quick to make friendships, therefore, and quick to drop them; for their friendship changes as the object which pleases them changes; and pleasure of this kind is liable to rapid alteration.

Moreover, young men are apt to fall in love; for love is, for the most part, a matter of impulse and based on pleasure: so they fall in love, and again soon cease to love, passing from one state to the other many times in one day.

Friends of this kind wish to spend their time together and to live together; for thus they attain the object of their friendship.

But the perfect kind of friendship is that of good men who resemble one another in virtue. For they both alike wish well to one another as good men, and it is their essential character to be good men. And those who wish well to their friends for the friends' sake are friends in the truest sense; for they have these sentiments towards each other as being what they are, and not in an accidental way: their friendship, therefore, lasts as long as their virtue, and that is a lasting thing.

Again, each is both good simply and good to his friend; for it is true of good men that they are both good simply and also useful to one another.

---

*A family of importance in a Greek state was usually connected by ties of hospitality with other families in other states: persons so connected were not, not strictly friends, since they lived apart; but, for which there is no English equivalent.

In like manner they are pleasant too; for good men are both pleasant in themselves and pleasant to one another: for every kind of character takes delight in the acts that are proper to it and those that resemble these; but the acts of good men are the same or similar.

This kind of friendship, then, is lasting, as we might expect, since it unites in itself all the conditions of true friendship. For every friendship has for its motive some good or some pleasure (whether it be such in itself or relatively to the person who loves), and is founded upon some similarity: but in this case all the requisite characteristics belong to the friends in their own nature; for here there is similarity and the rest, viz. what is good simply and pleasant simply, and these are the most lovable things: and so it is between persons of this sort that the truest and best love and friendship is found.

It is but natural that such friendships should be uncommon, as such people are rare. Such a friendship, moreover, requires long and familiar intercourse. For, as the proverb says, it is impossible for people to know one another till they have consumed the requisite quantity of salt together. Nor can they accept one another as friends, or be friends, till each show and approve himself to the other as worthy to be loved. Those who quickly come to treat one another like friends may wish to be friends, but are not really friends, unless they not only are lovable, but know each other to be so; a wish to be friends may be of rapid growth, but not friendship.

This kind of friendship, then, is complete in respect of duration and in all other points, and that which each gets from the other is in all respects identical or similar, as should be the case with friends.

The friendship of which pleasure is the motive bears some resemblance to the foregoing; for good men, too, are pleasant to each other. So also does that of which the useful is the motive; for good men are useful also to one another. And in these cases, too, the friendship is most likely to endure when that which each gets from the other is the same (*e.g.* pleasure), and not only the same, but arising from the same source—a friendship between two wits, for instance, rather than one between a lover and his beloved. For the source of pleasure in the latter case is not the same for both: the lover delights to look upon his beloved, the beloved likes to have attentions paid him; but when the bloom of youth is gone, the friendship sometimes vanishes also; for the one misses the beauty that used to please him, the other misses the attentions. But, on the other hand, they frequently continue friends, *i.e.* when their intercourse has brought them to care for each other's characters, and they are similar in character.

Those who in matters of love exchange not pleasure but profit, are less truly and less permanently friends. The friendship whose motive is profit ceases when the advantage ceases; for it was not one another that they loved, but the profit.

For pleasure, then, or for profit it is possible even for bad men to be friends with one another, and good men with bad, and those who are neither with people of any kind, but it is evident that the friendship in which each loves the other for himself is only possible between good men; for bad men take no delight in each other unless some advantage is to be gained.

The friendship of good men, again, is the only one that can defy calumny; for people are not ready to accept the testimony of any one else against him whom themselves have tested. Such friendship also implies mutual trust, and the certainty that neither would ever wrong the other, and all else that is implied in true friendship; while in other friendships there is no such security.

For since men also apply the term friends to those who love one another for profit's sake, as happens with states (for expediency is thought to be the ground on which states make alliances), and also to those who love one another for pleasure's sake, as children do, perhaps we too ought to apply the name to such people, and to speak of several kinds of friendship—firstly, in the primary and strict sense of the word, the friendship of good men as such; secondly, the other kinds that are so called because of a resemblance to this: for these other people are called friends in so far as their relation involves some element of good, which constitutes a resemblance; for the pleasant, too, is good to those who love pleasant things. But these two latter kinds are not apt to coincide, nor do the same people become friends for the sake both of profit and pleasure; for such accidental properties are not apt to be combined in one subject.

Now that we have distinguished these several kinds of friendship, we may say that bad men will be friends for the sake of pleasure or profit, resembling one another in this respect, while good men, when they are friends, love each other for what they are, *i.e.* as good men. These, then, we say, are friends simply; the others are friends accidentally and so far as they resemble these.

But just as with regard to the virtues we distinguish excellence of character or faculty from excellence manifested, so is it also with friendship: when friends are living together, they take pleasure in, and do good to, each other; when they are asleep or at a distance from one another, they are not acting as friends, but they have the disposition which, if manifested, issues in friendly acts; for distance does not destroy friendship simply, but the manifestation of friendship. But if the absence be prolonged, it is thought to obliterate even friendship; whence the saying—

"Full many a friendship hath ere now been loosed By lack of converse."

. . . Those who accept each other's company, but do not live together, seem to be rather well-wishers than friends. For there is nothing so characteristic of friendship as living together:* those who need help seek it thus, but even those who are happy desire company; for a solitary life suits them least of all men. But people cannot live together unless they are pleasant to each other, nor unless they take delight in the same things, which seems to be a necessary condition of comradeship.

The truest friendship then, is that which exists between good men, as we have said again and again. For that, it seems, is lovable and desirable which is good or pleasant in itself, but to each man that which is good or pleasant to him; and the friendship of good men for one another rests on both these grounds.

But it seems that while love is a feeling, friendship is a habit or trained faculty. For inanimate things can equally well be the object of love, but the love of friends for one another implies purpose, and purpose proceeds from a habit or trained faculty. And in wishing well for their sakes to those they love, they are swayed not by feeling, but by habit. Again, in loving a friend they love what is good for themselves; for he who gains a good man for his friend gains something that is good for himself. Each then, loves what is good for himself, and what he gives in good wishes and pleasure is equal to what he gets; for love and equality, which are joined in the popular saying are found in the highest degree in the friendship of good men. . . .

It is impossible to have friendship, in the full sense of the word, for many people at the same time, just as it is impossible to be in love with many persons at once (for it seems to be something intense, but intense feeling implies a single object); and it is not easy for one man to find at one time many very agreeable persons, perhaps not many good ones. Moreover, they must have tested and become accustomed to each other, which is a matter of great difficulty. But in the way of profit or pleasure, it is quite possible to find many† agreeable persons; for such people are not rare, and their services can be rendered in a short time.

---

*To a Greek, of course, this does not necessarily imply living under the same roof, as it does to us with our very different conditions of life.

†Reading πολλωὶς.

Of these other kinds, that which more nearly resembles true friendship
is that whose motive is pleasure, when each renders the same service to the
other, and both take pleasure in one another, or in the same things, such as
young men's friendships are wont to be; for a generous spirit is commoner
in them than in others. But the friendship whose motive is utility is the
friendship of sordid souls. Those who are happy do not need useful, but
pleasant friends; it is people to live with that they want, and though they
may for a short time put up with what is painful, yet no one could endure
anything continually, not even the good itself, if it were painful to him; so
they require that their friends shall be pleasant. But they ought, we may say,
to require that they shall be good as well as pleasant, and good for them;
then all the characteristics of a friend will be combined.

EPICURUS
_____

# Of Friendship

*Epicurus (342–270 B.C.E.) was a Greek philosopher born and educated on the
island of Samos in the Aegean Sea. Although he was a prolific writer, only a few
letters and fragments of his writings are extant. In this selection we learn that
disturbances in life are to be avoided at all costs for Epicurus. He believes that
association with friends who are similar to us intellectually and otherwise
brings about the best life.*

To the exercise of this Virtue (the last of all those, that retain to Justice)
all are obliged, who Love, and and beloved again by the same persons. And
well may we make it the Crown of this our Discourse upon the Virtues or
means to make life happy; when nothing that lies in the power of Wisdom
to obtain, doth afford more Comfort, more Delight, than true Friendship:
and the same Reason that confirms the mind not to fear any lasting or eternal Evil; doth also assure, that during life there is no Sanctuary, so safe, no
protection so secure, as that of true Friendship which together with that
Security, doth adfer also very great pleasures.

II. FOR, as Enmity, Hate, Envy, Despite, are adverse to and inconsistent
with Pleasures; so are Friendships, and Amities not only the most faithful

Conservers, but also the most effectual and certain Causers of Pleasures, and that as well to ones Friend, as to one self: in that thereby men do not only enjoy the Good things of the present more fully but are erected and animated with hope of such as are to succeed in the future. And, since Solitude and want of Friends exposeth a man to dangers and fears; certainly it must be very highly rational in us, to procure Friendships whereby the mind may be confirmed in the present, and possessed with lively hopes of enjoying very great Pleasures in the future.

III. BUT, in the choice of our Friends, we are to be exceeding cautious and prudent: for it concerns us to be more circumspect with whom we eat; than about what we eat: To eat ones meat alone, and spend ones days in solitude; indeed, is to live the life of a Lion or a Wolf: and yet no friend is better than such a one, that is not as well pleasant, as faithful, so that his Conversation may be the best sawce to our meat. Such a friend, therefore, is to be sought for, to whom nothing is more in esteem, than candor, Simplicity and Verity; and who is not morose, querulous and murmuring at all things, but full of Complacency, Alacrity, and pleasant Hopes, that so his Conversation may not sowre, but sweeten the occurrences of life.

IV. FRIENDSHIP, we acknowledge, doth consist in, and is kept alive by the mutual participation of Pleasures, or Goods; and yet we cannot admit it to be therefore necessary, that betwixt Friends there should be a Community of the Goods of Fortune: as that Philosopher conceived, who was the Author of that saying, that *among Friends all things are Common*. And our Reason is, that Community of Estates implies mutual diffidence or distrust of each others Constancy, in case of Adversity or Poverty on one part: and Distrust is wholly inconsistent with friendship. They only are friends, who can with full Confidence and freedom take and make use of so much of their friends Goods or Estate, as the necessity of their present condition doth require; and this no otherwise, than as if it were absolutely their own, though each partly still reserves a propriety in the full of his own Estate.

V. THIS, we are assured, will sound strange in the ears of the Vulgar; but, what are the Common People to us, seeing that no Faith or Constancy is to be found in their Kindness and Friendship? For, being wholly uncapable of any part of Wisdom, that might render their Conversation commendable and grateful; and as uncapable of either understanding what is privately, what publickly profitable, or what's the difference betwixt Good Manners and Bad; it is impossible they should have any Sentiments of the Goods of Amity and Friendship; and consequently that they should in any measure fulfill the duties thereof.

VI. WE speak, therefore, of Wise men only, among whom there is as it were a firm Covenant and League, not to love their friends less than themselves. Reason dictating, that it may, and should be so; and Experience assuring that it frequently hath been so. So that it is most evident; as well that such a perfect Conjunction (you may call it Union) may be made betwixt Wise men; as that nothing doth more conduce to the Quiet and Pleasure of life; than such a Conjunction once made and conserved.

VII. FOR, as it is impossible for us, to conserve the sweetness and security of our lives firm and lasting, without the influence of friendship; so it is equally impossible to conserve Friendship firm and lasting, without that Cement of Loving our Friends, at the same rate, as we do ourselves. This, therefore, and Pleasure are the inseparable. Adjuncts of Friendship: and who so doth not hold so full a Sympathy with his Friend, as to rejoyce at his joy, and condole with him in his sorrow; doth but pretend to the noble title of a Friend.

VIII. CONSIDERING this, the Wise man will be sure, to stand equally affected toward himself, and his Friend; what labours and pains he undergoes for his own Security and Pleasures, the same will he undergo for the Security and Pleasures of his Friend: and as he rejoiceth to think, that he hath one, with whom he may sit, and to whom he may administer in his sickness, whom he may visit and assist in case of imprisonment, and whom he may relieve in case of want; so will it rejoice him to be confident that he hath one, who will stick close to him, in sickness, imprisonment, want and all other Calamities. And not only this; but his love will be so great to him, as to oblige him to suffer the greatest of torments, nay, if occasion be, even Death it self for his Friends sake.

IX. WE have known, Certainly (and from our Fathers, in whose memories it was fresh) that many of those Wise and Good men, who had the happiness of procuring to themselves full Confidence and Security in the Society of men, living in one and the same opinion, and the self-same affections with themselves; have lived in a most pleasant and mutually comfortable League of Friendship, and been conjoined with so absolute a Neerness each to other, as that they could heartily, and without the least of reluctancy, wish to suffer death in the place of their friend destined to die.

## CRITICAL THINKING QUESTIONS

1. Examine and analyze Epicurus' theory on an ethical friendship.
2. Epicurus believes that happiness is achieved through the simple and harmonious pleasures that preserve peace of mind and bodily health. How do these traits fit within an ideal friendship?

3. Can friendship with those not similar to us bring the best in life? Support your point of view.
4. Write and analyze a case involving escape from a worldly existence to a place where one spends time with friends in philosophical deliberation.

LAURA TRACY

# INTIMACY AND JUDGMENT AMONG SISTERS AND FRIENDS

*Laura Tracy is an author and scholar. In this 1991 excerpt from her book,* The Secret Between Us: Competition Among Women, *Tracy details relationships between sisters and friends. She sees many similarities between the two friendships. One similarity is a problem with competition between females.*

## INTIMACY AND JUDGMENT AMONG SISTERS AND FRIENDS

As we have seen, "sisterhood" in friendships and families is a conflicted experience, in which women forge powerful bonds—both loving and hateful. "Sisters" can be the best of friends or the worst enemies.

This is important information for women. It allows us to understand who our friends are and why we chose them. It allows us to see that we choose our friends to confirm our view of the world—perspectives we developed as older and younger sisters. It also allows us to understand why the relationships with the men in our lives often seem so difficult, while our friendships seem so easy. Frequently the men we choose to love replicate the relationships we experienced with our sisters, *not* with our fathers and mothers.

For example, all too often, sisters are unable to talk to each other about their competition. Instead of a relationship based on disagreement and resolution, they are locked into one based on judgment and evaluation.

"I don't know how to tell her how I feel about her feeling judged," said Hallie, forty-nine, about her younger sister. "I want to say, 'You don't have to defend yourself; we're different,' but something stops me. The words aren't there. And I guess my defensiveness is equally high."

Like Hallie, most of the sisters I talked to revealed that when they thought about their sisters, they judged them as they would not dream of judging their friends.

Almost without exception, too, these were the same sorts of judgments they made about the men in their lives.

Libby, forty-seven, expressed it well. "When I'm at a party with my husband," she said, "at some level I expect the other people there to judge me according to how they perceive him. I've discovered that indirectly I monitor his behavior, watching to see whether he's being too loud or too quiet, whether he's offending anyone. I know this is wrong, but it's hard to let go of the feeling that when they react to him, they also wonder how I could have married someone like that."

Libby describes a confusion of identity shared by many women. Unlike men, as women grow up they are encouraged to form identities based on connection with other people. As Nancy Chodorow writes, women develop fluid, permeable ego boundaries. Women feel that who they are is connected intricately with the other people in their lives. While such connection can be a real strength, it also can be a liability in adult life.

Emotionally, we can feel joined at the hip to our husbands and children, and to our sisters. Our joint identities can make us feel that the actions and behavior, even the personalities, of our families tacitly comment on ourselves.

Yet at the same time, most women also believe that correcting a disturbed relationship with a sister means getting closer to her. We think that the problem is intimacy. We believe that intimacy means more, rather than less, closeness. However, when sisters get closer to each other, often they increase their secret judgments.

In contrast, genuine intimacy depends on knowing that another person is separate, really other. It depends on respecting another person's difference, on tolerating her faults because they belong to her, not to oneself.

Although it is very difficult to change our relationships with our sisters, knowing that *we* are judging *them* can have direct impact on relationships with husbands and lovers.

Sometimes, in fact, focusing on sister relationships produces unexpected illumination. For example, June, forty-five, told me how, after several years of bitter anger, she finally came to understand her relationship with her husband's former wife.

"I knew something was wrong—wrong with me," said June, "because I was the one who stayed so angry at Helene, long after Neil had let go. Finally, I realized that I was relating to Helene just like I had related to my own sister putting Neil between us even though he was clear about his love and loyalty to me.

"I was the one who couldn't let go," June continued, "not until I could recognize that the hate I felt for Helene was a version of the anger I felt toward my sister. First, of course, I had to admit that I *was* so angry at my sister. Then I could recognize that it was the same emotion I felt toward Helene. I still feel it, but now I don't also feel so desperate about acting on it. When Neil talks to Helene now about the kids, I'm able to separate my feelings from the realty—the reality that he loves me, not her. In a funny way, now I feel like Helene is really my 'sister.' I don't think I'll ever love or even like her, but at least I'm able to accept her as part of the family." ...

But sisters judge each other. They feel defined by each other; they often spend years trying to be different because they fear that other people will judge *them* as *they* judge their sisters.

Ironically, when sisters compete with each other for difference, they are competing to evade the judgments they themselves are making about each other. They are competing to not judge themselves. Psychologists call this dynamic projective identification, meaning that we see in other people all the qualities we loathe about ourselves.

We are more comfortable, emotionally and psychologically, when we can believe that the parts of ourselves we hate are not part of us at all. They belong to our sisters.

However, recognizing our own judgmentalism toward our sisters can have a profound effect on our relationships both with our sisters *and* with women who are not our sisters. . . .

## NO EXIT: MORALITY AND LOYALTY BETWEEN SISTERS AND FRIENDS

When we dream of "sisterhood," I no longer believe we are thinking about our relationships with biological sisters. Instead, relationships between adult sisters constitute a trail, not a core. What sisters really see when they look at each other is historical research. The competition between adult sisters provides the most visible traces of the cauldron in which they began to be formed.

The naturalist Loren Eiseley writes that when he goes out to discover the "secret of life," he does so in the autumn. "Of late years," Eiseley says, "I have come to suspect that the mystery may just as well be solved in a carved and intricate seed case out of which life has flown, as in the seed itself."

The competition between adult sisters, making each despair and often despise her sister, is exactly such a seed case. It is the husk remaining of the intense life sisters once shared. In it, as Eiseley writes, "there is an unparalleled opportunity to examine in sharp and beautiful angularity the shape of life, without its disturbing muddle of juices and leaves." But it is the rare sister who can get enough emotional distance to realize she deals with a dry husk rather than a raging volcano. . . .

The competition between adult sisters, no matter what age they are, keeps them their parents' children. It keeps their parents alive in the present, and it keeps the present in bondage to the past.

Sometimes the competition between sisters lasts only as long as their parents are alive. But for others sisters, their competition is all they feel toward each other. Giving it up would mean giving each other up. . . .

The intensity of their voices and their serious expressions told me that competition between female friends was far more significant than a simple fact of relationship; it was a point of honor, the equivalent of masculine insistence on courage or honesty. Like men admitting cowardice, women, when they faced their competitiveness toward their friends, felt their integrity was in question. They felt fragmented, as though they had failed to live up to an ideal of themselves they carried around in their imagination. . . .

Carol Gilligan tells us in *Mapping the Moral Domain* (page 151) that for women, "the willingness and the ability to care become a source of empowerment and a standard of self-evaluation."

Care, for women, takes on a moral dimension. It signals our ability to perceive another person in her own terms and to respond to need. In contrast, the failure to care, or detachment, feels somehow immoral to most women. Women believe that when they "don't care," they are bad people—unethical and dishonorable. Since women are loyal to other people rather than to social institutions, not caring signals disloyalty.

In a way, we can think about competition between women, particularly women who are friends, as the stage on which women act out moral and ethical decisions.

The disloyalty most women associate with competition feels like a failed morality. That's why recognizing our competition with our friends is so painful. Loyal friends don't compete with each other, not simply out of emotional desire, but also from a deeply rooted perception of moral rightness. Ironically, this means that when biological sisters openly compete with each other, we fail each other morally and ethically. We demonstrate *disloyalty*.

Most sisters know this, however, we may conceal the knowledge from ourselves and from our sisters. We know that the blood bond between us feels more like a facade of loyalty. We know it is not the real thing, the thing we dream of creating with our friends, but, even more ironically, the morality women associate with noncompetition does not belong to us. We have not created it.

Moral action inherently means self-determination. We act morally and ethically when we choose, with self-awareness and with consciousness of consequences, what we do. Women have not chosen noncompetition—it has been chosen for them.

In our society, there is a real division between the morality expected of men and the morality expected of women. Traditionally, women were not asked to demonstrate physical courage or adhere to a ritualized code of ethics. Instead, they were encouraged to practice "situational" ethics, making moral decisions based on human relationships, not impersonal standards of justice. Thus, most women developed an "ethic of care." For women, basing action on impersonal standards *feels* unethical and immoral.

However, this large division between men and women conceals the fact that women have not *chosen* to develop an ethic of care. It was formed by the traditional division of labor, aligning women with home and family, historically denying them access to public endeavor.

Especially now that Carol Gilligan's work allows us to realize how valuable is the ethic of care, it becomes even more difficult to recognize that it restricts women in the same way the ethic of justice restricts men. Through the ethic of care, women have developed intensely negative feelings about *not* caring. But women associate not caring with a wide variety of actions that can, in reality, produce "not-caring" behavior.

For example, when we link loyalty with noncompetition, we actually become disloyal. Our definition of loyalty is restricted to the narrow assumption that loyalty means agreement. Loyalty means no difference. When we refuse to compete with our friends, we really imply that we don't *trust* our friends to be different from us, nor do we trust ourselves to be loyal in the face of difference. Tacitly, we imply that we can be loyal only when our friends are like us.

In an ironic and terribly destructive way, many of us practice the morality of slaves and masters. Slaves always know more about their masters than masters know about slaves. Without complex information about masters, slaves would not survive their condition. Furthermore, slaves are certain—and right—that whatever information about them their masters possess will be used against them.

When we practice noncompetition with our friends, we unconsciously transfer into our relationships almost a parody of the master-slave relationship. When we don't tell our friends what we are really thinking, when we believe that competition signals disloyalty instead of disagreement, we act like slaves. When we fail to recognize our friends' difference and disagreement, when we assume that a competitive friend is no friend at all, we are masters.

Noncompetition as the basis for friendship conflicts with genuine friendship. Noncompetition means that we exclude *ourselves*—our own opinions, desires, and ideas—from our friendships. It is actually unethical: when we practice it, the connection between us is violated just as much as when we are excessively competitive—the fear we inherited from life with our biological sisters.

The way out of this dilemma for women is very difficult, but there is a way out, a way for us to *choose* our moral standard.

The answer is contained in work done by Albert Hirschman. Concerned about how people behaved in deteriorating organizations, Hirschman contrasted two strategies used for remedy: exit and voice.

Exit, exactly as the term implies, means that one leaves a sinking ship before going under with it. Exit is neat, clean, practical. It coincides with an ethic of justice supporting a consumer economy in which buyers are encouraged to switch from one product to another version made by a different company. When we use exit as a strategy for remedy, we do not stick around to try to change things.

In contrast, voice is messy, complicated, and personal. Hirschman writes that voice is located on a continuum "all the way from grumbling to violent protest." Using voice means that open, personal encounters are more valuable than private, secret, and impersonal action. Voice insists on community and on the sort of personal engagement inherently present in the concept of community. In terms of loyalty, voice operates to hold exit at bay. It enforces the loyalty of "hanging in there" in the face of disagreement and dissension.

People who use voice to solve problems in their relationships feel that real disloyalty is located in exit—leaving too soon to work things out, running away, escaping.

## CRITICAL THINKING QUESTIONS

1. Examine Tracy's notions of friendship and competition between friends and sisters.
2. What does Tracy believe is unique to relationships between sisters and friends? Why would these traits not exist in female-male relationships?
3. Write and analyze a case that involves competition in friendship between women.


WILLIAM K. RAWLINS

# ADULT FRIENDSHIPS

*William K. Rawlins, an associate professor of communication at Purdue University, has published extensively about tensions of communicating in friendships. In this 1992 excerpt from* Friendship Matters Communication, Dialectics and the Life Source, *Rawlins focuses on the importance of the private relationship in preference to the public persona.*

People disagree on the precise criteria or boundaries announcing the transition from young to mature adulthood. Even so, in providing some broad age-related parameters for this chapter, I view adult friendships as spanning Neugarten's (1968) time periods of maturity (from around 30 to 40 years old) and middle age (from 40 to around 65 years old), with later adulthood and old age approaching thereafter.

Like other periods of life, adulthood involves an ongoing configuring of self with others through communicating in diverse roles and relationships. As the adult years unfold, numerous choices regarding marital, parental, family, work, and community roles and performance define one's day-to-day possibilities and responsibilities while also restricting one's options for alternative life paths. Deciding to marry, have children, and pursue a specific career, for example, result in obligations, benefits, challenges, and frustrations that differ markedly from those of single or married persons without children and in other occupations. Further, many decisions emerging within the specific "life structure" (Levinson et al., 1979) fashioned by these earlier adult choices produce consequences affecting individuals profoundly (like children, spouse, close friends, partners, and employees) and a range of others to various degrees (like kin, in-law, co-workers, and acquaintances). Consequently, one's continuing life choices during most of adulthood are not simple functions of age or linear development. Instead, they compose an increasingly complex array of contigencies produced by previous selections in conjunction with one's social environment (Atchley, 1982).

However, in recognizing individual praxis, we must also acknowledge how little control many individuals have over their field of concrete options. To a great extent, each person's opportunities and obstacles are socially and culturally patterned according to gender, socioeconomic status (including educational and occupational advantages and disadvantages), marital status, as well as age (Pearlin, 1980). And the significance of one's age interacts with the other factors. Giele (1980) observes how those with privileged educations and better jobs experience changes occurring across adult life more favorably than those lacking such chances. Further, Neugarten (1968, p. 146) argues that the major events punctuating an "orderly and sequential" adulthood (for example, marriage, the arrival and departure of children, occupational promotions, and retirement) are understood through superimposing social and cultural "time clocks" onto biological ones. Thus, one's chronological age is not inherently meaningful, though it does readily represent "events that occur with the passage of time" (Neugarten et al. 1964, p. 197) that must be interpreted further in terms of specific contextual features.

In examining the forms and functions of friendships across the broad expanse of middle to later adulthood, I will employ Hess's (1972) conception that once configurations of personal and social roles begin to diversify during adulthood:

> the number and type of friendships open to an individual at particular stages of his [sic] life depend less upon explicit age criteria for the friendship role itself than upon the *other* roles that he plays. As his total cluster of roles changes over his lifetime, so do his friendship relations undergo change. (Hess, 1972, p. 361)

Studying friendships throughout adulthood involves deciphering their fit and ramifications within the friends' overall arrangements of roles and relationships, which are not strictly tied to age. Accordingly, this chapter will not present a comprehensive chronological series of adult developmental stages as its central focus: other depictions are available (Sheehy, 1974; Levinson et al., 1979). Instead, it is organized thematically around modal patterns and communicative exigencies of the social domains of work, marriage, parenthood, kinship, and neighborhood as they affect and reflect friendship processes, while mindful of various broad trends, contigencies, and changes which transpire over time (Basseches, 1984). Further, I will primarily discuss middle-class male and female patterns and practices of managing friendships across these interpenetrated realms.

One final matter is important in analyzing the friendships of adulthood. As dialectical totalities composed of multiple contradictory processes, adults' existential milieus constantly interweave stability and flux. In Pearlin's (1980, p. 174) words, "Adulthood is not a quiescent stretch interspersed with occasional change; it is a time in which change is continuous, interspersed with occasional quiescent interludes." Basseches (1984, p. 312) notes basic accord among authors on adult development regarding this "fundamental dialectical idea." Adults cultivate reasonably stable configurations of relationships of self with others, termed "life structures" by Levinson et al. (1979). However, inevitable periods of flux, questioning, and critical reflection trigger and reveal changes within oneself and in relations with one's spouse, family, friends, work associates, and/or the larger society. Consequently, individuals find themselves facing or avoiding the requirements of negotiating alternative internal and external arrangements. Viewed in this way, the daily events of adulthood continually present both incipient and undeniable practical and emotional challenges.

Farrell and Rosenberg (1981) suggest that adults typically experience their social nexus as blending worthwhile and confirming aspects with irritating, demeaning, and limiting ones. These features are taken for granted much of the time although events may coalesce to accentuate a person's awareness of them. Farrell and Rosenberg argue, "In this sense, adult development can be seen as an episodic heightening and diminishing of self-consciousness" (1981, p. 46). When consciously dissatisfied, a person may struggle to comprehend or change his or her self, situation or both (Farrell & Rosenberg, 1981). Such activity may include constructive, energetic engagement or detrimental, yet equally vigorous alienation, or some combination of these stances. During stable phases when disturbing issues are less salient, adults may adjust favorably to their circumstances or become unconsciously resigned, "an alienation that is not even aware of itself" (Farrell & Rosenberg, 1981, p. 46).

People continually face the urges and demands for change and adaptation as well as for stability and integrity in managing the internal, interpersonal, and public stresses and pleasures of adult life (Giele, 1980; Fiske, 1980). Living a full life, accomplishing and maintaining personal integrity and self-respect while getting along with others, and perceiving some meaningful continuity in one's existence are important goals throughout adulthood (Giele, 1980; Fiske, 1980). The ongoing achievement or subversion of these aims takes place in one's private and public relationships. How adult friendships figure in this process is the principal concern below.

## WORK LIFE AND ADULT FRIENDSHIPS

In considering work as the paramount organizing principle for middle class adult life, two types of work emerge: home making and money making. However, as cultural critics note, the requirements, rewards, punishments, and symbols of money making work dominate and saturate the public and private moments of middle class existence (Henry, 1971). For Americans in the work force, positively meeting the challenges of one's occupation favorably defines self; shirking them or failing threatens viable personhood. Our cultural image of "making something of oneself" is, for the most part, making money.

Even so, most people making money also like a home to return to, which necessitates home making work. Married and cohabiting couples, to varying degrees of shared and individual consciousness, arrange their work lives in different ways. Some modes include (1) both partners work full time to make money or develop their talents in ways to eventually produce income, with housework evenly divided or mutually paid for; (2) both partners work full time for or toward eventual income, with housework unevenly divided; (3) one person does money making while the other does home making work full time; and (4), resembling (3), only the homemaker also does part-time money-making work. A couple may shift from one mode to another as their family's internal and external circumstances change.

However, the gender alignments of these modes tend to skew in certain directions, especially when a couple has children. In the dual career couple (#2), the female frequently does the most home making work, which now includes taking care of children. Gilbert reports, "Fathers provide on the average about a third of the child care when mothers are employed full-time" (1988, p. 80). In mode (#3) she typically manages the home and raises children full time, and in (#4) also supplements the family income. My point here is to recognize that someone has to accomplish both types of work on an ongoing basis, though women have tended to embrace primary responsibilities for home making work (Oliker, 1989). I also want to stress that references to "work" or "occupation" in describing the middle class usually refer to those activities, which, in addition to other possible benefits, generate the income necessary for appropriate life-styles, thereby ignoring the labor of home making (Lopata, 1971; Bellah et al., 1985). In the words of a midlife, middle-class male I spoke with, "I never apologize for having to work. Work makes it all possible." The ramifications of this pervasive and privileged though narrowly conceived world of work for adult friendships is the subject of this section.

It is difficult to overstate the centrality of money-making work in composing the lives of middle-class Americans. The nature of one's work shapes adult self-images and values. According to Gould:

> When we attach ourselves to particular work, we are likely to stay with it because, if we are successful, it confirms our status as adults. In return for this gift of adultness, we tend to accept the explicit and implicit value system of the particular organization or career, becoming narrower in relation to our full potential while becoming deeper in relation to a specific real-life complacency. The work becomes us, not just our activity of choice, (1980, p. 228).

Work articulates one's sense of time, including the general contours and rhythms of one's waking hours, weekly and yearly calendars. Even one's biological age is experienced differently in various jobs. Many sales jobs and management positions expect considerable achievement and advancement by the early thirties; meanwhile, persons in occupations requiring extensive formal education beyond college, like professors, lawyers, and physicians, are typically just getting established at this age (Levinson et al., 1979). Moreover, how and with whom persons spend their time at work determines their place in society in two senses: first, with regard to their income and status (Levinson et al., 1979); and second, in terms of the multiple geographic relocations associated with upward mobility in their careers (Bellah et al., 1985). The recurring enterprise of making new friends and relinquishing old ones is a basic repercussion of pursuing occupational success, reconstructing interrelated senses of identity, and social connection for both adults and children (Maines, 1978).

For employed men and women, the workplace constitutes a primary pool and setting for making friends of varying degrees of closeness. People in similar jobs often share physical proximity, overlapping work schedules, common interests and projects, and allied values, which, taken together, can facilitate routine contact and friendship formation. Further, the culture and traditions of an organization may enhance its affiliative climate by permitting or encouraging joking relations, convivial break times, and lighthearted lunches, and by sponsoring ceremonies and activities outside of work, such as picnics, seasonal parties, and company sports teams (Fine, 1986).

Even so, several matters complicate the likelihood and nature of work friendships. First, people's overall attitudes toward their jobs say much about whether they will form friendships with fellow workers (Parker, 1964). Parker (1964, p. 217) found that people who considered their work "a central life interest," identified with it positively, and would choose to do it "even without financial necessity" were significantly more likely to report between two-thirds and all of their six closest friends as doing identical or associated work. Parker concluded, "If work experiences are not valued, friendships are less likely to arise there" (1964, p. 217). Indeed, if people are involved in, dedicated to, and derive personal esteem and/or social prestige from their occupation, working with others and talking shop afterward are likely to combine self-expression and emotional catharis with instrumental accomplishment. Such relationships may become close friendships.

But other factors further mediate professional attachments. The inherent goals of the actual work or the employing organization may affect how relationships are developed or experienced. For example, the people described above may be strongly committed to jobs ambodying inherently self-serving, divisive, and/or highly competitive aims or values. As a result, the time they spend together doing or discussing work ultimately serves an overarching agenda antithetical to close or real friendship. The more they agree on certain objectives or strategies, the more likely they are to be wary of one another. By comparison, other occupations may intrinsically strive for more edifying and/or encompassing goals not directly or simply reduced to dollars or profit. Accomplishment here includes the workers' contributions to the development and well-being of others and a shared social and/or natural environment. The inherently humane and collective values mutually enacted in doing and discussing such work may serve to draw individuals closer together as friends.

Such distinctions in the activities and moral visions of occupations and organizations are seldom so clearcut. Specific organizational cultures and subcultures may develop reward structures encouraging ethics of cooperation that subdue a rigidly competitive orientation among their workers. Likewise, people involved in seemingly primarily altruistic, aesthetic, or service-oriented pursuits may be organized or rewarded in ways that promote competition, greed, and material gain. To a degree, a culture encouraging genuine cooperation and concern for others amongs its members engenders and reflects friendship practices that a culture thriving on its participants' competition ultimately limits. But these tentative generalizations masks further ironies and tensions involved in the situated and ongoing achievement of friendships in work settings.

The duration and overlap of the time people spend working is a critical concern for developing friendships. If persons do little else but work, most of their socializing is likely to occur there or be associated with it. However, regular and extended interactions are contingent on both parties' work schedules and the amount of solitary and uninterrupted labor required by their jobs (Fine, 1986). Meeting at breaks or during and after work also depends on the degree of autonomy in one's job and ability to control one's own schedule. Thus, positions in the organizational hierarchy also pattern work affiliations. Co-workers who are relative equals and prime candidates for friendship are frequently accessible but also in direct competition for recognition, resources, and opportunities for advancement. By comparison, two parties' unequal status and power in an organization can normatively constrain a mutually negotiated friendship and strongly affect other company members' perceptions of it. Frequent or extended private conversations may be encouraged or discouraged by the schedules, norms, and physical and hierarchical arrangements of a workplace. And the sociability and "occupational community" associated with certain jobs may be voluntary and incidental to the work itself or fairly essential for competent performance in the organization (Parker, 1964).

Thus, several structural contingencies affect the possibility of two persons meeting on the job and becoming friends. Among other matters, these include (1) their attitudes toward and the nature of their occupation, (2) the amount of mutual competition versus cooperation or independence associated with their jobs, (3) the extent of freedom versus constraint in their daily interaction patterns, (4) their degree of equality versus inequality within the organization's hierarchy, and (5) their overall regularity and amount of time spent together during and after work.

Assuming some initial mutual interest, attraction, and/or liking, various relational scenarios emerge from different combinations of these elements. When relative equals do not primarily see themselves as competitors, compulsory time together on the job may involve "friendly relations" that could lead to friendship depending partly on the nature of their work, enjoyment of each other, degree of mutual assistance, and other time commitments (Kurth, 1970). People in professions requiring shared knowledge and cooperation in the specialized and collective handling of work-related challenges and problems often negotiate the relationship of "colleagues," a term ideally connoting mutual respect and good will, notably informed by the objective standards and conventions of the field involved (Lepp, 1966). Positive affiliations with colleagues resemble friendships and may develop into them over time, though collegiality does not require the voluntary interaction, person-qua-person orientation or depth of mutual concern of friendship. In light of their experiences in working together and observing each other's actions, personal qualities, and values, colleagues may also become close friends, indifferent work associates, or bitter enemies, thereby exceeding, affirming, or barely meeting the minimal requirements of professional collegiality.

Though its pervasiveness and intensity varies by organizational culture and the individuals' personal inclinations, most equals at work must compete with one another, especially earlier in their careers when they are "on the make" (Wilensky, 1968). If their schedules permit only occasional contact, they may maintain the simultaneous distance and "friendliness" characterizing the appropriate demeanor of cordial American business practice. But if compelled to interact frequently and/or for long periods, they may further personalize their encounters, enact "friendly relations," and become acquaintances, or even friends (Kurth, 1970; Paine, 1969). Burt (1983) found that as income and education increased and age decreased, individuals were more likely to report co-worker friends, but these were the most ambiguous relationships he studied. By comparison, Wilensky (1968) found high-seniority colleagues to report more stable friendships at work than the "lightly-held attachments" of the young. Equal status in the older group probably reflects more shared work experiences, acceptance of diminishing upward horizons, and common ground than active competition, whereas equal status among the young implies and incites competition. If competing equals can control their contact, its nature and extent will depend on their joint affinity, emphasis on comparative performance, perceptions of potential career impact, and other time constraints.

Since a spirit of equality pervades friendship, the inequality and unilateral control of one person over another dictated by organizational authority structures typically inhibits truly mutual friendships. Yet friendships are privately negotiated, and a superior and subordinate may become friends if they like each other, some common interests or facets of their relationship function as levelers, and they are able to separate suitably their professional and personal relationships. In such cases it is usually the superior's privilege to initiate the friendship outside or as part of work and to monitor how much it intrudes on "getting the job done." Because subordinates have much to gain by befriending a superior, they may be seen as apple-polishing, seeking favors, social climbing, or otherwise patently attempting to further their own careers through such affiliations.

For their part, senior work associates have few career-related incentives encouraging friendships with juniors. They acquire minimal status or upwardly influential connections; attributions of favoritism, compromised administrative "muscle," or conflicts of interest may tarnish perceptions of their decisions involving particular others; and they may be suspected of taking undue advantage of close subordinates, especially in cross-sex relationships (Fine, 1986). The type of arrangement advocated by Levinson et al. (1979) in these circumstances is a mentor relationship, which openly acknowledges structural inequality and the junior person's career development as its primary aim. Though intrinsically gratifying in many cases, and ultimately rewarding to both participants if the protege thrives in the organization and reflects well on his or her mentor, most mentor relationships are too fundamentally shaped by inequality and extrinsic considerations to be considered friendships. When capably, caringly and mutually negotiated, and if the junior is able to succeed and stand alone, however, the mentorship may eventually be renegotiated as a friendship (Levinson et al., 1979).

## CRITICAL THINKING QUESTIONS

1. Examine Rawlins's notions of communication beween friends.
2. What are the differences between the dialectic in the private and public relationship?
3. Write and analyze a case that involves friendship within both the private and public spheres.

## REFERENCES

Allan, G. A. (1979) *A sociology of friendship and kinship.* London: Allen and Unwin.

Atchley, R. C. (1975). Dimensions of widowhood in later life. *The Gerontologist, 15,* 176–178.

Bakan, D. (1966). *The duality of human existence.* Boston: Beacon.

Basseches, M. (1984). *Dialectical theory and adult development.* Norwood, NJ: Ablex.

Bellah, R. N., Madsen, R., Sullivan, W. M., Swidler, A., & Tipton, S. M. (1985). *Habits of the heart: Individualism and commitment in American life.* Berkeley: University of California Press.

Burt, R. S. (1983). Distinguishing relational contents. In R. S. Burt & M. J. Minor (Eds.), *Applied network analysis* (pp. 35–74). Beverly Hills: Sage.

Corwin, R., Taves, M. J., & Haas, E. J. (1960). Social requirements for occupational success: Internalized norms and friendship. *Social Forces, 39,* 135–140.

Farrell, M. P., & Rosenberg, S. D. (1981). *Men at midlife.* Boston: Auburn House.

Fine, G. A. (1986). Friendships in the work place. In V. J. Derlega & B. A. Winstead (Eds.), *Friendship and social interaction* (pp. 185–206). New York: Springer-Verlag.

Fiske, M. (1980). Changing hierarchies of commitment in adulthood. In N. J. Smelser & E. H. Erikson (Eds.), *Themes of work and love in adulthood* (pp 238–264). Cambridge, MA: Harvard University Press.

Giele, J. Z. (1980). Adulthood as transcendence of age and sex. In N. J. Smelser & E. H. Erikson (Eds.), *Themes of love and work in adulthood* (pp. 151–173). Cambridge, MA: Harvard University Press.

Gilbert, L. A. (1988). *Sharing it all: The rewards and struggles of two-career families.* New York: Plenum Press.

Gilligan, C. (1982). *In a different voice.* Cambridge: Harvard University Press.

Gould, R. L. (1980). Transformations during early and middle adult years. In N. J. Smelser & E. H. Erikson (Eds.), *Themes of love and work in adulthood,* (pp. 213–237). Cambridge, MA: Harvard University Press.

Gouldner, H., & Strong, M. S. (1987). *Speaking of friendship: Middle-class women and their friends.* New York: Greenwood Press.

Granovetter, M. S. (1974). *Getting a job.* Cambridge, MA: Harvard University Press.

Hellman, L. (1973). *Pentimento.* New York: Signet.

Henry, J. (1971). *Pathways to madness.* New York: Vintage Books.

Henry, W. E. (1971). The role of work in structuring the life cycle. *Human Development, 14,* 125–131.

Hess, B. (1972). Friendship. In M. W. Riley, M. Johnson, & A. Foner (Eds.), *Aging and Society: A sociology of age stratification* (Vol. 3, pp. 357–393). New York: Russell Sage Foundation.

Jacobson, D. (1976). Fair weather friend: Label and context in middle class friendships. In W. Arens & S. P. Montague (Eds.), *The American dimension* (pp. 149–160). New York: Alfred Publishing Co.

Kurth, S. B. (1970). Friendships and friendly relations. In G. J. McCall, M. M. McCall, N. K. Denzin, G. D. Suttles, & S. Kurth (Eds.), *Social relationships* (pp. 136–170). Chicago: Aldine.

Laumann, E. O. (1973). *Bond of pluralism: The form and substance of urban social networks,* New York: John Wiley.

Lepp, I. (1966). *The ways of friendship.* New York: Macmillan.

Levinson, D. J., Darrow, C. N., Klein, E. B., Levinson, M. H., & McKee, B. (1979). *The seasons of a man's life.* New York: Alfred A. Knopf.

Lewis, M., Young, G., Brooks, J., & Michalson, L. (1975). The beginning of friendship. In M. Lewis & L. A. Rosenblum (Eds.), *Friendship and peer relations* (pp. 27–66). New York: John Wiley.

Lewis, R. A. (1978). Emotional intimacy among men. *Journal of Social Issues, 34,* 108–121.

Lincoln, J. R., & Miller, J. (1979). Work and friendship ties in organizations: A comparative analysis of relational networks. *Administrative Science Quarterly, 24,* 181–199.

Lopata, H. Z. (1971). *Occupation: Housewife.* New York: Oxford.

Madden, T. R. (1987). *Women vs. women.* New York: Amacom.

Maines, D. R. (1978). Bodies and selves: Notes on a fundamental dilemma in demography. In N. Denzin (Ed.), *Studies in symbolic interaction* (Vol, 1, pp. 241–265). Greenwich, CT: JAI.

May, W. F. (1967). The sin against the friend: Betrayal. *Cross Currents, 17,* 158-170.

Neugarten, B. L. (Ed.) (1968). *Middle age and aging: A reader in social psychology.* Chicago: University of Chicago Press.

Neugarten, B. L., and associates. (1964). *Personality in middle and late life.* New York: Atherton.

Oliker, S. J. (1989). *Best friends and marriage: Exchange among women.* Berkeley University of California Press.

Paine, R. (1969). In search of friendship: An exploratory analysis in "middle class" culture. *Man, 4,* 505-524.

Parker, S. R. (1964). Type of work, friendship patterns, and leisure. *Human Relations, 17,* 215-220.

Pearlin, L. I. (1980). Life strains and psychological distress among adults. In N. J. Smelser & E. H. Erikson (Eds.), *Themes of work and love in adulthood* (pp. 174-192). Cambridge, MA: Harvard University Press.

Reisman, J. M. (1981). Adult friendships. In S. Duck & R. Gilmour (Eds.), *Personal relationships 2: Developing personal relationships* (pp. 205-230). London: Academic Press.

Sheehy, G. (1974). *Passages: Predictable crises of adult life.* New York: Dutton.

Wilensky, H. L. (1968). Orderly careers and social participation: The impact of work history on social integration in the middle mass. In B. L. Neugarten (Ed.), *Middle age and aging: A reader in social psychology* (pp. 321-340). Chicago & London: University of Chicago Press.

Williams, R. M., Jr., (1959). Friendship and social values in a suburban community: An exploratory study. *The Pacific Sociological Review, 2,* 3-10.

Wright, P. (1989). Gender differences in adults' same- and cross-gender friendships. In R. G. Adams & R. Blieszner (Eds.), *Older adult friendship* (pp. 197-221). Newbury Park: Sage.

M A Y A   A N G E L O U

## Mama and the Dentist

*Maya Angelou is the author of numerous books, including short stories, essays, poetry, and other writings. In 1982 she was awarded the lifetime appointment as the Reynolds Professor of American Studies at Wake Forest University in Winston-Salem, North Carolina. She was selected to read her poem "On the Pulse of Morning" at the inauguration of President Bill Clinton. "Mama and the Dentist," published in 1969 in* I Know Why the Caged Bird Sings, *details the experiences of discrimination in the friendship between a white dentist and a black woman whose granddaughter suffers because of the discrimination.*

The Angel of the candy counter had found me out at last, and was exacting excruciating penance for the stolen Milky Ways, Mounds, Mr. Goodbars and Hersheys with Almonds. I had two cavities that were rotten to the gums. The pain was beyond the bailiwick of crushed aspirins or oil of cloves. Only one thing could help me, so I prayed earnestly that I'd be allowed to sit under the house and have the building collapse on my left jaw. Since there was no Negro dentist in Stamps, nor doctor either, for that matter, Momma had dealt with previous toothaches by pulling them out (a string tied to the tooth while the other end looped over her fist), pain killers and prayer. In this particular instance the medicine had proved ineffective; there wasn't enough enamel left to hook a string on, and the prayers were being ignored because the Balancing Angel was blocking their passage.

I lived a few days and nights in blinding pain, not so much toying with as seriously considering the idea of jumping in the well, and Momma decided I had to be taken to a dentist. The nearest Negro dentist was in Texarkana, twenty-five miles away, and I was certain that I'd be dead long before we reached half the distance. Momma said we'd go to Dr. Lincoln, right in Stamps, and he'd take care of me. She said he owed her a favor.

I knew there were a number of whitefolks in town that owed her favors. Bailey and I had seen the books which showed how she had lent money to Blacks and whites alike during the Depression, and most still owed her. But I couldn't aptly remember seeing Dr. Lincoln's name, nor had I ever heard of a Negro's going to him as a patient. However, Momma said we were going, and put water on the stove for our baths. I had never been to a doctor, so she told me that after the bath (which would make my mouth feel better) I had to put on freshly starched and ironed underclothes from inside out. The ache failed to respond to the bath, and I knew then that the pain was more serious than that which anyone had ever suffered.

Before we left the Store, she ordered me to brush my teeth and then wash my mouth with Listerine. The idea of even opening my clamped jaws increased the pain, but upon her explanation that when you go to a doctor you have to clean yourself all over, but most especially the part that's to be examined, I screwed up my courage and unlocked my teeth. The cool air in my mouth and the jarring of my molars dislodged what little remained of my reason. I had frozen to the pain, my family nearly had to tie me down to take the toothbrush away. It was no small effort to get me started on the road to the dentist. Momma spoke to all the passers-by, but didn't stop to chat. She explained over her shoulder that we were going to the doctor and she'd "pass the time of day" on our way home.

Until we reached the pond the pain was my world, an aura that haloed me for three feet around. Crossing the bridge into whitefolks' country, pieces of sanity pushed themselves forward. I had to stop moaning and start walking straight. The white towel, which was drawn under my chin and tied over my head, had to be arranged. If one was dying, it had to be done in style if the dying took place in whitefolks' part of town.

On the other side of the bridge the ache seemed to lessen as if a white-breeze blew off the whitefolks and cushioned everything in their neighborhood—including my jaw. The gravel road was smoother, the stones smaller and the tree branches hung down around the path and nearly covered us. If the pain didn't diminish then, the familiar yet strange sights hypnotized me into believing that it had.

But my head continued to throb with the measured insistence of a bass drum, and how could a toothache pass the calaboose, hear the songs of the prisoners, their blues and laughter, and not be changed? How could one or two or even a mouthful of angry tooth roots meet a wagonload of powhitetrash children, endure their idiotic snobbery and not feel less important?

Behind the building which housed the dentist's office ran a small path used by servants and those tradespeople who catered to the butcher and Stamps' one restaurant. Momma and I followed that lane to the backstairs of Dentist Lincoln's office. The sun was bright and gave the day a hard reality as we climbed up the steps to the second floor.

Momma knocked on the back door and a young white girl opened it to show surprise at seeing us there. Momma said she wanted to see Dentist Lincoln and to tell him Annie was there. The girl closed the door firmly. Now the humiliation of hearing Momma describe herself as if she had no last name to the young white girl was equal to the physical pain. It seemed terribly unfair to have a toothache and a headache and have to bear at the same time the heavy burden of Blackness.

It was always possible that the teeth would quiet down and maybe drop out of their own accord. Momma said we would wait. We leaned in the harsh sunlight on the shaky railings of the dentist's back porch for over an hour.

He opened the door and looked at Momma. "Well, Annie, what can I do for you?"

He didn't see the towel around my jaw or notice my swollen face.

Momma said, "Dentist Lincoln. It's my grandbaby here. She got two rotten teeth that's giving her a fit."

She waited for him to acknowledge the truth of her statement. He made no comment, orally or facially.

"She had this toothache purt' near four days now, and today I said, 'Young lady, you going to the Dentist.'"

"Annie?"

"Yes, sir, Dentist Lincoln."

He was choosing words the way people hunt for shells. "Annie, you know I don't treat nigra, colored people."

"I know, Dentist Lincoln. But this here is just my little grandbaby, and she ain't gone be no trouble to you ..."

"Annie, everybody has a policy. In this world you have to have a policy. Now, my policy is I don't treat colored people."

The sun had baked the oil out of Momma's skin and melted the Vaseline in her hair. She shone greasily as she leaned out of the dentist's shadow.

"Seem like to me, Dentist Lincoln, you might look after her, she ain't nothing but a little mite. And seems like maybe you owe me a favor or two."

He reddened slightly. "Favor or no favor. The money has all been repaid to you and that's the end of it. Sorry, Annie." He had his hand on the doorknob. "Sorry." His voice was a bit kinder on the second "Sorry," as if he really was.

Momma said, "I wouldn't press on you like this for myself but I can't take No. Not for my grandbaby. When you come to borrow my money you didn't have to beg. You asked me, and I lent it. Now, it wasn't my policy. I ain't no moneylender, but you stood to lose this building and I tried to help you out."

"It's been paid, and raising your voice won't make me change my mind. My policy ..." He let go of the door and stepped nearer Momma. The three of us were crowded on the small landing. "Annie, my policy is I'd rather stick my hand in a dog's mouth than in a nigger's."

He had never once looked at me. He turned his back and went through the door into the cool beyond. Momma backed up inside herself for a few minutes. I forgot everything except her face which was almost a new one to me. She leaned over and took the doorknob, and in her everyday soft voice she said, "Sister, go on downstairs. Wait for me. I'll be there directly."

Under the most common of circumstances I knew it did no good to argue with Momma. So I walked down the steep stairs, afraid to look back and afraid not to do so. I turned as the door slammed, and she was gone.

*Momma walked in that room as if she owned it. She shoved that silly nurse aside with one hand and strode into the dentist's office. He was sitting in his chair, sharpening his mean instruments and putting extra sting into his medicines. Her eyes were blazing like live coals and her arms had doubled themselves in length. He looked up at her just before she caught him by the collar of his white jacket.*

*"Stand up when you see a lady, you contemptuous scoundrel." Her tongue had thinned and the words rolled off well enunciated. Enunciated and sharp like little claps of thunder.*

*The dentist had no choice but to stand at R.O.T.C. attention. His head dropped after a minute and his voice was humble. "Yes, ma'am, Mrs. Henderson."*

*"You knave, do you think you acted like a gentleman, speaking to me like that in front of my granddaughter?" She didn't shake him, although she had the power. She simply help him upright.*

*"No, ma'am, Mrs. Henderson."*

*"No, ma'am, Mrs. Henderson, what?" Then she did give him the tiniest of shakes, but because of her strength the action set his head and arms to shaking loose on the ends of his body. He stuttered much worse than Uncle Willie. "No, ma'am, Mrs. Henderson, I'm sorry."*

*With just an edge of her disgust showing, Momma slung him back in his dentist's chair. "Sorry is as sorry does, and you're about the sorriest dentist I ever laid my eyes on." (She could afford to slip into the vernacular because she had such eloquent command of English.)*

*"I didn't ask you to apologize in front of Marguerite, because I don't want her to know my power, but I order you, now and herewith. Leave Stamps by sundown."*

*"Mrs. Henderson, I can't get my equipment . . ." He was shaking terribly now.*

*"Now, that brings me to my second order. You will never again practice dentistry. Never! When you get settled in your next place, you will be a vegetarian caring for dogs with the mange, cats with the cholera and cows with the epizootic. Is that clear?"*

*The saliva ran down his chin and his eyes filled with tears. "Yes, ma'am. Thank you for not killing me. Thank you, Mrs. Henderson."*

*Momma pulled herself back from being ten feet tall with eight-foot arms and said, "You're welcome for nothing, you varlet, I wouldn't waste a killing on the likes of you."*

*On her way out she waved her handkerchief at the nurse and turned her into a crocus sack of chicken feed.*

Momma looked tired when she came down the stairs, but who wouldn't be tired if they had gone through what she had. She came close to me and adjusted the towel under my jaw (I had forgotten the toothache; I only knew that she made her hands gentle in order not to awaken the pain). She took my hand. Her voice never changed. "Come on, Sister."

I reckoned we were going home where she would concoct a brew to eliminate the pain and maybe give me new teeth too. New teeth that would grow overnight out of my gums. She led me toward the drugstore, which was in the opposite direction from the Store. "I'm taking you to Dentist Baker in Texarkana."

I was glad after all that I had bathed and put on Mum and Cashmere Bouquet taclum powder. It was a wonderful surprise. My toothache had quited to solemn pain, Momma had obliterated the evil white man, and we were going on a trip to Texarkana, just the two of us.

On the Greyhound she took an inside seat in the back, and I sat beside her. I was so proud of being her granddaughter and sure that some of her magic must have come down to me. She asked if I was scared. I only shook my head and leaned over on her cool brown upper arm. There was no chance that a dentist, especially a Negro dentist, would dare hurt me then. Not with Momma there. The trip was uneventful, except that she put her arm around me, which was very unusual for Momma to do.

The dentist showed me the medicine and the needle before he deadened by gums, but if he hadn't I wouldn't have worried. Momma stood right behind him. Her arms were folded and she checked on everything he did. The teeth were extracted and she bought me an ice cream cone from the side window of a drug counter. The trip back to Stamps was quiet, except that I had to spit into a very small empty snuff can which she had gotten for me and it was difficult with the bus humping and jerking on our country roads. At home, I was given a warm salt solution, and when I washed out my mouth I showed Bailey the empty holes, where the clotted blood sat like filling in a pie crust. He said I was quite brave, and that was my cue to reveal our confrontation with the peckerwood dentist and Momma's incredible powers.

I had to admit that I didn't hear the conversation, but what else could she have said than what I said she said? What else done? He agreed with my analysis in a lukewarm way, and I happily (after all, I'd been sick) flounced into the Store. Momma was preparing our evening meal and Uncle Willie leaned on the door sill. She gave her version.

"Dentist Lincoln got right uppity. Said he'd rather put his hand in a dog's mouth. And when I reminded him of the favor, he brushed it off like a piece of lint. Well, I sent Sister downstairs and went inside. I hadn't never been in his office before, but I found the door to where he takes out teeth, and him and the nurse was in there thick as thieves. I just stood there till he caught sight of me." Crash bang the pots on the stove. "He jumped just like he was sitting on a pin. He said, 'Annie, I done tole you, I ain't gonna mess around in no niggah's mouth.' I said, 'Somebody's got to do it then,' and he said, 'Take her to Texarkana to the colored dentist' and that's when I said, 'If you paid me my money I could afford to take her.' He said, 'It's all been paid.' I tole him everything but the interest been paid. He said ''Twasn't no interest.' I said ''Tis now. I'll take ten dollars as payment in full.' You know, Willie, it wasn't no right thing to do, 'cause I lent that money without thinking about it.

"He tole that little snippity nurse of his'n to give me ten dollars and make me sign a 'paid in full' receipt. She gave it to me and I signed the papers. Even though by rights he was paid up before, I figger, he gonna be that kind of nasty, he gonna have to pay for it."

Momma and her son laughed and laughed over the white man's evilness and her retributive sin.

I preferred, much preferred, my version.


## CRITICAL THINKING QUESTIONS

1. Examine the concept of a white and a black part of town. Interpersonally how are these traditions set and kept in place?

2. Why would a white dentist refuse to help a black child in extreme pain? What are other problems with discrimination in this story?
3. Give an example of someone you know who has suffered discrimination of any kind. How was the conflict managed? Explain how the perceptions differed and how you might have tried to manage the situation.
4. Write and analyze a case involving ethics and interpersonal communication to correct a severe discrimination situation.

## CONTEMPORARY CASE

### *Betrayal in Friendship: Linda and Monica*

A classic relationship betrayal could have been the impetus behind the impeachment of President William Jefferson Clinton. At the center were two women, supposed friends. The younger of the women had confessed her sexual liaison with "a certain married man" to the older woman. It was a story with extraordinary characters and details—too extraordinary for the older woman to keep in confidence. The older woman didn't just tell another friend the juicy information, she went to the highest sources possible to spread information, a book publicist and Special Prosecutor Kenneth Starr. Linda Tripp taped over 20 hours of conversation in which Monica Lewinsky, sobbed about her unrequited love affair with the president. Later Linda Tripp defined and defended herself by saying, "Who am I? I'm you—an average American."

Monica Lewinsky believed she could trust the older woman to keep confidential the details she imparted to Tripp. One of Tripp's famous quotes on tape to Monica is, "The beauty of (the affair) is it has stayed internal, and it will never taint you down the road." One of Lewinsky's famous quotes is, "I just want my life back." Had Lewinsky not confided in Tripp, would the result of the impeachment hearings have been different?

For Tripp the political stakes were much higher than the relationship duties. She had always enjoyed political favor with the Bush administration but found herself on the outs with the Clinton group. In 1997, Clinton attorney Robert Bennett questioned Tripp's credibility in a *Newsweek* article. Monica's lovelorn tales were perfect for Tripp to get back at the Clinton group. In fact, Tripp knew about evidence that could fully prove that Monica had an affair with the President—the blue Gap dress. Lewinsky told Tripp about the stain on the dress and that she needed to get the dress cleaned for Thanksgiving dinner. Friend Linda Tripp told her she looked fat in the dress. It was never cleaned and the evidence of sexual contact between the president and Lewinsky remained when Starr's team confiscated the dress. The words "it makes you look fat," (implying she shouldn't wear it) helped lead to an impeachment.

Monica had certainly betrayed the president. On the occasions of their sexual encounters, the agreement had been made not to tell anyone about their relationship. Monica could not uphold her end of this agreement and told 11 people about the affair. After her grand jury testimony, Lewinsky vowed that she never meant to get the president in trouble. She added that he never told her to lie and was never promised a job for her cooperation. In grand finale she stated, "And I hate Linda Tripp."

1. Analyze at least three ethical problems involved in this very complicated relationship.
2. Is betrayal in a friendship ever warranted? Was it warranted in this case? Explain.
3. How would Aristotle characterize the betrayal of Lewinsky and the betrayal of Clinton?
4. Under extreme pressure, such as that from Starr's investigative team, should a person divulge friendship confidences?

# 4

## DEVELOPMENT AND STABILITY IN INTERPERSONAL RELATIONSHIPS

### CAROL GILLIGAN

### IMAGES OF RELATIONSHIP

*Carol Gilligan is a professor in the Graduate School of Education at Harvard University and is highly regarded for her work in relationship ethics. In this 1982 excerpt from* In a Different Voice, *Gilligan emphasizes the problems of research in moral psychology centered only on males.*

In 1914, with his essay "On Narcissism," Freud swallows his distaste at the thought of "abandoning observation for barren theoretical controversy" and extends his map of the psychological domain. Tracing the development of the capacity to love, which he equates with maturity and psychic health, he locates its origins in the contrast between love for the mother and love for the self. But in thus dividing the world of love into narcissism and "object" relationships, he finds that while men's development becomes clearer, women's becomes increasingly opaque. The problem arises because the contrast between mother and self yields two different images of relationships. Relying on the imagery of men's lives in charting the course of human growth, Freud is unable to trace in women the development of relationships, morality, or a clear sense of self. This difficulty in fitting the logic of his theory to women's experience leads him in the end to set women apart, marking their relationships, like their sexual life, as "a 'dark continent' for psychology" (1926, p. 212).

Thus the problem of interpretation that shadows the understanding of women's development arises from the differences observed in their experience of relationships. To Freud, though living surrounded by women and otherwise seeing so much and so well, women's relationships seemed increasingly mysterious, difficult to discern, and hard to describe. While this mystery indicates how theory can blind observation, it also suggests that development in women is masked by a particular conception of human relationships. Since the imagery of relationships shapes the narrative of human development, the inclusion of women, by changing that imagery, implies a change in the entire account.

The shift in imagery that creates the problem in interpreting women's development is elucidated by the moral judgments of two eleven-year-old children, a boy and a girl, who see, in the same dilemma, two very different moral problems. While current theory brightly illuminates the line and the logic of the boy's thought, it casts scant light on that of the girl. The choice of a girl whose moral judgments elude existing categories of developmental assessment is meant to highlight the issue of interpretation rather than to exemplify sex differences per se. Adding a new line of interpretation, based on the imagery of the girl's thought, makes it possible not only to see development where previously development was not discerned but also to consider differences in the understanding of relationships without scaling these differences from better to worse.

The two children were in the same sixth-grade class at school and were participants in the rights and responsibilities study, designed to explore different conceptions of morality and self. The sample selected for this study was chosen to focus the variables of gender and age while maximizing developmental potential by holding constant, at a high level, the factors of intelligence, education, and social class that have been associated with moral development, at least as measured by existing scales. The two children in question, Amy and Jake, were both bright and articulate and, at least in their eleven-year-old aspirations, resisted easy categories of sex-role stereotyping, since Amy aspired to become a scientist while Jake preferred English to math. Yet their moral judgments seem initially to confirm familiar notions about differences between the sexes, suggesting that the edge girls have on moral development during the early school years gives way at puberty with the ascendance of formal logical thought in boys.

The dilemma that these eleven-year-olds were asked to resolve was one in the series devised by Kohlberg to measure moral development in adolescence by presenting a conflict between moral norms and exploring the logic of its resolution. In this particular dilemma, a man named Heinz considers whether or not to steal a drug which he cannot afford to buy in order to save the life of his wife. In the standard format of Kohlberg's interviewing procedure, the description of the dilemma itself—Heinz's predicament, the wife's disease, the druggist's refusal to lower his price—is followed by the question, "Should Heinz steal the drug?" The reasons for and against stealing are then explored through a series of questions that vary and extend the parameters of the dilemma in a way designed to reveal the underlying structure of moral thought.

Jake, at eleven, is clear from the outset that Heinz should steal the drug. Constructing the dilemma, as Kohlberg did, as a conflict between the values of property and life, he discerns the logical priority of life and uses that logic to justify his choice:

> For one thing, a human life is worth more than money, and if the druggist only makes $1,000, he is still going to live, but if Heinz doesn't steal the drug, his wife is going to die. (*Why is life worth more than money?*) Because the druggist can get a thousand dollars later from rich people with cancer, but Heinz can't get his wife again. (*Why not?*) Because people are all different and so you couldn't get Heinz's wife again.

Asked whether Heinz should steal the drug if he does not love his wife, Jake replies that he should, saying that not only is there "a difference between hating and killing," but also, if Heinz were caught, "the judge would probably think it was the right thing to do." Asked about the fact that, in stealing, Heinz would be breaking the law, he says that "the laws have mistakes, and you can't go writing up a law for everything that you can imagine."

Thus, while taking the law into account and recognizing its function in maintaining social order (the judge, Jake says, "should give Heinz the lightest possible sentence"), he also sees the law as man-made and therefore subject to error and change. Yet his judgment that Heinz should steal the drug, like his view of the law as having mistakes, rests on the assumption of agreement, a societal consensus around moral values that allows one to know and expect others to recognize what is "the right thing to do."

Fascinated by the power of logic, this eleven-year-old boy locates truth in math, which, he says, is "the only thing that is totally logical." Considering the moral dilemma to be "sort of like a math problem with humans," he sets it up as an equation and proceeds to work out the solution. Since his solution is rationally derived, he assumes that anyone following reason would arrive at the same conclusion and thus that a judge would also consider stealing to be the right thing for Heinz to do. Yet he is also aware of the limits of logic. Asked whether there is a right answer to moral problems, Jake replies that "there can only be right and wrong in judgment," since the parameters of action are variable and complex. Illustrating how actions undertaken with the best of intentions can eventuate in the most disastrous of consequences, he says, "like if you give an old lady your seat on the trolley, if you are in a trolley crash and that seat goes through the window, it might be that reason that the old lady dies."

Theories of developmental psychology illuminate well the position of this child, standing at the juncture of childhood and adolescence, at what Piaget describes as the pinnacle of childhood intelligence, and beginning through thought to discover a wider universe of possibility. The moment of preadolescence is caught by the conjunction of formal operational thought with a description of self still anchored in the factual parameters of his childhood world—his age, his town, his father's occupation, the substance of his likes, dislikes, and beliefs. Yet as his self-description radiates the self-confidence of a child who has arrived, in Erikson's terms, at a favorable balance of industry over inferiority—competent, sure of himself, and knowing well the rules of the game—so his emergent capacity for formal thought, his ability to think about thinking and to reason things out in a logical way, frees him from dependence on authority and allows him to find solutions to problems by himself.

This emergent autonomy follows the trajectory that Kohlberg's six stages of moral development trace, a three-level progression from an egocentric understanding of fairness based on individual need (stages one and two), to a conception of fairness anchored in the shared conventions of societal agreement (stages three and four), and finally to a principled understanding of fairness that rests on the free-standing logic of equality and reciprocity (stages five and six). While this boy's judgments at eleven are scored as conventional on Kohlberg's scale, a mixture of stages three and four, his ability to bring deductive logic to bear on the solution of moral dilemmas, to differentiate morality from law, and to see how laws can be considered to have mistakes points toward the principled conception of justice that Kohlberg equates with moral maturity.

In contrast, Amy's response to the dilemma conveys a very different impression, an image of development stunted by a failure of logic, an inability to think for herself. Asked if Heinz should steal the drug, she replies in a way that seems evasive and unsure:

> Well, I don't think so. I think there might be other ways besides stealing it, like if he could borrow the money or make a loan or something, but he really shouldn't steal the drug—but his wife shouldn't die either.

Asked why he should not steal the drug, she considers neither property nor law but rather the effect that theft could have on the relationship between Heinz and his wife:

> If he stole the drug, he might save his wife then, but if he did, he might have to go to jail, and then his wife might get sicker again, and he couldn't get more of the drug, and it might not be good. So, they should really just talk it out and find some other way to make the money.

Seeing in the dilemma not a math problem with humans but a narrative of relationships that extends over time, Amy envisions the wife's continuing need for her husband and the husband's continuing concern for his wife and seeks to respond to the druggist's need in a way that would sustain rather than sever connection. Just as she ties the wife's survival to the preservation of relationships, so she considers the value of the wife's life in a context of relationships, saying that it would be wrong to let her die because, "if she died, it hurts a lot of people and it hurts her." Since Amy's moral judgment is grounded in the belief that, "if somebody has something that would keep somebody alive, then it's not right not to give it to them," she considers the problem in the dilemma to arise not from the druggist's assertion of rights but from his failure of response.

As the interviewer proceeds with the series of questions that follow from Kohlberg's construction of the dilemma, Amy's answers remain essentially unchanged, the various probes serving neither to elucidate nor to modify her initial response. Whether or not Heinz loves his wife, he still shouldn't steal or let her die; if it were a stranger dying instead, Amy says that "if the stranger didn't have anybody near or anyone she knew," then Heinz should try to save her life, but he should not steal the drug. But as the interviewer conveys through the repetition of questions that the answers she gave were not heard or not right, Amy's confidence begins to diminish, and her replies become more constrained and unsure. Asked again why Heinz should not steal the drug, she simply repeats, "Because it's not right." Asked again to explain why, she states again that theft would not be a good solution, adding lamely, "if he took it, he might not know how to give it to his wife, and so his wife might still die." Failing to see the dilemma as a self-contained problem in moral logic, she does not discern the internal structure of its resolution; as she constructs the problem differently herself, Kohlberg's conception completely evades her.

Instead, seeing a world comprised of relationships rather than of people standing alone, a world that coheres through human connection rather than through systems of rules, she finds the puzzle in the dilemma to lie in the failure of the druggist to respond to the wife. Saying that "it is not right for someone to die when their life could be saved," she assumes that if the druggist were to see the consequences of his refusal to lower his price, he would realize that "he should just give it to the wife and then have the husband pay back the money later." Thus she considers the solution to the dilemma to lie in making the wife's condition more salient to the druggist or, that failing, in appealing to others who are in a position to help.

Just as Jake is confident the judge would agree that stealing is the right thing for Heinz to do, so Amy is confident that, "if Heinz and the druggest [sic] had talked it out long enough, they could reach something besides stealing." As he considers the law to "have mistakes," so she sees this drama as a mistake, believing that "the world should just share things more and then people wouldn't have to steal." Both children thus recognize the need for agreement but see it as mediated in different ways—he impersonally through systems of logic and law, she personally through communication in relationship. Just as he relies on the conventions of logic to deduce the solution to this dilemma, assuming these conventions to be shared, so she relies on a process of communication, assuming connection and believing that her voice will be heard. Yet while his assumptions about agreement are confirmed by the convergence in logic between his answers and the questions posed, her assumptions are belied by the failure of communication, the interviewer's inability to understand her response.

Although the frustration of the interview with Amy is apparent in the repetition of questions and its ultimate circularity, the problem of interpretation is focused by the assessment of her response. When considered in the light of Kohlberg's definition of the stages and sequence of moral development, her moral judgments appear to be a full stage lower in maturity than those of the boy. Scored as a mixture of stages two and three, her responses seem to reveal a feeling of powerlessness in the world, an inability to think systematically about the concepts of morality or law, a reluctance to challenge authority or to examine the logic of received moral truths, a failure even to conceive of acting directly to save a life or to consider that such action, if taken, could possibly have an effect. As her reliance on relationships seems to reveal a continuing dependence and vulnerability, so her belief in communication as the mode through which to resolve moral dilemmas appears naive and cognitively immature.

Yet Amy's description of herself conveys a markedly different impression. Once again, the hallmarks of the preadolescent child depict a child secure in her sense of herself, confident in the substance of her beliefs, and sure of her ability to do something of value in the world. Describing herself at eleven as "growing and changing," she says that she "sees some things differently now, just because I know myself really well now, and I know a lot more about the world." Yet the world she knows is a different world from that refracted by Kohlberg's construction of Heinz's dilemma. Her world is a world of relationships and psychological truths where an awareness of the connection between people gives rise to a recognition of responsibility for one another, a perception of the need for response. Seen in this light, her understanding of morality as arising from the recognition of relationship, her belief in communication as the mode of conflict resolution, and her conviction that the solution to the dilemma will follow from its compelling representation seem far from naive or cognitively immature. Instead, Amy's judgments contain the insights central to an ethic of care, just as Jake's judgments reflect the logic of the justice approach. Her incipient awareness of the "method of truth," the central tenet of nonviolent conflict resolution, and her belief in the restorative activity of care, lead her to see the actors in the dilemma arrayed not as opponents in a contest of rights but as members of a network of relationships on whose continuation they all depend. Consequently her solution to the dilemma lies in activating the network by communication, securing the inclusion of the wife by strengthening rather than severing connections.

But the different logic of Amy's response calls attention to the interpretation of the interview itself. Conceived as an interrogation, it appears instead as a dialogue, which takes on moral dimensions of its own, pertaining to the interviewer's uses of power and to the manifestations of respect. With this shift in the conception of the interview, it immediately becomes clear that the interviewer's problem in understanding Amy's response stems from the fact that Amy is answering a different question from the one the interviewer thought had been posed. Amy is considering not *whether* Heinz should act in this situation ("*should* Heinz steal the drug?") but rather *how* Heinz should act in response to his awareness of his wife's need ("Should Heinz *steal* the drug?"). The interviewer takes the mode of action for granted, presuming it to be a matter of fact; Amy assumes the necessity for action and considers what form it should take. In the interviewer's failure to imagine a response not dreamt of in Kohlberg's moral philosophy lies the failure to hear Amy's question and to see the logic in her response, to discern that what appears, from one perspective, to be an evasion of the dilemma signifies in other terms a recognition of the problem and a search for a more adequate solution.

Thus in Heinz's dilemma these two children see two very different moral problems—Jake a conflict between life and property that can be resolved by logical deduction, Amy a fracture of human relationship that must be mended with its own thread. Asking different questions that arise from different conceptions of the moral domain, the children arrive at answers that fundamentally diverge, and the arrangement of these answers as successive stages on a scale of increasing moral maturity calibrated by the logic of the boy's response misses the different truth revealed in the judgment of the girl. To the question, "What does he see that she does not?" Kohlberg's theory provides a ready response, manifest in the scoring of Jake's judgments a full stage higher than Amy's in moral maturity; to the question, "What does she see that he does not?" Kohlberg's theory has nothing to say. Since most of her responses fall through the sieve of Kohlberg's scoring system, her responses appear from his perspective to lie outside the moral domain.

Yet just as Jake reveals a sophisticated understanding of the logic of justification, so Amy is equally sophisticated in her understanding of the nature of choice. Recognizing that "if both the roads went in totally separate ways, if you pick one, you'll never know what would happen if you went the other way," she explains that "that's the chance you have to take, and like I said, it's just really a guess." To illustrate her point "in a simple way," she describes her choice to spend the summer at camp:

> I will never know what would have happened if I had stayed here, and if something goes wrong at camp, I'll never know if I stayed here if it would have been better. There's really no way around it because there's no way you can do both at once, so you've got to decide, but you'll never know.

In this way, these two eleven-year-old children, both highly intelligent and perceptive about life, though in different ways, display different modes of moral understanding, different ways of thinking about conflict and choice. In resolving Heinz's dilemma, Jake relies on theft to avoid confrontation and turns to the law to mediate the dispute. Transposing a hierarchy of power into a hierarchy of values, he defuses a potentially explosive conflict between people by casting it as an impersonal conflict of claims. In this way, he abstracts the moral problem from the interpersonal situation, finding in the logic of fairness an objective way to decide who will win the dispute. But this hierarchical ordering, with its imagery of winning and losing and the potential for violence which it contains, gives way in Amy's construction of the dilemma to a network of connection, a web of relationships that is sustained by a process of communication. With this shift, the moral problem changes from one of unfair domination, the imposition of property over life, to one of unnecessary exclusion, the failure of the druggist to respond to the wife.

## CRITICAL THINKING QUESTIONS

1. According to Gilligan, notions of personal autonomy are privileged over interpersonal relationship in the interviews with Jake and Amy. Explain how Gilligan finds this a major flaw in Kohlberg's work.
2. An ethical approach based on caring, sharing and relationship is being called an "emerging ethic." Cite thinkers in the past who have recognized the need for relationship in the making of ethical decisions.
3. Write and analyze a case based on the networking of relationships that can be used when confronted with one of life's tough problems.

NEL NODDINGS

## AN ETHICS OF CARE

*Nel Noddings is a professor of education, Emeriti, at Stanford University, and a professor of philosophy and education at Teachers College, Columbia University. She has written nine books and numerous articles. This excerpt is from the 1984 work* Caring: A Feminine Approach to Ethics and Moral Education. *Noddings theorizes that ethics cannot neatly be placed in categories of duties, rights, and so on, but that often acts are performed because of relationships.*

There are moments for all of us when we care quite naturally. We just do care; no ethical effort is required. "Want" and "ought" are indistinguishable in such cases. I want to do what I or others might judge I ought to do. But can there be a "demand" to care? There can be, surely, no demand for the initial impulse that arises as a feeling, an inner voice saying "I must do something," in response to the need of the cared-for. This impulse arises naturally, at least occasionally, in the absence of pathology. We cannot demand that one have this impulse, but we shrink from one who never has it. One who never feels the pain of another, who never confesses the internal "I must" that is so familiar to most of us, is beyond our normal pattern of understanding. Her case is pathological, and we avoid her.

But even if I feel the initial "I must," I may reject it. I may reject it instantaneously by shifting from "I must do something" to "Something must be done," and removing myself from the set of possible agents through whom the action should be accomplished. I may reject it because I feel that there is nothing I can do. If I do either of these things without reflection upon what I might do in behalf of the cared-for, then I do not care. Caring requires me to respond to the initial impulse with an act of commitment: I commit myself either to overt action on behalf of the cared-for (I pick up my crying infant) or I commit myself to thinking about what I might do. In the latter case, as we have seen, I may or may not act overtly in behalf of the cared-for. I may abstain from action if I believe that anything I might do would tend to work against the best interests of the cared-for. But the test of my caring is not wholly in how things turn out; the primary test lies in an examination of what I considered, how fully I received the other, and whether the free pursuit of his projects is partly a result of the completion of my caring in him.

But am I obliged to embrace the "I must"? In this form, the question is a bit odd, for the "I must" carries obligation with it. It comes to us as obligation. But accepting and affirming the "I must" are different from feeling it, and these responses are what I am pointing to when I ask whether I am obliged to embrace the "I must." The question nags at us; it is a question that has been asked, in a variety of forms, over and over by moralists and moral theorists. Usually, the question arises as part of the broader question of justification. We ask something of the sort: Why must I (or should I) do what suggests itself to reason as "right" or as needing to be done for the sake of some other? We might prefer to supplement "reason" with "and/or feeling." This question is, of course, not the only thorny question in moral theory, but it is one that has plagued theorists who see clearly that there is no way to derive an "I ought" statement from a chain of facts. I may agree readily that "things would be better"—that is, that a certain state of affairs commonly agreed to be desirable might be attained—if a certain chain of events were to take place. But there is still nothing in this intellectual chain that can produce the "I ought." I may choose to remain an observer on the scene.

Now I am suggesting that the "I must" arises directly and prior to consideration of what it is that I might do. The initial feeling is the "I must." When it comes to me indistinguishable from the "I want," I proceed easily as one-caring. But often it comes to me conflicted. It may be barely perceptible, and it may be followed almost simultaneously by resistance. When someone asks me to get something for him or merely asks for my attention, the "I must" may be lost in a clamor of resistance. Now a second sentiment is required if I am to behave as one-caring. I care about myself as one-caring and, although I do not care naturally for the person who has asked something of me—at least not at this moment—I feel the genuine moral sentiment, the "I ought," that sensibility to which I have committed myself.

Let me try to make plausible by contention that the moral imperative arises directly.[4] And, of course, I must try to explain how caring and what I am calling the "moral imperative" are related. When my infant cries in the night, I not only feel that I must do something but I want to do something. Because I love this child, because I am bonded to him, I want to remove his pain as I would want to remove my own. The "I must" is not a dutiful imperative but one that accompanies the "I want." If I were tied to a chair, for example, and wanted desperately to get free, I might say as I struggled, "I must do something; I must get out of these bonds." But this "must" is not yet the moral and ethical "ought." it is a "must" born of desire.

The most intimate situations of caring are, thus, natural. I do not feel that taking care of my own child is "moral" but, rather, natural. A woman who allows her own child to die of neglect is often considered sick rather than immoral; that is, we feel that either she or the situation into which she has been thrust must be pathological. Otherwise, the impulse to respond, to nurture the living infant, is overwhelming. We share the impulse with other creatures in the animal kingdom. Whether we want to consider this response as "instinctive" is problematic, because certain patterns of response may be implied by the term and because suspension of reflective consciousness seems also to be implied (and I am not suggesting that we have no choice), but I have no difficulty in considering it as innate. Indeed, I am claiming that the impulse to act in behalf of the present other is itself innate. It lies latent in each of us, awaiting gradual development in a succession of caring relations. I am suggesting that our inclination toward and interest in morality derives from caring. In caring, we accept the natural impulse to act on behalf of the present other. We are engrossed in the other. We have received him and feel his pain or happiness, but we are not compelled by this impulse. We have a choice; we may accept what we feel, or we may reject it.

If we have a strong desire to be moral, we will not reject it, and this strong desire to be moral is derived, reflectively, from the more fundamental and natural desire to be and to remain related. To reject the feeling when it arises is either to be in an internal state of imbalance or to contribute willfully to the diminution of the ethical ideal.

But suppose in a particular case that the "I must" does not arise, or that it whispers faintly and disappears, leaving distrust, repugnance, or hate. Why, then, should I behave morally toward the object of my dislike? Why should I not accept feelings other than those characteristic of caring and, thus, achieve an internal state of balance through hate, anger, or malice?

The answer to this is, I think, that the genuine moral sentiment (our second sentiment) arises from an evaluation of the caring relation as good, as better than, superior to, other forms of relatedness. I feel the moral "I must" when I recognize that my response will either enhance or diminish my ethical ideal. It will serve either to increase or decrease the likelihood of genuine caring. My response affects me as one-caring. In a given situation with someone I am not fond of, I may be able to find all sorts of reasons why I should not respond to his need. I may be too busy. He may be undiscerning. The matter may be, on objective analysis, unimportant. But, before I decide, I must turn away from this analytic chain of thought and back to the concrete situation. Here is this person with this perceived need to which is attached this importance. I must put justification aside temporarily. Shall I respond? How do I feel as a duality about the "I" who will not respond?

I am obliged, then, to accept the initial "I must" when it occurs and even to fetch it out of recalcitrant slumber when it fails to awake spontaneously.[5] The source of my obligation is the value I place on the relatedness of caring. This value itself arises as a product of actual caring and being cared-for and my reflection on the goodness of these concrete caring situations.

Now, what sort of "goodness" is it that attaches to the caring relation? It cannot be a fully moral goodness, for we have already described forms of caring that are natural and require no moral effort. But it cannot be a fully nonmoral goodness either, for it would then join a class of goods many of which are widely separated from the moral good. It is, perhaps, properly described as a "premoral good," one that lies in a region with the moral good and shades over into it. We cannot always decide with certainty whether our caring response is natural or ethical. Indeed, the decision to respond ethically as one-caring may cause the lowering of barriers that previously prevented reception of the other, and natural caring may follow.

I have identified the source of our obligation and have said that we are
obligated to accept, and even to call forth, the feeling "I must." But what exactly must I do? Can my obligation be set forth in a list or hierarchy of principles? So far, it seems that I am obligated to maintain an attitude and, thus,
to meet the other as one-caring and, at the same time, to increase my own
virtue as one-caring. If I am advocating an ethic of virtue, do not all the
usual dangers lie in wait: hypocrisy, self-righteousness, withdrawal from the
public domain? We shall discuss these dangers as the idea of an ethical ideal
is developed more fully. . . .

Many of us in education are keenly aware of the distortion that results
from undue emphasis on moral judgments and justification. Lawrence
Kohlberg's theory, for example, is widely held to be a model for moral education, but it is actually only a hierarchical description of moral reasoning.[10]
It is well known, further, that the description may not be accurate. In particular, the fact that women seem often to be "stuck" at stage three might call
the accuracy of the description into question. But perhaps the description
is accurate within the domain of morality conceived as moral justification.
If it is, we might well explore the possibility that feminine nonconformity
to the Kohlberg model counts against the justification/judgment paradigm
and not against women as moral thinkers.

Women, perhaps the majority of women, prefer to discuss moral problems in terms of concrete situations. They approach moral problems not as
intellectual problems to be solved by abstract reasoning but as concrete human problems to be lived and to be solved in living. Their approach is
founded in caring. Carol Gilligan describes the approach:

> . . . women not only define themselves in a context of human relationship
> but also judge themselves in terms of their ability to care. Woman's place
> in man's life cycle has been that of nurturer, caretaker, and helpmate, the
> weaver of those networks of relationships on which she in turn relies.[11]

Faced with a hypothetical moral dilemma, women often ask for more
information. It is not the case, certainly, that women cannot arrange principles hierarchically and derive conclusions logically. It is more likely that
they see this process as peripheral to or even irrelevant to moral conduct.
They want more information, I think, in order to form a picture. Ideally,
they need to talk to the participants, to see their eyes and facial expressions, to size up the whole situation. Moral decisions are, after all, made
in situations; they are qualitatively different from the solution of geome-
try problems. Women, like act-deontologists in general, give reasons for
their acts, but the reasons point to feelings, needs, situational conditions,

and their sense of personal ideal rather than universal principles and their application.

As we have seen, caring is not in itself a virtue. The genuine ethical commitment to maintain oneself as caring gives rise to the development and exercise of virtues, but these must be assessed in the context of caring situations. It is not, for example, patience itself that is a virtue but patience with respect to some infirmity of a particular cared-for or patience in instructing a concrete cared-for that is virtuous. We must not reify virtues and turn our caring toward them. If we do this, our ethic turns inward and is even less useful than an ethic of principles, which at least remains indirectly in contact with the acts we are assessing. The fulfillment of virtue is both in me and in the other.

A consideration of caring and an ethic built upon it give new meaning to what Kohlberg assesses as "stage three" morality. At this stage, persons behave morally in order to be thought of—or to think of themselves as—"good boys" or "good girls." Clearly, it makes a difference whether one chooses to be good or to be thought of as good. One who chooses to be good may not be "stuck," as Kohlberg suggests, in a stage of moral reasoning. Rather, she may have chosen an alternative route to moral conduct.

It should be clear that my description of an ethic of caring as a feminine ethic does not imply a claim to speak for all women nor to exclude men. As we shall see in the next chapter, there is reason to believe that women are somewhat better equipped for caring than men are. This is partly a result of the construction of psychological deep structures in the mother-child relationship. A girl can identify with the one caring for her and thus maintain relation while establishing identity. A boy must, however, find his identity with the absent one—the father—and thus disengage himself from the intimate relation of caring.[12]

There are many women who will deplore my insistence on locating the source of caring in human relations. The longing for something beyond is lovely—alluring—and it persists. It seems to me quite natural that men, many of whom are separated from the intimacy of caring, should create gods and seek security and love in worship. But what ethical need have women for God? I do not mean to suggest that women can brush aside an actually existing God but, if there is such a God, the human role in its maintenance must be trivial. We can only contemplate the universe in awe and wonder, study it conscientiously, and live in it conservatively. Women, it seems to me, can accept the God of Spinoza and Einstein. What I mean to suggest is that women have no need of a conceptualized God, one wrought in the image of man. All the love and goodness commanded by such a God can be generated from the love and goodness found in the warmest and best human relations. . . .

## The Toughness of Caring

An ethic built on caring is thought by some to be tenderminded. It does involve construction of an ideal from the fact and memory of tenderness. The ethical sentiment itself requires a prior natural sentiment of caring and a willingness to sustain tenderness. But there is no assumption of innate human goodness and, when we move to the construction of a philosophy of education, we shall find enormous differences between the view developed here and that of those who find the child innately good. I shall not claim that the child is "innately wise and good," or that the aim of life is happiness, or that all will be well with the child if we resist interfering in its intellectual and moral life.[15] We have memories of caring, of tenderness, and these lead us to a vision of what is good—a state that is good-in-itself and a commitment to sustain and enhance that good (the desire and commitment to be moral). But we have other memories as well, and we have other desires. An ethic of caring takes into account these other tendencies and desires; it is precisely because the tendency to treat each other well is so fragile that we must strive so consistently to care.

### CRITICAL THINKING QUESTIONS

1. Examine Nodding's approach to ethics. Do you agree or disagree with her descriptions and definitions of morality?
2. When someone needs help because of a car accident, do you help them out of a sense of duty, or do you assist them because they are in need? Defend your response in relation to Nodding's views.
3. Write and analyze a case based on a morality of caring, sharing, and relationship.

## Notes

4. The argument here is, I think, compatible with that of Philippa Foot, "Reasons for Action and Desires," in *Virtues and Vices,* ed. Philippa Foot (Berkeley: University of California Press, 1978), pp. 148–156. My argument, however, relies on a basic desire, universal in all human beings, to be in relation—to care and be cared for.
5. The question of "summonability" is a vital one for ethicists who rely on good or altruistic feelings for moral motivation. Note treatment of this problem in

Lawrence R. Blum, *Friendship, Altruism, and Morality* (London: Routledge & Kegan Paul, 1980), pp. 20–23 and pp. 194–203. See, also, Henry Sidgwick, *The Methods of Ethics* (Indianapolis: Hackett, 1981), and Philip Mercer, *Sympathy and Ethics* (Oxford: Clarendon Press, 1962).

10. See Lawrence Kohlberg and R. Kramer, "Continuities and Discontinuities in Childhood and Adult Moral Development," *Human Development* 12 (1969), 93–120. See also Lawrence Kohlberg, "Stages in Moral Development as a Basis for Moral Education," in *Moral Education: Interdisciplinary Approaches,* ed. C. M. Beck, B. S. Crittenden, and E. V. Sullivan (Toronto: Toronto University Press, 1971).

11. Carol Gilligan, "Woman's Place in Man's Life Cycle," *Harvard Educational Review* 49(1979), 440.

12. See Nancy Chodorow, *The Reproduction of Mothering* (Berkeley, Los Angeles, London: University of California Press, 1978).

15. For a lovely exposition of this view, see A. S. Neill, *Summerhill* (New York: Hart Publishing Company, 1960).

MARCIA DIXSON AND STEVE DUCK

# UNDERSTANDING THE RELATIONSHIP PROCESS: UNCOVERING THE HUMAN SEARCH FOR MEANING

*Marcia Dixson is associate professor of communication at Indiana/Purdue University in Fort Wayne, Indiana. She is an interpersonal communication researcher and scholar. Steven Duck is a professor of communication studies at the University of Sheffield, UK. He is the editor of a series of texts researching relationship development and disintegration. This 1992 excerpt explains the symbolic structure of communication in interpersonal relationships. Past and present symbols can be misinterpreted to cause interpersonal relationship difficulties.*

There is a curiosity about relationships: They are composed of individuals, yet are more than the sum of their parts. In understanding relationship processes, one therefore is faced with understanding not only what it is that individuals think, know, and do in relationships but also what they share and how they come to share it. Our analysis of this curiosity focuses on symbols and meaning because both of these entities can be "owned" by individuals for themselves and also can be shared with others (Baxter, 1987b). Individuals can see symbolism and meaning in idiosyncratic ways that they have constructed for themselves. In relationships, partners also experience a commonality of meaning and symbolism between themselves on a variety of topics and concerns, and this experience "goes beyond" simple similarity in it effects.

We focus on this overlooked curiosity in a number of ways—sometimes looking at the ways two persons create, establish, and share meaning with one another as relaters, and sometimes looking at the ways researchers do exactly the same thing by developing terminologies and ways of experiencing the world that can be shared by colleagues. Threaded through this analysis is the notion that both examples are instances of a fundamental human tendency to use symbols, to seek, create, and develop meaning, and to analyze experience. Duck (1991) has developed the basis of this argument elsewhere, and here we go further and apply an analysis of this fundamental human tendency proposed by Kenneth Burke, a rhetorical theorist who focused on the human use of symbols and the ways this use structures thought and explanation—whether at the level of relationships or at the level of scholarly discourse. We also see connections with the work of personality psychologist George Kelly (1955, but especially, 1969), who also focused on the ways humans construct meanings as a way to deal with the "constantly unforeseen originality" (Shotter, 1987) of their lives.

It has been traditional to point to the fact that humans are able to live—actually cannot avoid living—simultaneously in reference to all three dimensions of time (past, present, and future). Thus our past, as we have accounted for it, echoes in the present and in the future; our present makes sense because of our images of the past and the future; and our anticipations of the future often recast the past and direct our behaviors of the moment. All three are always present, and all three are humanly, symbolically constructed. Use of symbols represents a parallel between social actors and researchers: All of us seek to describe (represent) and explain past and present happenings both for their own sake and to control and predict future events. Both Burke (1966) and Kelly (1955, 1969), however, retranslate these views into a future orientation; that is, they see humans as evaluating and interpreting the past in order to give it a meaning that helps one cope with it in the future if similar events happen again. Thus both theorists emphasize the importance, in understanding human behavior, of noting that humans are driven by a need to cope with the future that is unpredictable unless people develop categories of expectation ("constructs" for Kelly;

"symbols" for Burke). Although meaning is often apparently retrospective, for Kelly constructs are personal creations developed and tested quasiscientifically to deal with the future (Duck & Condra, 1989). Burke wrote of symbols as human devices and schemes for comprehending life as a whole; they are not inherent in the phenomena that humans experience. Kelly wrote of the "anticipation of events by construing of their replications"; Burke (1966, p. 16) wrote, more opaquely, that humans are "rotten with perfection," meaning that humans place order on the phenomena they encounter, so as to organize their experience. Such activity inevitably provokes a restless hunt for the best way to do this organizing and creates a search for perfection or completeness (a tendency to continually revise, update, and regard as unfinished the business of their application and extension). In one sense, then, "rotten with perfection" is yet another way of saying that more research needs to be done!

The theme of dealing with change and the future has been a part of human thought about human behavior since at least the early Greek philosophers (e.g., Heraclitus) and takes its modern form in the emphasis on prediction and control that is found in many recent models of relationships (e.g., Kelley et al., 1983). We share the view that it is an important channeler of human thinking but feel that more can be said about its implications for the study and conduct of relationships. . . .

. . . *Symbols* and *meaning* are essentially motivating entities that exist in individual minds but about which two individual minds can (come to) agree. They are examples of important forms of cognitive overlap in relationships, in culture, and indeed in the professional terminologies that researchers develop and use among themselves. One important question, then, is how people come to *develop* such meaning systems. . . . A second question is how such systems relate to cultural and social milieus . . . a third question is how people come to share such symbols and meanings . . . and a fourth is how people use and can develop them once they are shared-issues that we cover here. . . .

. . . We argue that partners in relationships are using shared meaning systems or shared working models of the world to conduct the relational endeavor, just as scholars use shared specialized symbol systems or working models to conduct the collegial research endeavor. Indeed there are striking parallels between the theoretical activities of scholars in different disciplines once one focuses on that activity as examples of human "effort after meaning" (Bartlett, 1932). . . .

. . . Just as two individuals bring their own individual systems of thinking into any relationship, so to researchers and scholars come to the study of relationships with their own patterns of thought, training, method, theory, perspective, and so on. Such patterns of thought, necessarily and ex hypothesi, influence the choice of phenomena selected for inquiry and inspection as the individual researchers take different perspectives on the phenomena. Sociologists will gravitate toward patterns of structure and power as issues to be explained. Social psychologists will focus on the individual or social cognitions that are evident to them in relationships and their participants. Communication scholars will look for the structures of messages or the construction of relationships that they imply. Developmentalists will ask how persons and their beliefs or skills change across time in relationships. In short, each discipline will take a perspective that focuses characteristically on those things that make most sense within its own frame of reference or terminological geography (agreed meaning systems). Although, for example, the differences between disciplines often are exaggerated at the expense of the similarities, such differences often are seen as little more than foibles caused by training, rather than as examples of human choices based on meaning systems. Nevertheless there is a deeper structural point about the human mind here, showing a common element that runs through most human action: that a fundamental structure of human minds is based on choice in the context of *meaning* and that this structure expresses itself in human behavior of all kinds, including the activities of scholars in various disciplines.

The reader already may be ahead of us in seeing that individuals who come to relationships are also examples of this same fact about the human mind. The anxious persons focus on likely evidence of rejection by others (Erickson, Sroufe, & Egeland, 1985; Raush, Barry, Hertel, & Swain, 1974); the extravert explores opportunities for social interaction, while the introvert seeks to avoid them in favor of quiet solitude; women typically notice the progress of intimate talk in relationships, while men are alerted to different aspects of social experience (Duck, Rutt et al, 1991).

The fundamental human commonality evident in all of these examples is that people choose to focus on things that make sense within their preexisting frames of reference, their system of meaning, about which deductions can be made on the basis of evident choices (Duck, 1991). Burke, a rhetorical theorist, put it thus:

> We can say that people interpret natural sequences in terms of cause and effect not because of something in the natural scene requiring this interpretation but because humans are the sort of agents that see things in terms of necessary relations. In this view we do not derive our ideas of cause and effect from experience; all that we can derive from experience is the observation that certain happenings seem likely to follow certain other

happenings. But our ideas of cause and effect are derived from the nature of the mind. (Burke, 1945/1969, p. 187)

Natural phenomena do not scream out at us to be interpreted in a particular way; they make rather subliminal whispers that different people choose to hear in slightly different ways, as make sense to them within their frames of reference of meaning.

## MEANING AND SHARING OF MEANING IN TALK

We believe that such a view connects easily with several lines of thinking in psychology (e.g., personality psychology), as well as in communication studies (e.g., study of rhetoric and persuasion) and sociology (e.g., symbolic interaction). It also demonstrates the relevance of choice in the human endeavor. Choice of discipline, of structure for a series, of topics for a volume, of methodology, of research problem, friends, affiliative strategies, and many others are all expressions of a general human tendency to make choices within a framework of meanings accepted by the chooser (who also may be "a researcher," "a partner," "an author," "an editor," or "a person").

The notion of *meaning* has proven difficult in the history of ideas. By focusing, as the rest of this volume does, on what an individual knows about relating, we are emphasizing the way the person organizes, for him- or herself, knowledge about relationships and partners; but his is only a part of the picture, even if it clearly ties in with work in this and other fields. . . . [S]everal authors adopt Bowlby's (1988) term *working models* to refer to a similar concept. For us, *meaning* is an organizational concept too and refers to the way a person organizes knowledge about relationships in the context of what else he or she knows about the world. We believe that, having constructed organized knowledge about relationships in the ways discussed in other chapters in this volume, individuals represent that knowledge to other people by the language they use, as an invitation to those others to share and adopt that organization of knowledge. The formation of a dyadic relationship thus confronts the two partners with the organizational challenge of resolving any differences that exist between their respective working models or meaning systems. We follow Duck and Pond (1989) in seeing the formation, maintenance, and conduct of relationships as processes in which such organization and reconciliation of meaning systems is carried out, usually through talk—and everyday talk at that. But such talk is not to be dismissed as a trivial thing. One of our goals is to show that talk is not an idle medium in social (or scholarly) life: It represents, "constructs," and sustains (and perhaps helps develop and change) a person's system of meaning. It also represents the operation of cognition as choice, not just in the selection of terms and styles but also as reflected in the emphasis given to different terms in the presence of different audiences or for different purposes—or circumstances of human life not given the attention they truly deserve (cf. Billig, 1987). Finally it represents a *persuasive* activity with the effect of prodding other people into acceptance of the proffered organization of meaning.

### CRITICAL THINKING QUESTIONS

1. How do individuals create common meanings? How is communication interwoven in this process?
2. What are some barriers to effective communication? How can these be remedied?
3. How do you use symbols to describe and explain past and present happenings? How does this create a relationship process.
4. Write and analyze a case based on how humans live simultaneously in the three dimensions of time—past, present, and future.

BARBARA HERMAN

# THE PRACTICE OF MORAL JUDGMENT

*Barbara Herman, a professor of philosophy at the University of California, Los Angeles, is currently chair of the Philosophy Department. This excerpt from* Mind of One's Own: Feminist Essays on Reason and Objectivity *(1993) asserts that the practice of moral judgment is vital in every interpersonal interaction.*

We begin then with acknowledgment that intimacy and connection are necessary not just to a happy human life but to the form of life we call human. (This is to be understood in the sense that deprivation of the possibility of intimacy and connection threatens a person's humanity—thus the peculiar violence of solitary confinement.[9]) And the relationships between parents and children, between friends, lovers, neighbors, are essentially partial. It is because someone is *my* neighbor, lover, or child that I have reasons for action of a certain sort. Having these relationships is to have these reasons. They are reasons of considerable strength and priority, and they are reasons such that acting on them (and not on other reasons that can produce the same outcomes) is important to maintaining the relationships that generate them. The importance of these reasons derives from connections of feeling, familiarity, love.

If my child is among those who are at risk, I do not act for my child as a moral agent but as a mother. That is to say, even when morality permits mothers to act for their children first among others (and it will not always do this), I do not act for my child because morality permits it, but because I am his mother. To be a parent is to be a person constituted by a set of motives and reasons for action. This is a matter of personal identity. The strength of these reasons, their priority and the fact that acting on them gives expression to constitutive commitments, all add to the sense that moral reasons—reasons that do not arise directly from the natural affective connection between parent and child—are out of place here.[10]

There have been different philosophical responses to these facts.[11] Some suppose they show the limits of morality as regulative of our concerns.[12]

Not only are moral reasons not ubiquitous, but they must stand aside when they conflict with personal commitments that are constitutive of selves. Others do not find in the facts reason to question the authority of morality but rather the claim of impartial morality to be the paradigm of moral concern. So, it may be claimed, just these sorts of reasons, with their grounding in feeling and connection, provide the model for a "morality of

---

[9] That someone might choose a solitary life or live well without intimate connection to others no more undermines this fact about human beings than extreme physical stoicism or a high pain threshold undermines the fact that physical assault interferes with successful human activity.

[10] Thus Freud identifies an antisocial rather than a presocial role for the family in the "origins of society." But then, as he sees it, there is a primal antagonism between the partiality of family and the sociality of "fraternal" bonds. See his *Civilizaiton and Its Discontents* (New York: Norton, 1962), chap. 3.

[11] I view them as facts about feelings we take to be reasons.

[12] Williams' influential notion of constitutive "ground projects" provides the most direct version of this view (see his "Persons, Character and Morality," in *Moral Luck)*.

care" or, as some have argued, for the distinctive moral perspective of women.[13] With either response, any claim for the priority of impartial morality is rejected as a devaluing of constitutive human concerns.

Such arguments against impartial morality are based on the feeling that our commitments and relationships of connection are sometimes of greater or deeper importance than those of impartial morality. But because it feels this way is a reason to take such feelings seriously, not a reason to give their claims automatic authority. For example, part of what growing up as a parent involves is the recognition of the place and point of such feelings. I think it is generally true that you feel like hurting anyone who causes your child undeserved pain, but that is not sufficient reason to do it. That someone close to you may suffer terribly in failing to get what he wants is not reason to make it happen when that is inappropriate. Sometimes it is the welfare of the loved one that is jeopardized by what one would do out of feeling. So the feeling needs to mature (or we who have the feeling need to mature); we need to be able to ask whether a particular expression of love is good for the one loved. And we sometimes need to let changes in those we love change our feelings (or what will count as expression of those feelings).

Since accepting limits set by autonomy, maturation, and change do not necessarily interfere with the way our supporting actions give expression to our connection with others, why should we be so easily disposed to accept that morality will interfere? We mistake the nature of feelings and their role in constituting our character to think that they are "original existences" whose modification cannot or should not be tolerated.

Let us look a little closer at the moral dimension of a relationship of connection. In addition to involving a deep bond of connection, parent-to-child is a relationship of *trust* between unequals: an essential kind of moral relationship that Annette Baier has argued cannot be expressed in impartial morality. Trust, as Baier describes it, is a noncontractual moral relationship between persons where there is vulnerability on the one hand and an implied reliance on good will and caring on the other (explicit or not, conscious or not). Because they are centered on cool, voluntary relationships between equals, Baier contends that moral theories such as Kant's cannot provide guidance in these regions. Yet, as we must agree, "a complete moral

---

[13] In addition to Gilligan and some of the essays in the Kittay and Myers volume, see also Nel Noddings, *Caring: A Feminine Approach to Ethics and Moral Education* (Berkeley: University of California Press, 1984).

HERMAN: THE PRACTICE OF MORAL JUDGMENT

philosophy would tell us how and why we should act and feel toward others in relationships of shifting and varying power asymmetry and shifting and varying intimacy."[14]

If there is tension between trust and the morality of impartiality, there is no secure alliance between trust and partiality.[15] From the fact that my child trusts that my concern for him will lead me to guard and preserve his well-being as I can, it does not follow that I violate his trust if I refrain from doing some things that will benefit him (because they are wrong or unfair) or if I act for someone else first, as when I tend to the younger child hurt in the playground or expend finite resources on a needier sibling. What my son has reason to trust is that I am committed to his well-being: among the things that matter to me most and what will determine how I act is that he do well and flourish. But, as I must often remind him (and myself), his interests are not the only ones I care about (there are not only my friends, my spouse, my students, and myself, but sometimes complete strangers or causes that claim my attention and resources), and further he will do fine, indeed he will often do better, if he relies on me less and if my life is increasingly separate from his.[16] Because I care about him, he can trust that I will count his well-being as among the basic facts that determine what I do, not as special reasons at work when I have to choose between his and someone's equal or greater claim, but as a set of changing needs that will partially determine the shape of my life.

How we understand the role of impartial morality here depends on how we represent its place in deliberation. I want to suggest that failure to recognize two quite different models of practical concern and deliberation leads to serious distortion of the problem thought to be posed by impartial morality to concerns of trust and connection. I will call them, for reasons that should become clear, the "plural interest" and the "deliberative field" models.

According to the plural-interest model, where there is connection, there are those I care about, and the effect of my caring is to give their interests greater deliberative weight: for me. They matter more. And they matter more

---

[14] Annette Baier, "Trust and Anti-Trust," *Ethics* 96 (1986), 252.

[15] This is just an extension of Baier's point, reinforcing the claim that a moral theory must have the means to talk about connection, inequality, power, and such. A moral theory that cannot get it right about these relationships cannot generate the appropriate regulative norms.

[16] Of course I would not have said this when he was six months old. But that is just the point.

to me because I care about them. When I need to balance or weigh interests—should I do some good for my son or his friend—my son counts more. Of course I have a variety of interests and concerns, and they have different weights (as I care about them and as they matter directly or instrumentally). The interests of my child weigh more than the next career step, which weighs more than my enjoyment of movies, and morality (if it has regulative priority) weighs more than all of the above. Deliberation involves further weighing and balancing. Interinterest comparisons of various sorts will be necessary. The descriptions of interests will often need to be more qualified and situationally explicit: a minor desire of my child won't count against going to a film I've waited years to see. There will be tension between looking to get the most interests satisfied and getting the most important interests satisfied. Over all these differently weighted interests loom the requirements of impartial morality in which I am not only supposed to have an interest, but an interest sufficient to support its supremely regulative role.[17]

On the plural-interest model, when morality contends with attachments it forces one against the grain, attacking the immediacy of connection. It would be natural to feel hostile to or alienated from the requirements of morality if they in this way denied a deeply felt claim of partiality. I do not mean to suggest that one would necessarily feel alienated whenever one acts for morality in a context in which connection draws you in a different direction. There are many times, especially with children, when the fact that a choice must be made impartially provides the occasion for useful moral lessons. In such circumstances, acting impartially expresses trustworthiness. The problem arises when it looks like "over here" is what I most care about, what I want to happen (and cannot not want to happen), but "over there" is what impartial morality demands. There is then deep conflict and tension. And when impartial morality wins, it is not only at the expense of what I most care about, but it provides no deliberative space even to acknowledge my concerns. The fact that I care about my son in no way affects the deliberative outcome.

If this is the way I see it, I can learn to take these losses, even to believe they are necessary. They are the price you pay for . . . and then some account of the role of morality that presumably justifies such losses by pointing to greater

---

[17] It is not a necessary feature of the model that impartial morality have this role. I present it in this form because some such version of the plural-interest model is commonly introduced in preparation for criticism of the implausibility of the demands of impartial morality. Although I am primarily concerned with the limits of this model to represent that claim of morality, the causes of its failure in this area suggest more general inadequacies.

gains elsewhere. What other kind of justification of morality could work, given the imposition of losses? And if I am unmoved by the greater gains to be had elsewhere, often gains to be had by those other than myself or those I care about—not because I am selfish, but because of who I am (a person who cares about such and such)—then my life will not seem to be valued from the moral point of view. I will act either morally badly or against myself. Clearly, so long as we stick with the plural-interest model, we will have difficulty negotiating the terrain between impartial morality and attachment.

Among the elements of a full moral theory, we should find an account of how one is to integrate the requirements of morality into one's life. One could be someone whose interest in morality was an interest (if a very strong or strongest interest) among others. But such a connection to morality is not in itself morally neutral; it will follow from the substantive nature of moral requirements. There is no unique atheoretic model of a morally serious or committed moral agent. Depending on how this feature of a moral theory is elaborated, there will be more than one answer to the question of the effects of moral requirements on the motives of connection. Since on the plural-interest model, commitment to morality is at the expense of other commitments, especially attachments, there will be reason to favor a different model if it is better able to integrate these elements in a morally good life.

On the second model, deliberation addresses a field only partially shaped by those commitments, concerns, and relationships that determine my conception of the good. They stand there as myself—as interests that I need no further or instrumental reason to care about. It is not that I care about my son and therefore, when interests are to be weighed, his weighs more. Rather, because I care about my son—because of the way I care about my son—his interests (his good) are part of my good: *the* good as I see it. But just as I know in advance that I cannot do whatever will promote my own well-being, so I know in advance and as part of my caring that I may not be able to promote his good in circumstances where it is inappropriate to determine the effective practical weight of interests by how much I care about them.

According to this deliberative-field model, the practical self does not have as its major task negotiating a settlement among independent competing claims. Insofar as one has interests and commitments, one is a human self. But a human life is not the result of a "bundle" of competing interests (among which is an interest in morality). One's interests are present on a deliberative field that contains everything that gives one reasons. Thus, in addition to interests and attachments, there are also grounds of obligation, principles of prudential rationality, and, depending on the individual, a more or less complex conception of the Good. Not everything that may seek a place on my deliberative field is good for me to have there: bad habits, destructive relationships, incompatible goals and projects. And if there is a real question about what enters (or remains on) the deliberative field—this is often a question about ends—the conditions for accepting desires or interests as ends may (and often will) shape the result.

An agent with a deliberative field partly constructed by moral principles recognizes from the outset, in the adoption of ends, that pursuit of important goals may unforeseeably lead one to means that are morally inappropriate (not permissible). The commitment to pursue an end is always conditional; this is so whether the ends are ends of interest or necessary ends. In this way ends are absorbed into a moral structure as they enter the deliberative field.

This resetting of ends in the deliberative field is not unique to moral requirements. Something analogous occurs because of potential practical conflict between different nonmoral goals. Wanting both to have a career and a family, I can pursue both and hope for the best, or I can give one end priority (absolute or weighted) over the other, or I can make action on one conditional on noninterference with the other. With other ends—say, teaching and writing—I have additional possibilities, including the revision of each of these ends to include aspects of the other (I value my teaching as an integral part of the process that leads me to successful writing, or vice versa). These need not be once and for all decisions: my sense of the relative importance of ends may change, the likelihood of conflict may diminish, still other relevant interests may come on the scene. But having set ends in a complex deliberative framework, my sense of loss on abandoning one is different than it would be if I thought of myself simply as acting for diverse and separate goals, having to give up or limit or frustrate one for the sake of another. Acting from a deliberative framework, I am in a better position to accept the outcome. This is not a matter of resignation so much as acknowledgment. Without such a framework, the decision will seem more contingent—more a matter of bad luck—and the outcome arbitrary.[18]

---

[18] I do not mean to imply that desire must be understood to have its practical effect only in one of these two ways—in the deliberative field or as an intensity-weighted reason. There are accounts of desire that build reasons into them. In the tradition of Kant criticism, however, the simpler Humean model of desire has been thought to suffice in showing the weaknesses of the Kantian account of practical activity. The deliberative-field model is intended both to describe more accurately Kantian practical deliberation and activity and to show certain limits of the Humean model.

To make sense of the deliberative-field model (and so, I believe, of Kantian ethics[19]), we must resist the tendency to think of the Good—an agent's conception of what is good—as a composite cluster of objects of desire, perhaps structured by priority principles and other success-oriented practical devices external to the ends we have because of the desires we have. This leaves the desire-object relation too much intact, with the agent passive with respect to her bundle of desires. Desires do not give reasons for action: they may explain why such and such is a reason for action, or even why something can be an effective reason for action, but the desire itself is not a reason. One can take the fact of a desire to be a reason, but that just is to hold that desire, or this desire, is good.[20] Nor is it enough to replace desire with "end that it is rational or good to have." That still suggests discrete sets of interests and ends. What is missing—what you are supposed to learn as a maturing agent—is the integration and transformation of the ends in light of one another, of one's practical situation, and of one's conception of place and importance understood through the regulative principles—aesthetic, moral, prudential—one accepts. One has, or tries to have, a good life.

We will be inclined to view deliberation differently as we take ourselves to be either active or passive with respect to our desires. If we take the paradigmatic deliberative situation to be either means-end calculation or the resolution of conflict between ends, it will look as if our starting point is the pursuit of discrete goods (the objects of desires or interests) whose compatibility is a matter of luck. Now sometimes this is just the way things are. Circumstances can sharpen conflict, as they can make deliberation look like a search for the least costly compromise. But focusing on these cases reinforces a sense of our passivity as agents: what Kant meant, I believe, by a heteronomy of the will.

Our sense of things is different if we look instead at the ways we are or can be active with respect to our desires. We have desires we do not want to act on; we have desires we act on but do not value; we come to discover that some of what we want is caused by needs that would be better met some other way (as when an underlying insecurity leads to placing excessive demands on others). Refusing desires of the last two types is importantly not

---

[19] Textual and other support for this claim can be found in Chapter 8.

[20] I have borrowed this way of putting things from Phillipa Foot (unpublished manuscript, 1988), who sees confusion about this occurring because often it is reasonable to satisfy desires. If we imagine a very different sort of creature who had desires that were not in general good (for it) to satisfy, it is not clear how we would then regard desires.

like restraining one's desire for sweets: a kind of desire we like to think we can turn our back on at will (or fail at controlling because of "weakness of will," a kind of muscular insufficiency). Activity involves more than effective second-order wants.

When, for example, I hear my mother's parental anxieties in my own voice as I criticize my son, I cannot resolve the problem I discover just by abandoning some end or disowning some desire, however much distress I feel about what I am doing. Part of what I discover in these moments is who I am—or who I am as a parent. I listen and find out what I desire. But then it is not enough to say that I do not want to act on these desires, and also not enough to say that I do not want to have them. I want them not to have a place in the complex of desires and thoughts that constitute myself as a parent. This may be no easy thing, for the very desires I would disavow may hold together things I like about myself as a parent.

Someone who is otherwise a good friend cannot come through when there is illness involved; he simply cannot see what there is to do. Suppose he comes to believe that he acts inadequately in these circumstances. What can he do? He wants to act as a good friend. He has the relevant ends. The problem is that illness makes him panic. Perhaps as a child he was made to feel responsible for a sick parent. Now, confronted with illness in others, he feels inadequate; he withdraws in the face of what he feels will be certain failure.

When we discover that with our children or our friends we are acting in ways that do not match our values or ideals, the practical task involves special difficulties, in the sense that we must come to see why we would do what we do not seem to want to do (this is *not* weakness of will). Success at this task may still leave us trying to figure out what to do with, or what we are able to do with, what we find. This is a function of what we might think of as the enmeshedness or even geology of desire.

Encountering (or more often stumbling against) such a complex, we may be enlightened or transformed, or moved to therapy, or despair. Affective disorders alert us to inertial features of character. We cannot just choose to care (about some things), and we cannot just prize out an unwanted desire by identifying and rejecting its object. So also we come to see that you cannot just add ends: not only because there may be conflict in realizing ends but also because the adoption of some ends resonates in the deliberative field. For the good friend to lose his panic in the face of illness, he may have to revise his relations with his mother (now and in the past).

The point here is not to argue for therapy or discuss the relative merits of deep versus shallow psychological change, but to let the difficulty of these matters direct us to a different picture (or set of pictures) about the Good as the complex object not of desire, but of practical agency.

If the attempt to abandon ends may draw us into more complexity than expected, we should not suppose that adopting an end is any simple matter. Ends are not adopted in isolation from one another. It is not only that their joint pursuit may not be possible. Adopting an end is (or can be) wanting some interest to be effective in my life. This may alter other ends I already have and affect what ends I may come to have. Wanting friendship to play a greater role in my life does not just mean creating more time for friends (and so less for the pursuit of other ends). It may make me see in my present attachment to other ends a lack of concern for others. Or vice versa: coming to take my work more seriously may reveal a will to distraction in my absorption with others. (When everything works for the best, this kind of insight need not lead to a conflict with friendship: it can make me a better friend.)

Because of the complexity of relations among ends, it can be difficult to predict the outcome of deliberation—for another agent, but equally sometimes for ourselves. We may not know in advance what impact circumstances will have on ends. When situations are new or complex, what an agent wants can depend on her response to the situations she finds herself in and on the way she makes use of whatever knowledge and sensitivity she can bring to bear. Some deliberative outcomes will reshape ends; others can lead her to see the world in a different way. Deliberation itself will then reshape or reconfigure the deliberative field.

Deliberation structured by *substantive* regulative principles involves still more. If in all of my relationships I am to treat people as ends, then as this conception has deliberative priority, what is possible for me in relationships will be different. My ends of friendship and intimacy will not be what they would have been otherwise. It is not that I must replace motives of connection with moral motives; I will have *different* motives of connection. Perhaps I will be more sensitive to problems of exclusion or of fairness. Perhaps I will be less tempted to interfere "for the best." It does not follow from the interpenetration of motives of connection with moral concerns that these will be the changes: what the changes are will depend on what I discover about the structure and tendencies of my relationships.

This transformational process does not go only one way. Commitment to treat others as ends (or in accordance with the dictates of some moral conception or ideal) does not by itself guide deliberation. As I come to understand more of what is involved in friendship and intimacy, so I also come to see more of what the moral requirement amounts to. Without knowledge of how intimacy engages vulnerabilities, I cannot see that or how certain behaviors which could be acceptable among strangers are impermissibly manipulative among intimates, and vice versa. Where power and inequality mix with intimacy, questions of exploitation and abuse are raised. Such questions are not part of the concept of treating persons as ends. They are what we discover treating persons as ends amounts to, given what human relationships tend to be like, or what particular relationships involve. Without such knowledge, moral judgment is not possible.[21]

Let us briefly retrace our steps. The sense of conflict and loss that we think follows from the regulation of relationships and attachments by impartial moral principles might instead be a function of the way we understand the connection between ends and deliberative principles. My discussion of the difference between activity and passivity with respect to our desires and ends was aimed, on the one hand, to defeat a picture of an autarchy of ends slotted into a legalistic or merely formal deliberative framework and, on the other hand, to replace that picture with the idea of the Good as a constructed object of practical agency.[22] Locating attachments in a deliberative field, we uncover a mutual practical dependence between formal moral principle (as it applies to us) and the structure of attachment.

Some resistance to this move may come from a presumed tension between moral and personal reasons that follows from a split in the practical between the moral and the natural. There is the thought that personal attachments—and especially what is good in them—are in some special way natural or spontaneous or pure. So one might worry that moral transformation might involve loss of this natural good. This concern is to be met with the reminder that "natural" relationships are, among other things, the locales of abuse, infantilization, exploitation, and other sins of intimacy. Intimacy may be a natural need, or arise from natural motives, but the relationships among adults usually are, when healthy, complex and mediated descendants of spontaneous or natural attachments.

When there is moral criticism of a relationship, we should not think that morality aims to replace the structure of attachment. Love for another may be necessary to change a relationship whose premises or practices are morally faulty. Morality alone can do no more than indicate the fault and give reason not to accept terms of relationship in which the fault is embod-

---

[21] A more general conclusion of this sort if argued for in Chapter 4, section III.

ied; it cannot by itself direct the parties to a satisfactory resolution *within* the framework of intimacy.

As our conception of the Good becomes increasingly complex (involving morality but also work and children and the various kinds of intimacy), our understanding of our activities and attachments should reflect that complexity. This is not a loss of innocence that we have reason to reject (or rationally regret).

## CRITICAL THINKING QUESTIONS

1. How does Herman outline the practice of moral judgment?
2. What are Herman's views on treating persons as ends? Examine this in light of your own practices.
3. Give an example of a time when you made a moral decision in an interpersonal relationship. What made the decision difficult? What motivated you to make the decisions that you did?
4. Write and analyze a case based on moral deliberation within a close, personal relationship.

## SIMONE DE BEAUVOIR

# MYTH AND REALITY

*Simone de Beauvoir (1908–1986), a French philosopher best known for her extensive contributions to the development of feminist thought, has published several books in feminism and discrimination. She was the longtime companion of Jean-Paul Sartre. This 1952 article explains the myths that have often controlled the interpersonal behaviors of women and how harmful many of these controlling myths and behaviors are to the self and others.*

The myth of woman plays a considerable part in literature, but what is its importance in daily life? To what extent does it affect the customs and conduct of individuals? In replying to this question it will be necessary to state precisely the relations this myth bears to reality.

There are different kinds of myths. This one, the myth of woman, sublimating an immutable aspect of the human condition—namely, the "division" of humanity into two classes of individuals—is a static myth. It projects into the realm of Platonic ideas a reality that is directly experienced or is conceptualized on a basis of experience; in place of fact, value, significance, knowledge, empirical law, it substitutes a transcendental Idea, timeless, unchangeable, necessary. This idea is indisputable because it is beyond the given: it is endowed with absolute truth. Thus, as against the dispersed, contingent, and multiple existences of actual women, mythical thought opposes the Eternal Feminine, unique and changeless. If the definition provided for this concept is contradicted by the behavior of flesh-and-blood women, it is the latter who are wrong: we are told not that Femininity is a false entity, but that the women concerned are not feminine. The contrary facts of experience are impotent against the myth. In a way, however, its source is in experience. Thus it is quite true that woman is other than man, and this alterity is directly felt in desire, the embrace, love; but the real relation is one of reciprocity; as such it gives rise to authentic drama. Through eroticism, love, friendship, and their alternatives, deception, hate, rivalry, the relation is a struggle between concious beings each of whom wishes to be essential, it is the mutual recognition of free beings who confirm one another's freedom, it is the vague transition from aversion to participation. To pose Woman is to pose the absolute Other, without reciprocity, denying against all experience that she is a subject, a fellow human being.

In actuality, of course, women appear under various aspects; but each of the myths built up around the subject of woman is intended to sum her up *in toto;* each aspires to be unique. In consequence, a number of incompatible myths exist, and men tarry musing before the strange incoherencies manifested by the idea of Femininity. As every woman has a share in a majority of these archetypes—each of which lays claim to containing the sole Truth of woman—men of today also are moved again in the presence of their female companions to an astonishment like that of the old sophists who failed to understand how man could be blond and dark at the same time! Transition toward the absolute was indicated long ago in social phenomena: relations are easily congealed in classes, functions in types, just as relations, to the childish mentality, are fixed in things. Patriarchal society, for example, being centered upon the conservation of the patrimony, implies necessarily, along with those who own and transmit wealth, the existence of men and women who take property away from its owners and put it into circulation. The men—adventurers, swindlers, thieves, speculators—

are generally repudiated by the group; the women, employing their erotic attraction, can induce young men and even fathers of families to scatter their patrimonies, without ceasing to be within the law. Some of these women appropriate their victims' fortunes or obtain legacies by using undue influence; this role being regarded as evil, those who play it are called "bad women." But the fact is that quite to the contrary they are able to appear in some other setting—at home with their fathers, brothers, husbands, or lovers—as guardian angels; and the courtesan who "plucks" rich financiers is, for painters and writers, a generous patroness. It is easy to understand in actual experience the ambiguous personality of Aspasia or Mme de Pompadour. But if woman is depicted as the Praying Mantis, the Mandrake, the Demon, then it is most confusing to find in woman also the Muse, the Goddess Mother, Beatrice.

As group symbols and social types are generally defined by means of antonyms in pairs, ambivalence will seem to be an intrinsic quality of the Eternal Feminine. The saintly mother has for correlative the cruel stepmother, the angelic young girl has the perverse virgin: thus it will be said sometimes that Mother equals Life, sometimes that Mother equals Death, that every virgin is pure spirit or flesh dedicated to the devil.

Evidently it is not reality that dictates to society or to individuals their choice between the two opposed basic categories; in every period, in each case, society and the individual decide in accordance with their needs. Very often they project into the myth adopted the institutions and values to which they adhere. Thus the paternalism that claims woman for hearth and home defines her as sentiment, inwardness, immanence. In fact every existent is at once immanence and transcendence; when one offers the existent no aim, or prevents him from attaining any, or robs him of his victory, then his transcendence falls vainly into the past—that is to say, falls back into immanence. This is the lot assigned to woman in the patriarchate; but it is in no way a vocation, any more than slavery is the vocation of the slave. The development of this mythology is to be clearly seen in Auguste Comte. To identify Woman with Altruism is to guarantee to man absolute rights in her devotion, it is to impose on women a categorical imperative.

The myth must not be confused with the recognition of significance; significance is immanent in the object; it is revealed to the mind through a living experience; whereas the myth is a transcendent Idea that escapes the mental grasp entirely. When in *L'Age d'homme* Michel Leiris describes his vision of the feminine organs, he tells us things of significance and elaborates no myth. Wonder at the feminine body, dislike for menstrual blood, come from perceptions of a concrete reality. There is nothing mythical in the experience that reveals the voluptuous qualities of feminine flesh, and it is not an excursion into myth if one attempts to describe them through comparisons with flowers or pebbles. But to say that Woman is Flesh, to say that the Flesh is Night and Death, or that it is the splendor of the Cosmos, is to abandon terrestrial truth and soar into an empty sky. For man also is flesh for woman; and woman is not merely a carnal object; and the flesh is clothed in special significance for each person and in each experience. And likewise it is quite true that woman—like man—is a being rooted in nature; she is more enslaved to the species than is the male, her animality is more manifest; but in her as in him the given traits are taken on through the fact of existence, she belongs also to the human realm. To assimilate her to Nature is simply to act from prejudice. . . .

To tell the truth, her situation makes woman very liable to such a view. Her physiological nature is very complex; she herself submits to it as to some rigmarole from outside; her body does not seem to her to be a clear expression of herself; within it she feels herself a stranger. Indeed, the bond that in every individual connects the physiological life and the psychic life— or better the relation existing between the contingence of an individual and the free spirit that assumes it—is the deepest enigma implied in the condition of being human, and this enigma is presented in its most disturbing form in woman.

But what is commonly referred to as the mystery is not the subjective solitude of the conscious self, nor the secret organic life. It is on the level of communication that the word has its true meaning: it is not a reduction to pure silence, to darkness, to absence; it implies a stammering presence that fails to make itself manifest and clear. To say that woman is mystery is to say, not that she is silent, but that her language is not understood; she is there, but hidden behind veils; she exists beyond these uncertain appearances. What is she? Angel, demon, one inspired, an actress? It may be supposed either that there are answers to these questions which are impossible to discover, or, rather, that no answer is adequate because a fundamental ambiguity marks the feminine being; and perhaps in her heart she is even for herself quite indefinable: a sphinx.

The fact is that she would be quite embarrassed to decide *what* she *is;* but this not because the hidden truth is too vague to be discerned: it is because in this domain there is no truth. An existent *is* nothing other than what he does; the possible does not extend beyond the real, essence does not precede existence: in pure subjectivity, the human being *is not anything.* He is to be measured by his acts. Of a peasant woman one can say that she is a good or a bad worker, of an actress that she has or does not have talent; but if one considers a woman in her immanent presence, her inward self, one can say absolutely nothing about her, she falls short of having any qualifications. Now, in amorous or conjugal relations, in all relations where the woman is the vassal, the other, she is being dealt with in her and the burdens that physiologically are women's lot, since these are "intended by Nature"; men use them as a pretext for increasing the misery of the feminine lot still further, for instance by refusing to grant to woman any right to sexual pleasure, by making her work like a beast of burden.[1]

Of all these myths, none is more firmly anchored in masculine hearts than that of the feminine "mystery." It has numerous advantages. And first of all it permits an easy explanation of all that appears inexplicable; the man who "does not understand" a woman is happy to substitute an objective resistance for a subjective deficiency of mind; instead of admitting his ignorance, he perceives the presence of a "mystery" outside himself: an alibi, indeed, that flatters laziness and vanity at once. A heart smitten with love thus avoids many disappointments: if the loved one's behavior is capricious, her remarks stupid, then the mystery serves to excuse it all. And finally, thanks again to the mystery, that negative relation is perpetuated which seemed to Kierkegaard infinitely preferable to positive possession; in the company of a living enigma man remains alone—alone with his dreams, his hopes, his fears, his love, his vanity. This subjective game, which can go all the way from vice to mystical ecstasy, is for many a more attractive experience than an authentic relation with a human being. What foundations exist for such a profitable illusion?

Surely woman is, in a sense, mysterious, "mysterious as is all the world," according to Maeterlinck. Each is *subject* only for himself; each can grasp in immanence only himself, alone: from this point of view the *other* is always a mystery. To men's eyes the opacity of the self-knowing self, of the *pour-soi*, is denser in the *other* who is feminine; men are unable to penetrate her special experience through any working of sympathy: they are condemned to ignorance of the quality of woman's erotic pleasure, the discomfort of

---

[1] Cf. Balzac: *Physiology of Marriage:* "Pay no attention to her murmurs, her cries, her pains; *nature has made her for our use* and for bearing everything: children, sorrows, blows and pains inflicted by man. Do not accuse yourself of hardness. In all the codes of so-called civilized nations, man has written the laws that ranged woman's destiny under this bloody epigraph: "Vae victis! Woe to the weak!"

menstruation, and the pains of childbirth. The truth is that there is mystery on both sides: as the *other* who is of masculine sex, every man, also, has within him a presence, an inner self impenetrable to woman; she in turn is in ignorance of the male's erotic feeling. But in accordance with the immanence. It is noteworthy that the feminine comrade, colleague, and associate are without mystery; on the other hand, if the vassal is male, if, in the eyes of a man or a woman who is older, or richer, a young fellow, for example, plays the role of the inessential object, then he too becomes shrouded in mystery. And this uncovers for us a substructure under the feminine mystery which is economic in nature.

A sentiment cannot be supposed to be anything. "In the domain of sentiments," writes Gide, "the real is not distinguished from the imaginary. And if to imagine one loves is enough to be in love, then also to tell oneself that one imagines oneself to be in love when one is in love is enough to make one forthwith love a little less." Discrimination between the imaginary and the real can be made only through behavior. Since man occupies a privileged situation in this world, he is in a position to show his love actively; very often he supports the woman or at least helps her; in marrying her he gives her social standing; he makes her presents; his independent economic and social position allows him to take the initiative and think up contrivances: it was M. de Norpois who, when separated from Mme. de Villeparisis, made twenty-four-hour trips to visit her. Very often the man is busy, the woman idle: he *gives* her the time he passes with her; she takes it: is it with pleasure, passionately, or only for amusement? Does she accept these benefits through love or through self-interest? Does she love her husband or her marriage? Of course, even the man's evidence is ambiguous: is such and such a gift granted through love or out of pity? But while normally a woman finds numerous advantages in her relations with a man, his relations with a woman are profitable to a man only in so far as he loves her. And so one can almost judge the degree of his affection by the total picture of his attitude.

But a woman hardly has means for sounding her own heart; according to her moods she will view her own sentiments in different lights, and as she submits to them passively, one interpretation will be no truer than another. In those rare instances in which she holds the position of economic and social privilege, the mystery is reversed, showing that it does not pertain to *one* sex rather than the other, but to the situation. For a great many women the roads to transcendence are blocked: because they *do* nothing, they fail to *make themselves* anything. They wonder indefinitely what they *could have* become, which sets them to asking about what they *are*. It is a vain question. If man fails to discover that secret essence of femininity, it is simply because it does not exist. Kept on the fringe of the world, woman cannot be objectively defined through this world, and her mystery conceals nothing but emptiness.

Furthermore, like all the oppressed, woman deliberately dissembles her objective actuality; the slave, the servant, the indigent, all who depend upon the caprices of a master, have learned to turn toward him a changeless smile or an enigmatic impassivity; their real sentiments, their actual behavior, are carefully hidden. And moreover woman is taught from adolescence to lie to men, to scheme, to be wily. In speaking to them she wears an artificial expression on her face; she is cautious, hypocritical, play-acting.

But the Feminine Mystery as recognized in mythical thought is a more profound matter. In fact, it is immediately implied in the mythology of the absolute Other. If it be admitted that the inessential conscious being, too, is a clear subjectivity, capable of performing the *Cogito*, then it is also admitted that this being is in truth sovereign and returns to being essential; in order that all reciprocity may appear quite impossible, it is necessary for the Other to be for itself an other, for its very subjectivity to be affected by its otherness; this consciousness which would be alienated as a consciousness, in its pure immanent presence, would evidently be Mystery. It would be Mystery in itself from the fact that it would be Mystery for itself; it would be absolute Mystery.

In the same way it is true that, beyond the secrecy created by their dissembling, there is mystery in the Black, the Yellow, in so far as they are considered absolutely as the inessential Other. It should be noted that the American citizen, who profoundly baffles the average European, is not, however, considered as being "mysterious": one states more modestly that one does not understand him. And similarly woman does not always "understand" man; but there is no such thing as a masculine mystery. The point is that rich America, and the male, are on the Master side and that Mystery belongs to the slave.

To be sure, we can only muse in the twilight byways of bad faith upon the positive reality of the Mystery; like certain marginal hallucinations, it dissolves under the attempt to view it fixedly. Literature always fails in attempting to portray "mysterious" women; they can appear only at the beginning of a novel as strange, enigmatic figures; but unless the story remains unfinished they give up their secret in the end and they are then simply consistent and transparent persons. The heroes in Peter Cheyney's books, for example, never cease to be astonished at the unpredictable caprices of women: no one can ever guess how they will act, they upset all calculations. The fact is that once the springs of their action are revealed to the reader, they are seen to be very simple mechanisms: this woman was a spy, that one a thief; however clever the plot, there is always a key; and it could not be otherwise, had the author all the talent and imagination in the world. Mystery is never more than a mirage that vanishes as we draw near to look at it.

We can see now that the myth is in large part explained by its usefulness to man. The myth of woman is a luxury. It can appear only if man escapes from the urgent demands of his needs; the more relationships are concretely lived, the less they are idealized. The fellah of ancient Egypt, the Bedouin peasant, the artisan of the Middle Ages, the worker of today has in the requirements of work and poverty relations with his particular woman companion which are too definite for her to be embellished with an aura either auspicious or inauspicious. The epochs and the social classes that have been marked by the leisure to dream have been the ones to set up the images, black and white, of femininity. But along with luxury there was utility; these dreams were irresistibly guided by interests. Surely most of the myths had roots in the spontaneous attitude of man toward his own existence and toward the world around him. But going beyond experience toward the transcendent Idea was deliberately used by patriarchal society for purposes of self-justification; through the myths this society imposed its laws and customs upon individuals in a picturesque, effective manner; it is under a mythical form that the group-imperative is indoctrinated into each conscience. Through such intermediaries as religions, traditions, language, tales, songs, movies, the myths penetrate even into such existences as are most harshly enslaved to material realities. Here everyone can find sublimation of his drab experiences: deceived by the woman he loves, one declares that she is a Crazy Womb; another, obsessed by his impotence, calls her a Praying Mantis; still another enjoys his wife's company: behold, she is Harmony, Rest, the Good Earth! The taste for eternity at a bargain, for a pocket-sized absolute, which is shared by a majority of men, is satisfied by myths. The smallest emotion, a slight annoyance, becomes the reflection of a timeless Idea—an illusion agreeably flattering to the vanity.

## CRITICAL THINKING QUESTIONS

1. What are some of the remarkable considerations in de Beauvoir's writing, particularly for 1952?

2. de Beauvoir states that the more relationships are concretely lived, the less they are idealized. Explain some of the problems associated with idealizing or making a mystery of another person.
3. What are some of the myths that traditionally have placed women in nurturant situations?
4. Write and analyze a case based on breaking through a conventional myth.

ANNETTE BAIER

# TRUST AND ANTITRUST

*Annette Baier was born in New Zealand and studied philosophy at Oxford University. She was a professor of philosophy at the University of Pittsburgh. She has written numerous articles for philosophical journals and is the author of the book* Postures of the Mind. *This 1986 article details the numerous implications of trust through a strong philosophical perspective.*

Whether or not everything which matters to us is the sort of thing that can thrive or languish (I may care most about my stamp collection) or even whether all the possibly thriving things we care about need trust in order to thrive (does my rubber tree?), there surely is something basically right about Bok's claim. Given that I cannot myself guard my stamp collection at all times, nor take my rubber tree with me on my travels, the custody of these things that matter to me must often be transferred to others, presumably to others I trust. Without trust, what matters to me would be unsafe, unless like the Stoic I attach myself only to what can thrive, or be safe from harm, *however* others act. The starry heavens above and the moral law within had better be about the only things that matter to me, if there is no one I can trust in any way. Even my own Stoic virtue will surely thrive better if it evokes some trust from others, inspires some trustworthiness in them, or is approved and imitated by them.

To Bok's statement, however, we should add another, that not all the things that thrive when there is trust between people, and which matter, are things that should be encouraged to thrive. Exploitation and conspiracy, as much as justice and fellowship, thrive better in an atmosphere of trust. There are immoral as well as moral trust relationships, and trustbusting can be a morally proper goal. If we are to tell when morality requires the preservation of trust, when it requires the destruction of trust, we obviously need to distinguish different forms of trust, and to look for some morally relevant features they may possess. In this paper I make a start on this large task.

It is a start, not a continuation, because there has been a strange silence on the topic in the tradition of moral philosophy with which I am familiar. Psychologists and sociologists have discussed it, lawyers have worked out the requirements of equity on legal trusts, political philosophers have discussed trust in governments, and there has been some discussion of trust when philosophers address the assurance problem in Prisoner's Dilemma contexts. But we, or at least I, search in vain for any general account of the morality of trust relationships. The question, Whom should I trust in what way, and why? has not been the central question in moral philosophy as we know it. Yet if I am right in claiming that morality, as anything more than a law within, itself requires trust in order to thrive, and that immorality too thrives on some forms of trust, it seems pretty obvious that we ought, as moral philosophers, to look into the question of what forms of trust are needed for the thriving of the version of morality we endorse, and into the morality of that and other forms of trust. A minimal condition of adequacy for any version of the true morality, if truth has anything to do with reality, is that it not have to condemn the conditions needed for its own thriving. Yet we will be in no position to apply that test to the trust in which morality thrives until we have worked out, at least in a provisional way, how to judge trust relationships from a moral point of view.

Moral philosophers have always been interested in cooperation between people, and so it is surprising that they have not said more than they have about trust. It seems fairly obvious that any form of cooperative activity, including the division of labor, requires the cooperators to trust one another to do their bit, or at the very least to trust the overseer with his whip to do his bit, where coercion is relied on. One would expect contractarians to investigate the forms of trust and distrust parties to a contract exhibit. Utilitarians too should be concerned with the contribution to the general happiness of various climates of trust, so be concerned to understand the nature, roots, and varieties of trust. One might also have expected those with a moral theory of the virtues to have looked at trustworthiness, or at willingness to give trust. But when we turn to the great moral philosophers, in our tradition, what we find can scarcely be said to be even a sketch of a moral theory of trust. At most we get a few hints of directions in which we might go.

Plato in the *Republic* presumably expects the majority of citizens to trust the philosopher kings to rule wisely and expects the elite to trust their underlings not to poison their wine, nor set fire to their libraries but neither proper trust nor proper trustworthiness are among the virtues he dwells on as necessary in the cooperating parties in his good society. His version of justice and of the "friendship" supposed to exist between ruler and ruled seems to *imply* such virtues of trust, but he does not himself draw out the implications. In the *Laws* he mentions distrust as an evil produced by association with seafaring traders, but it is only a mention.[2] The same sort of claim can also be made about Aristotle—his virtuous person, like Plato's, must place his trust in that hypothetical wise person who will teach him just how much anger and pride and fear to feel with what reasons, when, and toward which objects. Such a wise man presumably also knows just how much trust in whom, on what matters, and how much trustworthiness, should be cultivated, as well as who should show trust toward whom, but such crucial wisdom and such central virtues are not discussed by Aristotle, as far as I am aware. (He does, in the *Politics*, condemn tyrants for sowing seeds of distrust, and his discussion of friendship might be cited as one place where he implicitly recognizes the importance of trust; could someone one distrusted be a second self to one? But that is implicit only, and in any case would cover only trust between friends.) Nor do later moral philosophers do much better on this count.[3]

There are some forms of trust to which the great philosophers *have* given explicit attention. Saint Thomas Aquinas, and other Christian moralists, have extolled the virtue of faith and, more relevantly, of hope, and so have

---

[2] Plato, *Laws* 4.705a. I owe this reference to John Cooper, who found my charge that Plato and Aristotle had neglected the topic of trust ungenerous, given how much they fairly clearly took for granted about its value and importance. (But taking for granted is a form of neglect.)

[3] Besides Bok and Locke, whom I refer to, those who have said something about it include N. Hartmann, *Ethik* (Berlin: W. de Gruyter, 1962), pp. 468 ff.; Virginia Held, *Rights and Goods* (New York and London: Free Press, 1984), esp. chap 5. "The Grounds for Social Trust"; I). O. Thomas, "The Duty to Trust," *Aristotelian Society Proceedings* (1970), pp 89–101. It is invoked in passing by Aurel Kolnai in "Forgiveness," in *Ethics, Value and Reality*, ed. Bernard Williams and David Wiggins (Indianapolis: Macmillan Co., 1978): "Trust in the world, unless it is vitiated by hairbrained optimism and dangerous irresponsibility, may be looked upon not to be sure as the very starting point and very basis but perhaps is the epitome and culmination of morality" (p. 223): and by John R. S. Wilson in "In One Another's Power" *Ethics* 88 (1978): 303.

said something about trust in God. And in the modern period some of the great moral and political philosophers, in particular John Locke, looked at trust in governments and officials, and some have shown what might be called an obsessive trust in contracts and contractors, even if not, after Hobbes's good example here, an equal obsession with the grounds for such trust. It is selective attention then, rather than total inattention, which is the philosophical phenomenon on which I wish to remark, tentatively to explain, and try to terminate or at least to interrupt.

Trust, the phenomenon we are so familiar with that we scarcely notice its presence and its variety, is shown by us and responded to by us not only with intimates but with strangers, and even with declared enemies. We trust our enemies not to fire at us when we lay down our arms and put out a white flag. In Britain burglars and police used to trust each other not to carry deadly weapons. We often trust total strangers, such as those from whom we ask directions in foreign cities, to direct rather than misdirect us, or to tell us so if they do not know what we want to know; and we think we should do the same for those who ask the same help from us. Of course we are often disappointed, rebuffed, let down, or betrayed when we exhibit such trust in others, and we are often exploited when we show the wanted trustworthiness. We do in fact, wisely or stupidly, virtuously or viciously, show trust in a great variety of forms, and manifest a great variety of versions of trustworthiness, both with intimates and with strangers. We trust those we encounter in lonely library stacks to be searching for books, not victims. We sometimes let ourselves fall asleep on trains or planes, trusting neighboring strangers not to take advantage of our defenselessness. We put our bodily safety into the hands of pilots, drivers, doctors, with scarcely any sense of recklessness. We used not to suspect that the food we buy might be deliberately poisoned, and we used to trust our children to day-care centers.

We may still have no choice but to buy food and to leave our children in day-care centers, but now we do it with suspicion and anxiety. Trust is always an invitation not only to confidence tricksters but also to terrorists, who discern its most easily destroyed and socially vital forms. Criminals, not moral philosophers, have been the experts at discerning different forms of trust. Most of us notice a given form of trust most easily after its sudden demise or severe injury. We inhabit a climate of trust as we inhabit an atmosphere and notice it as we notice air, only when it becomes scarce or polluted.

We may have no choice but to continue to rely on the local shop for food, even after some of the food on its shelves has been found to have been poisoned with intent. We can still rely where we no longer trust. What is the difference between trusting others and merely relaying on them? It seems to be reliance on their good will toward one, as distinct from their dependable habits, or only on their dependably exhibited fear, anger, or other motives compatible with ill will toward one, or on motives not directed on one at all. We may rely on our fellows' fear of the newly appointed security guards in shops to deter them from injecting poison into the food on the shelves. Once we have ceased to trust them, we may rely on the shopkeeper's concern for his profits to motivate him to take effective precautions against poisoners and also trust him to *want* his customers not to be harmed by his products, at least as long as this want can be satisfied without frustrating his wish to increase his profits. Trust is often mixed with other species of reliance on persons. Trust which is reliance on another's good will, perhaps minimal good will, contrasts with the forms of reliance on others' reactions and attitudes which are shown by the comedian, the advertiser, the blackmailer, the kidnapper-extortioner, and the terrorist, who all depend on particular attitudes and reactions of others for the success of their actions. We all depend on one anothers' psychology in countless ways, but this is not yet to trust them. The trusting can be betrayed, or at least let down, and not just disappointed. Kant's neighbors who counted on his regular habits as a clock for their own less automatically regular ones might be disappointed with him if he slept in one day, but not let down by him, let alone had their trust betrayed. When I trust another, I depend on her good will toward me. I need not either acknowledge this reliance nor believe that she has either invited or acknowledged such trust since there is such a thing as unconscious trust, as unwanted trust, as forced receipt of trust, and as trust which the trusted is unaware of. (Plausible conditions for proper trust will be that it survives consciousness, by both parties, and that the trusted has had some opportunity to signify acceptance or rejection, to warn the trusting if their trust is unacceptable.)

Where one depends on another's good will, one is necessarily vulnerable to the limits of that good will. One leaves others an opportunity to harm one when one trusts, and also shows one's confidence that they will not take it. Reasonable trust will require good grounds for such confidence in another good will, or at least the absence of good grounds for expecting their ill will or indifference. Trust then, on this first approximation, is accepted vulnerability to another's possible but not expected ill will (or lack of good will) toward one.

What we now need to do, to get any sense of the variety of forms of trust, is to look both at varieties of vulnerability and at varieties of grounds for not expecting others to take advantage of it. One way to do the former, which I shall take, is to look at the variety of sorts of goods or things one values or cares about, which can be left or put within the striking power of others, and the variety of ways we can let or leave others "close" enough to what we value to be able to harm it. Then we can look at various reasons we might have for wanting or accepting such closeness of those with power to harm us, and for confidence that they will not use this power. In this way we can hope to explicate the vague terms "good will" and "ill will." If it be asked why the initial emphasis is put on the trusting's vulnerability, on the risks rather than the benefits of trust, part of the answer has already been given—namely, that we come to realize what trust involves retrospectively and posthumously, once our vulnerability is brought home to us by actual wounds. The other part of the answer is that even when one does become aware of trust and intentionally continues a particular case of it, one need not intend to achieve any particular benefit from it—one need not trust a person in order to receive some gain, even when in fact one does gain. Trusting, as an intentional mental phenomenon, need not be purposive. But intentional trusting does require awareness of one's confidence that the trusted will not harm one, although they could harm one. It is not a Hobbesian obsession with strike force which dictates the form of analysis. I have sketched but, rather, the natural order of consciousness and self-consciousness of trust, which progresses from initially unself-conscious trust to awareness of risk along with confidence that it is a good risk, on to some realization of why we are taking this particular risk, and eventually to some evaluation of what we may generally gain and what we may lose from the willingness to take such risks. The ultimate point of what we are doing when we trust may be the last thing we come to realize. . . .

The more extensive the discretionary powers of the trusted, the less clear-cut will be the answer to the question of when trust is disappointed. The truster, who always needs good judgment to know whom to trust and how much discretion to give, will also have some scope for discretion in judging what should count as failing to meet trust, either through incompetence, negligence, or ill will. In any case of a questionable exercise of discretion there will be room both for forgiveness of unfortunate outcomes and for tact in treatment of the question of whether there is anything to forgive. One thing that can destroy a trust relationship fairly quickly is the combination of a rigoristic unforgiving attitude on the part of the truster and a touchy sensitivity to any criticism on the part of the trusted. If a trust relationship is to continue, some tact and willingness to forgive on the part of the truster and some willingness on the part of the trusted both to be forgiven and to forgive unfair criticisms, seem essential.[5] The need for this will be greater the more discretion the trusted has.

If part of what the truster entrusts to the trusted are discretionary powers, then the truster risks abuse of those and the successful disguise of such abuse. The special vulnerability which trust involves is vulnerability to not yet noticed harm, or to disguised ill will. What one forgives or tactfully averts one's eyes from may be not well-meant but ill-judged or incompetent attempts to care for what is entrusted but, rather, ill-meant and cleverly disguised abuses of discretionary power. To understand the moral risks of trust, it is important to see the special sort of vulnerability it introduces. Yet the discretionary element which introduces this special danger is essential to that which trust at its best makes possible. . . .

It is fairly easy, once we look to see how this special vulnerability is involved in many ordinary forms of trust. We trust the mailman to deliver and not tamper with the mail, and to some extent we trust his discretion in interpreting what "tampering" covers. Normally we do not expect him to read our mail but to deliver it unread, even when the message is open, on a postcard. But on occasion it may be proper, or at least not wrong, for him to read it. I have had friendly mailmen (in Greek villages and in small Austrian towns) who tell me what my mail announces as they hand it over: "Your relatives have recovered and can travel now, and are soon arriving!" Such

---

[5] This point I take from the fascinating sociological analysis of trust given by Niklas Luhmann (*Trust and Power* [Chichester, N.Y., 1979]) which I discovered while revising this paper. In many ways my analysis agrees with his, insofar as I understand the implications of his account of it as "reduction of complexity," in particular of complex future contingencies. He makes much of the difference between absence of trust and distrust, and distinguishes trust from what it presupposes, a mere "familiarity," or taking for granted. I have blurred these distinctions. He treats personal trust as a risky investment and looks at mechanisms of establishing and maintaining trust. Tact is said to play an important role in both. It enables trust-offering overtures to be rejected without hostility ensuing, and it enables those who make false moves in their attempts to maintain trust to recover their position without too much loss of face. "A social climate . . . institutionalizes tact and knows enough escape routes for self presentation in difficult situations" (p 84). Tact is a virtue which needs to be added to delicacy of discrimination in recognizing *what* one is trusted with, good judgments as to whom to trust with what, and a willingness to admit and forgive fault, as all functional virtues needed in those who would sustain trust.

interest in one's affairs is not part of the normal idea of the role of mailman and could provide opportunity for blackmail, but in virtue of that very interest they could give much more knowledgeable and intelligent service—in the above case by knowing our plans they knew when and where we had moved and delivered to the new address without instructions. What do we trust our mailmen to do or not to do? To use their discretion in getting our mail to us, to take enough interest in us and in the nature of our mail, (compatibly with their total responsibility) to make intelligent decisions about what to do with it when such decisions have to be made. Similarly with our surgeons and plumbers—*just* what they should do to put right what is wrong is something we must leave to them. Should they act incompetently, negligently, or deliberately against our interests, they may conceal these features of their activities from us by pretense that whatever happened occurred as a result of an honest and well-meaning exercise of the discretion given to them. This way they may retain our trust and so have opportunity to harm us yet further. In trusting them, we trust them to use their discretionary powers competently and nonmaliciously, and the latter includes not misleading us about how they have used them.

Trust, on the analysis I have proposed, is letting other persons (natural or artificial, such as firms, nations, etc.) take care of something the truster cares about, where such "caring for" involves some exercise of discretionary powers. But not all the variables involved in trust are yet in view. One which the entrusting model obscures rather than highlights is the degree of explicitness. To entrust is intentionally and usually formally to hand over the care of something to someone, but trusting is rarely begun by making up one's mind to trust, and often it has no definite initiation of any sort but grows up slowly and imperceptibly. What I have tried to take from the notion of entrusting is not its voluntarist and formalist character but rather the possible specificity and restrictedness of *what* is entrusted, along with the discretion the trustee has in looking after that thing. Trust can come with no beginnings, with gradual as well as sudden beginnings, and with various degrees of self-consciousness, voluntariness, and expressness. My earlier discussion of the delicacy and tact needed by the truster in judging the performance of the trusted applied only to cases where the truster not merely realizes that she trusts but has some conscious control over the continuation of the trust relationship. The discussion of abuses of discretionary power applied only to cases where the trusted realizes that she is trusted and trusted with discretionary powers. But trust relationships need not be so express, and some important forms of them cannot be verbally acknowledged by the persons involved. Trust between infant and parent is such a case, and it is one which also reminds us of another crucial variable in trust relations to which so far I have only indirectly alluded. This is the relative power of the truster and the trusted, and the relative costs to each of a breakdown of their trust relationship. In emphasizing the toleration of vulnerability by the truster I have made attitudes to relative power and powerlessness the essence of trust and distrust; I have not yet looked at the varieties of trust we discern when we vary the power of the truster in relation to the power of the trusted, both while the trust endures and in its absence. Trust alters power positions, and both the position one is in without a given form of trust and the position one has within a relation of trust is sensible and morally decent. Infant trust reminds us not just of inarticulate and uncritical or blind trust, but of trust by those who are maximally vulnerable, whether or not they give trust. . . .

## TRUST AND VOLUNTARY ABILITIES

The child trusts as long as she is encouraged to trust and until the trust is unmistakably betrayed. It takes childhood innocence to be able to trust simply because of encouragement to trust. "Trust me!" is for most of us an invitation which we cannot accept at will—either we do already trust the one who says it, in which case it serves at best as reassurance,[9] or it is properly responded to with, "Why should and how can I, until I have cause to?"[10] The child, of course, cannot trust at will any more than experienced adults can—encouragement is a condition of not lapsing into distrust, rather than of a move from distrust to trust. One constraint on an account of trust which postulates infant trust as its essential seed is that it not make essential to trusting the use of concepts or abilities which a child cannot be

---

[9] My thoughts about the role of the words "Trust me!" are influenced by an unpublished paper on promising by T. M. Scanlon. Indeed Scanlon's talk on this topic to the University of Pittsburgh philosophy department in April 1984 was what, along with Hume's few remarks about it, started me thinking about trust in and out of voluntary exchanges.

[10] Luhmann says, "It is not possible to demand the trust of others; trust can only be offered and accepted" (p. 43).

reasonably believed to possess. Acts of will of any sort are not plausibly attributed to infants; it would be unreasonable to suppose that they can do at will what adults cannot, namely, obey the instruction to trust, whether it comes from others or is a self-instruction.

To suppose that infants emerge from the womb already equipped with some confidence in what supports them, so that no choice is needed to continue with that attitude, until something happens to shake or destroy such confidence, is plausible enough. My account of trust has been designed to allow for unconscious trust, for conscious but unchosen trust, as well as for conscious trust the truster has chosen to endorse and cultivate. Whereas it strains the concept of agreement to speak of unconscious agreements and unchosen agreements, and overstrains the concept of contract to speak of unconscious or unchosen contracts, there is no strain whatever in the concept of automatic and unconscious trust, and of unchosen but mutual trust. Trust between infant and parent, at its best, exhibits such primitive and basic trust. Once it is present, the story of how trust becomes self-conscious, controlled, monitored, critical, pretended, and eventually either cautious and distrustful of itself, or discriminatory and reflexive, so that we come to trust ourselves as trusters, is relatively easy to tell. What will need explanation will be the ceasings to trust, the transfers to trust, the restriction or enlargements in the fields of what is trusted, when, and to whom, rather than any abrupt switches from distrust to trust. Even if such occurrences do ever occur (when one suddenly falls in love or lust with a stranger or former enemy, or has a religious conversion), they take more than the mere invitation "Trust me."

In his famous account of what a promise (and a contract) involves, Hume strongly implies that it is an artificially contrived and secured case of mutual trust. The penalty to which a promisor subjects himself in promising, he says, is that of "never being trusted again in case of failure."[11] The problem which the artifice of promise solves is a generally disadvantageous "want of mutual confidence and security."[12] It is plausible to construe the offer whose acceptance counts as acceptance of a contract or a promise as at least implicitly including an invitation to trust. Part of what makes promises the special thing they are, and the philosophically intriguing thing they are, is that we *can* at will accept *this* sort of invitation to trust, whereas in general we cannot trust at will. Promises are puzzling because they seem to have the power, by verbal magic, to initiate real voluntary short-term trusting. They not merely create obligations apparently at the will of the obligated, but they create trust at the will of the truster. They present a very fascinating case of trust and trustworthiness, but one which, because of those very intriguing features, is ill suited to the role of paradigm. Yet in as far as modern moral philosophers have attended at all to the morality of trust, it is trust in parties to an agreement that they have concentrated on, and it is into this very special and artificial mold that they have tried to force other cases of trust, when they notice them at all.

## THE MALE FIXATION ON CONTRACT

The great moral theorists in our tradition not only are all men, they are mostly men who had minimal adult dealings with (and so were then minimally influenced by) women. With a few significant exceptions (Hume, Hegel, J. S. Mill, Sidgwick, maybe Bradley) they are a collection of gays, clerics, misogynists, and puritan bachelors. It should not surprise us, then, that particularly in the modern period they managed to relegate to the mental background the web of trust tying most moral agents to one another, and to focus their philosophical attention so single-mindedly on cool, distanced relations between more or less free and equal adult strangers, say, the members of an all male club, with membership rules and rules for dealing with rule breakers and where the form of cooperation was restricted to ensuring that each member could read his *Times* in peace and have no one step on his gouty toes. Explicitly assumed or recognized obligations toward others with the same obligations and the same power to see justice done to rule breakers then are seen as the moral norm.

Relations between equals and nonintimates will *be* the moral norm for adult males whose dealings with others are mainly business or restrained social dealings with similarly placed males. But for lovers, husbands, fathers, the ill, the very young, and the elderly, other relationships with their moral potential and perils will loom larger. For Hume, who had several strong-willed and manipulative women to cooperate or contend with in his adult life, for Mill, who had Harriet Taylor on his hands, for Hegel, whose domestic life was of normal complication, the rights and duties of equals to equals in a civil society which recognized only a male electorate could only be *part* of the moral story. They could not ignore the virtues and vices of family relationships, male-female relationships, master-slave, and employer-employee relationships as easily as could Hobbes, Butler, Bentham, or Kant. Nor could they as easily adopt the usual compensatory strategies of the moral philosophers who confine their attention to the rights and duties of free and equal adults to one another—the strategy of claiming, if pressed, that these rights are the *core* of all moral relationships and maybe also claiming that any other relationships, engendering additional or different rights and duties, come about only by an exercise of one of the core rights, the right to promise. Philosophers who remember what it was like to be a dependent child, or know what it is like to be parent, or to have a dependent parent, an old or handicapped relative, friend, or neighbor will find it implausible to treat such relations as simply cases of comembership in a kingdom of ends, in the given temporary conditions of one-sided dependence.

To the extent that these claims are correct (and I am aware that they need more defense than I have given them here)[18] it becomes fairly easy to see one likely explanation of the neglect in Western moral philosophy of the full range of sorts of trust. Both before the rise of a society which needed contract as a commercial device, and after it, women were counted on to serve their men, to raise their children to fill the roles they were expected to fill and not deceive their men about the paternity of these children. What men counted on one another for, in work and war, presupposed this background domestic trust, trust in women not merely not to poison their men (Nietzsche derides them for learning less than they might have in the kitchen), but to turn out sons who could trust and be trusted in traditional men's roles and daughters who would reduplicate their own capacities for trust and trustworthiness. Since the women's role did not include the writing of moral treatises, any thoughts they had about trust, based on their experience of it, did not get into our tradition (for did Diotima teach Socrates something about trust as well as love?). And the more powerful men, including those who did write the moral treatises, were in the morally awkward position of being, collectively, oppressors of women, exploiters of women's capacity for trustworthiness in unequal, nonvoluntary, and non-contract-based relationships. Understandably, they did not focus their attention on forms of trust and demands for trustworthiness which it takes a Nietzsche to recognize without shame. Humankind can bear only so much reality.

The recent research of Carol Gilligan has shown us how intelligent and reflective twentieth-century women see morality, and how different their picture of it is from that of men, particularly the men who eagerly assent to

---

[18] I defend them a little more in "What Do Women Want in a Moral Theory?" *Nous* 19 (march 1985): 53-64.

the claims of currently orthodox contractarian-Kantian moral theories.[19] Women cannot now, any more than they could when oppressed, ignore that part of morality and those forms of trust which cannot easily be forced into the liberal and particularly the contractarian mold. Men may but women cannot see morality as essentially a matter of keeping to the minimal moral traffic rules, designed to restrict close encounters between autonomous persons to self-chosen ones. Such a conception presupposes both an equality of power and a natural separateness from others, which is alien to women's experience of life and morality. For those most of whose daily dealings are with the less powerful or the more powerful, a moral code designed for those equal in power will be at best nonfunctional, at worst an offensive pretense of equality as a substitute for its actuality. But equality is not even a desirable ideal in all relationships—children not only are not but should not be equal in power to adults, and we need a morality to guide us in our dealings with those who either cannot or should not achieve equality of power (animals, the ill, the dying, children while still young) with those with whom they have unavoidable and often intimate relationships.

Modern moral philosophy has concentrated on the morality of fairly cool relationships between those who are deemed to be roughly equal in power to determine the rules and to instigate sanctions against rule breakers. It is not surprising, then, that the main form of trust that any attention has been given to is trust in governments, and in parties to voluntary agreements to do what they have agreed to do. . . .

## CRITICAL THINKING QUESTIONS

1. What are some of the morally relevant features of trust relationships according to Baier?
2. Why does Baier say that reliance on others is not the same as trusting them? Provide an example from your own experience that shows the difference between relying on someone and trusting someone.
3. Compare Baier's notions of parent/child trust with those of Noddings and Herman.
4. Write and analyze a case that demonstrates the morality of trust.

---

[19] Carol Gilligan, *In a Different Voice* (Cambridge, Mass.: Harvard University Press, 1982).

MARTIN LUTHER KING, JR.

## On Being a Good Neighbor

*Martin Luther King, Jr. (1929–1968) achieved national fame when he success-*
*fully led the boycott against segregated bus lines in Montgomery, Alabama. In*
*1964 he was awarded the Nobel Peace Prize; four years later he was assassi-*
*nated in Memphis, Tennessee. This writing comes from the 1963 work* Strength
to Love. *King expresses the importance of being neighborly nonracially based.*

> *And who is my neighbour?*
> Luke 10:29

I should like to talk with you about a good man, whose exemplary life
will always be a flashing light to plague the dozing conscience of mankind.
His goodness was not found in a passive commitment to a particular creed,
but in his active participation in a life-saving deed; not in a moral pilgrim-
age that reached its destination point, but in the love ethic by which he jour-
neyed life's highway. He was good because he was a good neighbor.

The ethical concern of this man is expressed in a magnificent little story,
which begins with a theological discussion on the meaning of eternal life
and concludes in a concrete expression of compassion on a dangerous road.
Jesus is asked a question by a man who had been trained in the details of
Jewish law: "Master, what shall I do to inherit eternal life?" The retort is
prompt: "What is written in the law? how readest thou?" After a moment the
lawyer recites articulately "Thou shalt love the Lord thy God with all thy
heart, and with all thy soul, and with all thy strength, and with all thy mind;
and thy neighbour as thyself." Then comes the decisive word from Jesus:
"Thou hast answered right: this do, and thou shalt live."

The lawyer was chagrined. "Why," the people might ask, "would an ex-
pert in law raise a question that even the novice can answer? Desiring to justify himself and to show that Jesus' reply was far from conclusive, the lawyer
asks, "And who is my neighbour?" The lawyer was now taking up the cud-
gels of debate that might have turned the conversation into an abstract theological discussion. But Jesus, determined not to be caught in the "paralysis

of analysis," pulls the question from mid-air and places it on a dangerous curve between Jerusalem and Jericho.

He told the story of "a certain man" who went down from Jerusalem to Jericho and fell among robbers who stripped him, beat him, and, departing, left him half dead. By chance a certain priest appeared, but he passed by on the other side, and later a Levite also passed by. Finally, a certain Samaritan, a half-breed from a people with whom the Jews had no dealings, appeared. When he saw the wounded man, he was moved with compassion, administered first aid, placed him on his beast, "and brought him to an inn, and took care of him."

Who is my neighbor? "I do not know his name," says Jesus in essence. "He is anyone toward whom you are neighborly. He is anyone who lies in need at life's roadside. He is neither Jew nor Gentile; he is neither Russian nor American; he is neither Negro nor white. He is 'a certain man'—any needy man—on one of the numerous Jericho roads of life." So Jesus defines a neighbor, not in a theological definition, but in a life situation.

What constituted the goodness of the good Samaritan? Why will he always be an inspiring paragon of neighborly virtue? It seems to me that this man's goodness may be described in one word—altruism. The good Samaritan was altruistic to the core. What is altruism? The dictionary defines altruism as "regard for, and devotion to, the interest of others." The Samaritan was good because he made concern for others the first law of his life.

## I

The Samaritan had the capacity for a *universal altruism*. He had a piercing insight into that which is beyond the eternal accidents of race, religion, and nationality. One of the great tragedies of man's long trek along the highway of history has been the limiting of neighborly concern to tribe, race, class, or nation. The God of early Old Testament days was a tribal god and the ethic was tribal. "Thou shalt not kill" meant "Thou shalt not kill a fellow Israelite, but for God's sake, kill a Philistine." Greek democracy embraced a certain aristocracy, but not the hordes of Greek slaves whose labors burn the city-states. The universalism at the center of the Declaration of Independence has been shamefully negated by America's appalling tendency to substitute "some" for "all." Numerous people in the North and South still believe that the affirmation, "All men are created equal," means "All white men are created equal." Our unswerving devotion to monopolistic capitalism makes us more concerned about the economic security of the captains of industry than for the laboring men whose sweat and skills keep industry functioning. What are the devastating consequences of this narrow, group-centered attitude? It means that one does not really mind what happens to the people outside this group. If an American is concerned only about his nation, he will not be concerned about the people of Asia, Africa, or South America. Is this not why nations engage in the madness of war without the slightest sense of penitence? Is this not why the murder of a citizen of your own nation is a crime, but the murder of the citizens of another nation in war is an act of heroic virtue? If manufacturers are concerned only in their personal interests they will pass by on the other side while thousands of working people are stripped of their jobs and left displaced on some Jericho road as a result of automation, and they will judge every move toward a better distribution of wealth and a better life for the working man to be socialistic. If a white man is concerned only about his race, he will casually pass by the Negro who has been robbed of his personhood, stripped of his sense of dignity, and left dying on some wayside road.

A few years ago, when an automobile carrying several members of a Negro college basketball team had an accident on a Southern highway, three of the young men were severely injured. An ambulance was immediately called, but on arriving at the place of the accident, the driver, who was white, said without apology that it was not his policy to service Negroes, and he drove away. The driver of a passing automobile graciously drove the boys to the nearest hospital, but the attending physician belligerently said, "We don't take niggers in this hospital." When the boys finally arrived at a "colored" hospital in a town some fifty miles from the scene of the accident, one was dead and the other two died thirty and fifty minutes later respectively. Probably all three could have been saved if they had been given immediate treatment. This is only one of thousands of inhuman incidents that occur daily in the South, an unbelievable expression of the barbaric consequences of any tribal-centered, national-centered, or racial-centered ethic.

The real tragedy of such narrow provincialism is that we see people as entities or merely as things. Too seldom do we see people in their true *humanness*. A spiritual myopia limits our vision to external accidents. We see men as Jews or Gentiles, Catholics or Protestants, Chinese or American, Negroes or whites. We fail to think of them as fellow human beings made from the same basic stuff as we, molded in the same divine image. The priest and the Levite saw only a bleeding body, not a human being like themselves. But the good Samaritan will always remind us to remove the cataracts of provincialism from our spiritual eyes and see men as men. If the Samaritan had considered the wounded man as a Jew first, he would not have stopped, for the Jews and the Samaritans had no dealings. He saw him as a human being first, who was Jew only by accident. The good neighbor looks beyond the external accidents and discerns those inner qualities that make all men human and, therefore, brothers.

## II

The Samaritan possessed the capacity for a *dangerous altruism*. He risked his life to save a brother. When we ask why the priest and the Levite did not stop to help the wounded man, numerous suggestions come to mind. Perhaps they could not delay their arrival at an important ecclesiastical meeting. Perhaps religious regulations demanded that they touch no human body for several hours prior to the performing of their temple functions. Or perhaps they were on their way to an organizational meeting of a Jericho Road Improvement Association. Certainly this would have been a real need, for it is not enough to aid a wounded man on the Jericho Road; it is also important to change the conditions which make robbery possible. Philanthropy is commendable, but it must not cause the philanthropist to overlook the circumstances of economic injustice which make philanthropy necessary. Maybe the priest and the Levite believed that it is better to cure injustice at the causal source than to get bogged down with a single individual effect.

These are probable reasons for their failure to stop, yet there is another possibility, often overlooked, that they were afraid. The Jericho Road was a dangerous road. When Mrs. King and I visited the Holy Land, we rented a car and drove from Jerusalem to Jericho. As we traveled slowly down that meandering, mountainous road, I said to my wife, "I can now understand why Jesus chose this road as the setting for his parable." Jerusalem is some two thousand feet above and Jericho one thousand feet below sea level. The descent made in less than twenty miles. Many sudden curves provide likely places for ambushing and exposes the traveler to unforeseen attack. Long ago the road was known as the Bloody Pass. So it is possible that the Priest and the Levite were afraid that if they stopped, they too would be beaten. Perhaps the robbers were still nearby. Or maybe the wounded man on the ground was a faker, who wished to draw passing travelers to his side for quick and easy seizure. I imagine that the first question which the priest and the Levite asked was: "If I stop to help this man, what will happen to me?" But by the very nature of his concern, the good Samaritan reversed the question: "If I do not stop to help this man, what will happen to him?" The good Samaritan engaged in a dangerous altruism. . . .

The ultimate measure of a man is not where he stands in moments of comfort and convenience, but where he stands at times of challenge and controversy. The true neighbor will risk his position, his prestige, and even his life for the welfare of others. In dangerous valleys and hazardous pathways, he will lift some bruised and beaten brother to a higher and more noble life.

### III

The Samaritan also possessed *excessive altruism*. With his own hands he bound the wounds of the man and then set him on his own beast. It would have been easier to pay an ambulance to take the unfortunate man to the hospital, rather than risk having his neatly trimmed suit stained with blood.

True altruism is more than the capacity to pity; it is the capacity to sympathize. Pity may represent little more than the impersonal concern which prompts the mailing of a check, but true sympathy is the personal concern which demands the giving of one's soul. Pity may arise from interest in an abstraction called humanity, but sympathy grows out of a concern for a particular needy human being who lies at life's roadside. Sympathy is fellow feeling for the person in need—his pain, agony, and burdens. . . . The Samaritan used his hands to bind up the wounds of the robbed man's body, and he also released an overflowing love to bind up the wounds of his broken spirit.

Another expression of the excessive altruism on the part of the Samaritan was his willingness to go far beyond the call of duty. After tending to the man's wounds, he put him on his beast, carried him to an inn, and left money for his care, making clear that if further financial needs arose he would gladly meet them. "Whatsoever thou spendest more, when I come again, I will repay thee." Stopping short of this, he would have more than fulfilled any possible rule concerning one's duty to a wounded stranger. He went beyond the second mile. His love was complete. . . .

More than ever before, my friends, men of all races and nations are today challenged to be neighborly. The call for a worldwide good-neighbor policy is more than an ephemeral shibboleth; it is the call to a way of life which will transform our imminent cosmic elegy into a psalm of creative fulfillment. No longer can we afford the luxury of passing by on the other side. Such folly was once called moral failure; today it will lead to universal suicide. We cannot long survive spiritually separated in a world that is geographically together. In the final analysis, I must not ignore the wounded man on life's Jericho Road, because he is a part of me and I am a part of him. His agony diminishes me, and his salvation enlarges me.

In our quest to make neighborly love a reality, we have, in addition to the inspiring example of the good Samaritan, the magnanimous life of our Christ to guide us. His altruism was universal, for he thought of all men, even publicans and sinners, as brothers. His altruism was dangerous, for he willingly traveled hazardous roads in a cause he knew was right. His altruism was excessive, for he chose to die on Calvary, history's most magnificent expression of obedience to the unenforceable.

## CRITICAL THINKING QUESTIONS

1. King states that race should not be a factor in being a good neighbor. Some changes in racial equality have been made since King's time. What ways can you further equality through the notion of a good neighbor?
2. Detail King's argument in furthering equality.
3. Write and analyze a case involving good neighbor concepts regardless of differences in race, religion, socioeconomic status, and so on.

## CONTEMPORARY CASE

### *Issues of Trust: First Rate Air*

In an effort to provide better response time and greater advertisement, First Rate Air, a local heating, ventilation, and air conditioning contractor, began allowing their service technicians to take home a company service truck. These trucks are equipped with virtually any tool a technician could need. Along with the change in policy concerning company trucks, First Rate Air instituted a no-compete policy; that is, technicians were not to moonlight doing private jobs that would compete with First Rate Air.

One weekend, Jill, a service technician for First Rate Air, got a call from her girlfriend, Debbie. Jill and Debbie had been friends since high school. When Debbie saw how successful Jill was at her job with First Rate Air, she decided to follow Jill's example and get a degree in air conditioning. Debbie was far enough along in the program that she could do some repairs, but she did not have all the tools she needed. Debbie asked Jill if she could use some of the tools provided by First Rate Air to do a job. Jill realized that the job Debbie was going to do would be in direct competition with First Rate Air. Jill knew that if she drove the truck over to Debbie's job that she might be seen and reported. She also knew that Debbie would not be covered by First Rate Air's insurance, so letting Debbie drive the truck was out of the question. However, she reasoned that First Rate Air had not said anything about loaning the equipment that was stored inside the truck. Besides, it would not be Jill doing the work anyway.

1. Is there any particular problem with Debbie using equipment owned by First Rate Air to do a private job? Explain the communication dynamics between the women in regard to the truck's tools.
2. Does the interpersonal relationship overrule First Rate Air's no compete policy? How could communication play a role?
3. According to Gilligan, would a networking of relationships find another solution for Debbie and Jill? Or, should Jill's response be based on duty, utility, virtue, or rights? Explain your position.
4. Is it important to take risks in interpersonal relationships? What if the risk could get you fired? What if the risk isn't ethical?
5. Are there problems of trust in this case? If so on whose part?
6. What nonverbal communication is present in this case?

# 5

# INTIMATE COMMUNICATION

ROBERT C. SOLOMON

## THE VIRTUE OF LOVE

*Robert C. Solomon, professor of philosophy at the University of Texas, Austin, is the author of numerous scholarly books and articles on relationship ethics. He is also a scholar in continental philosophy and a respected writer, thinker, and speaker. This 1988 article explains the many ethical dimensions of intimate relationships.*

In a famous—or infamous—passage, Kant off-handedly dismisses one of the most essential elements in ethics.

> Love out of inclination cannot be commanded; but kindness done from duty—although no inclination impels us, and even although natural and unconquerable disinclination stands in our way—is *Practical* and not *Pathological* love, residing in the will and not of melting compassion.[1]

In the *Symposium*, on the other hand, Phaedrus offers us one of many contrasting comments by Plato in honor of *erös*:

> That is why I say Love is the eldest of the gods and most honored and the most powerful for acquiring virtue and blessedness, for men both living and dead.[2]

This paper has two aims: to understand erotic (romantic, "pathological") love as itself a virtue, and to broaden our view of ethics.

## *ERÖS* AND ETHICS

It (love) does not hesitate to intrude with its trash. . . . It knows how to slip its love-notes and ringlets even into ministerial portfolios and philosophical manuscripts. Every day it brews and hatches the worst and most perplexing quarrels and disputes, destroys the most valuable relationships and breaks the strongest bonds. . . . Why all this noise and fuss? . . . It is merely a question of every Jack finding his Jill. (The gracious reader should translate this phrase into precise Aristophanic language.) Why should such a trifle play so important a role?[3]

Love as a virtue? Well, hardly, Motherly love, certainly; patriotism, perhaps. The love of humanity, to be sure, but romantic love? Sexual love? The passion that makes fools of us all and has led to the demise of Anthony, Cleopatra, young Romeo, Juliet, and King Kong? Love is nice, but it is not a virtue. Maybe it is not even nice. Hesiod in the *Theogony* warned against erös as a force contrary and antagonistic to reason. Sophocles and Euripides both denounced erös, in *Antigone* and *Hippolytus* respectively, and even Virgil had his doubts. Schopenhauer, much more recently, thought all love to be sexual and damnable, and today we are much more likely to invoke the cynical wit of Oscar Wilde or Kinglsey Amis than the saccharine pronouncements of our latter-day love pundits. Indeed, running through the history of ideas in the West one cannot but be struck by the ambivalence surrounding this central and celebrated concept. It is cursed as irrational and destructive and praised as the origin of everything. *Erös* is famous for its foolishness and at the same time elevated and venerated as a god, albeit at first a rather minor one, but by the time of early Christianity, nothing less than God as such.

Today, we find ourselves torn between such mundane considerations as dependency and autonomy, security and the dubious freedom to remain "uncommitted." It is hard to remind ourselves, therefore, that the history of love is intellectual warfare between bestiality on one side and divinity on the other. The word "love" has so often functioned as a synonym for lust that it is hard to take it seriously as a virtue. It has just as long been raised to cosmological status, by Parmenides, Empedocles, and Plotinus, for example, and it therefore seems somewhat small minded to reduce it to a mere source of human relationships. Most modern philosophers have, accordingly, ignored it, Schopenhauer here as elsewhere being a bit eccentric, while moralists have had a field day playing the one side (lust) against the other (divine grace, piety, and contempt for all bodily functions, but particularly those that are best when shared).

In any discussion of love as a virtue, it is necessary, if by now routine, to mention some different "kinds" of love. (The notion of "kinds" may already be question begging here, for the more difficult issue may be what links, rather than distinguishes, e.g., friendship, sexual love and parental affection.) In particular, it is essential that we distinguish *erös* and *agapé*, the former usually translated as sexual love, the latter as selfless and certainly sexless love for humanity. The distinction is often drawn crudely. For instance, *erös* is taken to be purely erotic and reduced to sexual desire, which it surely is not. Or *agapé* is characterized as selfless given, opposed by *erös* which thus becomes selfish taking (or at least craving). *Agapé* is idealized to the point where it becomes an attitude possible only to God, thus rendering it virtually inapplicable to common human fellow-feelings. *Erös* by contrast is degraded to the profanely secular and denied any hint of spirituality. To think of love as a virtue, therefore, is first of all to expand (once again) the domain of *erös*. (Romantic love, I am presuming, is one historical variant of *erös*.) One need not deny the desirability (or the possibility) of altruistic *agapé* to insist that erotic *erös* shares at least some of its virtues.

*Erös*, and what we now call "romantic love," should also be distinguished (carefully) from other forms of particular affection—for example, motherly, fatherly, brotherly, or sisterly love and friendship. I think that Schopenhauer was partly right when he suggested (with Freud following him) that all love is to some extent sexual. But to make this point one obviously needs a generously enlarged conception of sex and sexual desire, and I often fear that this insight is motivated as much by its titillating implications as by the impulse to clarify the nature of human bonding. A more modest thesis is that *erös* (not sex) encompasses almost all intimate, personal affections. What characterizes *erös* in general, we might then suggest, is an intense quasiphysical, even "grasping," affection for a particular person, a Buscaglian "urge to hug" if you will. (Plato often uses such desire-defined language in talking about *erös*, even when he is reaching for the Forms.) In romantic love, sexual desire is undeniably a part of this affection, though it is not at all clear whether this is the source of the affection or rather its vehicle. *Erös* differs from *agapé* in the prevalence of self-interested desire, but it is not thereby selfish and the desire is not just sexual. It also includes a much more general physical desire to "be with," such personal desires as "to be appreciated" and "to be happy together," such inspirational

desires as "to be the best for you" and such "altruistic" desires as "to do anything I can for you." As laRochefoucauld once put it, "in the soul . . . a thirst
for mastery; in the mind sympathy; in the body, nothing but a delicately desire to possess, after many mysteries."[4]
    It is a common mistake to think of the other person in sex as a mere "ob-
ject" of desire, which leads to the idea that *erös* too is degrading and seeks
only its own satisfaction. Consider Kant on the matter:

> Because sexuality is not an inclination which one human being has for an-
> other as such, but is an inclination for the sex of another, it is a principle
> of the degradation of human nature, in that it gives rise to the preference
> of one sex to the other, and to the dishonoring of that sex through the sat-
> isfaction of desire.[5]

But surely the question (as Plato raised it 2300 years earlier) is *what* one desires when one sexually desires another person. In the *Symposium,*
Aristophanes suggested that one desires not sex but permanent (re-)unifica-
tion with the other; Socrates insisted that one really wants the Forms. Even if
we consider such goals too fantastic for *erös*, it is clear that the Greeks—as
opposed to Kant and many moderns—saw that sexual desire was much,
much more than desire for sex and not at all opposed to virtuous desire. At
the very least, it is clear that sexual desire is some sort of powerful desire *for*
the other person *through* sex. The question is: a desire *for what?* And by no
means should we assume from the outset that the answer to this question has
anything to do with sexual *objects.* Indeed, taking our clue from Hegel and
Sartre, we might suggest rather that it has everything to do with the sexual
*subject,* and subjects by their very nature cannot be wholly sexual.
    The most obvious difference between erotic (romantic) and other par-
ticular forms of love is the centrality of sexual (do not read "genital") desire,
but there are two other differences that, philosophically, are much more illuminating. The first, though quite controversial, is the prerequisite of
*equality* between lovers. This may seem odd in the light of modern accusations against love as a vehicle for the degradation and oppression of women
(Shulamith Firestone, Marilyn French), but in historical perspective it becomes clear that—however far we may be from real equality—romantic
love emerges only with the relative liberation of women from traditional
subservient social and economic roles. Romantic love emerges only when
women begin to have more of a choice about their lives—and about their
lovers and husbands in particular. One thinks of John Milton's Adam, created early in the era of romantic love, who specifically requested from God

not a mere playmate or companion or a mirror image of himself but an *equal*, for "among unequals what society/Can sort, what harmony or true delight?"[6] Or, paraphrasing Stendhal, we might say that love tends to create equals even where it does not find them, for equality is as essential to romantic love as authority is to parenthood—whether or not this is adequately acknowledged or acted upon.

One other difference between *erös* and other loves is that romantic love, unlike familial love, for example, is unprescribed and often spontaneous. ("Romantic friendships" are especially worth noting in this context.) Critical to erotic, romantic love is the sense of *choice*. Family love, in this sense, is always prescribed. The love between husband and wife, or what such authors as de Rougemont call "conjugal love," might be considered prescribed in this sense too, including its sexuality. This is emphatically not to say that married love cannot be romantic, or that romantic love is characterized only by its novelty or by the excitement and anxiety consequent to that novelty. It is a common mistake to take the exhilaration of love as love—without asking what that exhilaration is *about*. Love and marriage often begin together even if they do not always remain together, and to separate them is just to say that love can be unhitched just as horses can, while carriages sit unmoving.

What could be virtuous about *erös*? One might rationalize sexual love as the slippery slope to marriage, but this faint praise only reinforces our image of romantic love as something in itself childish, foolish, and a kind of conspiracy of nature and society to trick self-consciously rebellious adolescents into maturity. One might celebrate *erös* as the often unrecognized source of many of our most beautiful creations, from Dante's poetry to the Taj Mahal, but this too is to demean love as a virtue and see it merely as a means, as Freud once saw anal retention as a means to great art. But it seems to me that *erös* is not considered a virtue for three general sorts of reasons:

(1) *Erös* is reduced to mere sexuality, and philosophers, insofar as they deign to dirty their minds with sex at all (*qua* philosophers, of course), tend to see sexuality as vulgar and not even a candidate for virtue. Part of this is the common perception of sex as either a form of recreation or a means to procreation, but in any case a set of desires constrained by ethics but hardly of ethical value in themselves.

(2) Love is an emotion and emotions are thought to be irrational, beyond our control, merely episodic instead of an essential aspect of character, products of "instinct" and intractable in the face of all evidence and objective consideration. Even Aristotle, one of the few

friends of the passions in the history of philosophy, insisted that only states of character, not passions, can count as virtues.

(3) *Erös* even insofar as it is not just sexual is self-love and the self-indulgence of desire, while an essential characteristic of the virtues is, in Hume's phrase, their utility, their being pleasing to others and based on such sentiments as compassion and sympathy. Romantic love, far from being "pleasing to others," tends to be embarrassing and sometimes harmful to others and self-destructive. It tends to be possessive, jealous, obsessive, antisocial, even "mad." Such drama is not the stuff of which virtue is made.

I obviously believe that each of these objections to erotic love as a virtue is just plain wrong, but it will take most of this paper to spell out an alternative view. Simply, for now, let me state that these objections demean and misunderstand the nature of sexuality, the nature of emotions, and the nature of love in particular. So that I do not appear overly irrationalist and romantic here, let me draw Plato to my side. He clearly saw *erös* as a virtue, and every one of the speakers in the *Symposium* agrees with this. Even Socrates, by far the most effete of the speakers, celebrates *erös* not as the disinterested appreciation of beauty and wisdom (as many Oxford commentaries would make it seem) but rather as a "grasping" sensuality, perhaps of the mind rather than the body, but erotic none the less for that. (Why did he so distrust beauty in art but yet celebrate it in *erös*?) In Plato's thinking, *erös* was a virtue just because it was (in part) a passion, filled with desire and—in that peculiarly noble Socratic sense—self-obsessed as well.

• • •

## WHAT IS ROMANTIC LOVE?

Love is the expression of an ancient need, that human desire was originally one and we were whole, and the desire and the pursuit of the whole is called love.[21]

Romantic love, we may need to remind ourselves, is an emotion—an ordinary and very common emotion. It is not a "force" or a "mystery." Like all emotions, it is largely learned, typically obsessive, peculiar to certain kinds of cultures with certain brands of philosophy. I will not here rehearse once again my usual analysis of emotion as a complex of judgments, desires, and values. Let me just claim, without argument, the weaker thesis that every emotion presupposes, if it is not composed of, a set of specifiable concepts (e.g., anger as offense, sadness as loss, jealousy as the threat of loss) and more or less specific desires and values, such as revenge in anger, care in sadness, possessiveness in jealousy. Love, accordingly, can and must be analyzed in terms of such a set of concept sand desires, some of which are obvious, the more interesting perhaps not so. It is evident enough that one set of desires in romantic love is the desire to be with, the desire to touch, the desire to caress, and here we are immediately reminded of Aristophanes' lesson: that which manifests itself as a sexual urge in love is actually something much more, a desire to be reunited with, to be one with, one's love. From this, I want to suggest what I take to be the dominant conceptual ingredient in romantic love, which is just this urge for *shared identity*, a kind of *ontological dependency*. The challenge, however, is to get beyond this familiar idea (and its kindred characterizations as a "union," "a merger of souls," etc.) and explain exactly what "identity" could possibly mean in this context. Aristophanes' wonderful metaphor is still a metaphor, and whether or not we would want Hephaestus to weld the two of us together, body and soul, the image does not do our understanding much good. Aristophanes claims that we want the impossible, indeed the unimaginable; he does not give us any indication of how we might in fact share an identity, over and above brief and not always well-coordinated unifications of the flesh.

More to the point, one might well quote Cathy's climactic revelation in *Wuthering Heights*: "I *am* Heathcliff—he's always, always in my mind—not as a pleasure, anymore than I am always a pleasure to myself—but as my own being." Here we have more than a hint of what is involved in shared identity, not a mystical union nor a frustrated physicality but a sense of presence, always "in mind," defining one's sense of self to one's self. Love is just this shared identity, and the desires of love—including especially the strong non-physiological desire for sexual intercourse—can best be understood with reference to this strange but not at all unfamiliar concept. I cannot do justice to this challenge here, but let me at least present the thesis: Shared this intended identity. This is not to deny or neglect sex but to give it a context. Nor does this give away too much to marriage (which is a legal identity) but it does explain how romantic love and marriage have come so close together, the latter now considered to be the culmination of the former.

Before we say any more, however, let me express a Socratic caveat: I think that it is necessary to display love as it is by itself, without confusing it with all of the other Good Things we would like and expect to go with it—companionship, great sex, friendship, someone to travel with, someone who really cares, and, ultimately, marriage. Of course we want these things, and preferably all in the same package, but love can and must be understood apart from all of them. Without being depressing, let us remind ourselves that love often goes wrong, that love can be unrequited, that love can interfere with or at least it does not assure satisfying sex, that love and friendship are sometimes opposed, that love can be very lonely, that love can be not only obsessive but insane. Not that love must be or often is all of these, but it can be, and so let us look at the virtues of love itself, as Socrates insisted, not in terms of its consequences or its most desirable embellishments.

The nature of identity in love, briefly described, is this. (You will note, no doubt, a certain debt to Hegel and Sartre in what follows.) We define ourselves, not just in our own terms (as adolescent existentialists and pop-psychologists may argue) but in terms of each other. The virtues, in a society such as Aristotle's, are defined and assigned communally; the idea of "private" virtues would be incomprehensible. But we distinguish public and private with a vengeance, and we typically value our private, personal character more highly than our public persona, which is sometimes thought to be superficial, impersonal, "plastic," and merely manipulative, instrumental. A person's character is best determined by those who "really know him," and it is not odd to us that a person generally known as a bastard might be thought to be a good person just on the testimony of a wife, a husband, or a close friend. ("But if you knew Johnny as I do, you would see that . . . .") In a fragmented world so built on intimate privacies, love even more than family and friendship determines selfhood. Love is just this determining of selfhood. When we talk about "the real self" or "being true to ourselves," what we often mean is being true to the image of ourselves that we share with those we love most. We say, and are expected to say, that the self we display in public performance, the self we present on the job, the self we show to acquaintances, is not real. We sometimes take great pains to prove that the self we share with our family (a historical kind of love) is no longer the self that we consider real. Nor is it any surprise that the self we would like to think of as most real is the self that emerges in intimacy, and its virtues are the typically private virtues of honesty in feeling and expression, interpersonal passion, tenderness, and sensitivity.

The idea of an Aristophanic union—the reunification of two halves that already belong together—is charming and suggestive, but it is only half of the story. The other half starts with the fact of our differences and our stubbornness, and how we may ill fit together even after years of compromise and cohabitation. The freedom of choice that allows us virtually unrestricted range for our romantic intentions also raises the possibility—which was one of the suppositions of courtly love as well—that our choice will often be difficult, if not socially prohibited. (Who was the one girl in Verona that young Romeo should not have chosen? And the one woman wholly forbidden to Lancelot?) The process of mutual self-identification runs into conflict with one of its own presuppositions—the ideal of autonomous individualism. The selves that are to merge do not have the advantage of having adjusted to and complemented each other when the self was still flexible and only partially formed—as in societies where families arrange marriages between children who have grown up together. And whatever the nostalgic popularity of "first love" and the Romeo and Juliet paradigm, the truth is that most of us fall in love well advanced in our development, even into old age, when the self is full-formed and complementarity is more often an exercise in compromise. The development of love is consequently defined by a *dialectic*, often tender but sometimes ontologically vicious, in which each lover struggles for control over shared and reciprocal self-images, resists them, revises them, rejects them. For this reason, love—unlike many other emotions—takes time. It does not make sense to say of love, as it does of anger, that one was in love for fifteen minutes but then calmed down. But neither is this to say that there is no such thing as unrequited love, or that unrequited love is not love, for the dialectic, complete with resistance and conflict, can go on just as well in one soul as in two. Granted that the drama may be a bit impoverished, but as Stendhal often argued, the imagination may be enriched thereby. Or as Goethe once said, "If I love you, what business is that of yours?"

## IN PURSUIT OF A PASSION (CONCLUSION)

> True love, whatever is said of it, will always be honored by men; for although its transports lead us astray, although it does not exclude odious qualities from the heart that feels it—and even produces them—it nevertheless always presupposes estimable qualities without which one would not be in a condition to feel it.[22]

Love, briefly summarized, is a dialectical process of (mutually) reconceived selfhood with a long and varied history. As such, it is much more than a feeling and it need not be at all capricious or unintelligent or disruptive. But the idea that love is concerned with selfhood might suggest that love is essentially self-love, casting love in the role of a vice rather than a virtue. And the suggestion that love is essentially the reconception and determination of oneself through another looks dangerously similar to some familiar definitions of narcissism. But self-reference entails neither cynicism nor narcissism. Although one does see oneself through the other on this analysis, and although as in narcissism the idea of "separation of subject and object" is greatly obscured, love as mutual self-defining reflection does not encourage either vicious or clinical conclusions. Unlike narcissism, love takes the other as its standard, not just as its mirror, which is why the courtly lovers called it "devotion" (as in devoting oneself to God) and why Stendhal—himself an accomplished narcissist—called "passion-love" the one wholly unselfish experience. Love is not selfless but it is nevertheless the antithesis of selfishness. It embodies an expansion of self, modest, perhaps, but what it lacks in scope it more than makes up for in motivation.

## Notes

1. J. Kant, *The Groundwork of the Metaphysics of Morals,* translated by H. J. Paton (New York, 1964), 67 (p. 13 of the standard German edition).
2. Plato, *The Symposium,* translated by W. Hamilton (London, 1951), 43.
3. A. Schopenhauer, *The World as Will and Representation,* translated by E. Payne (New York, 1958), quoted in *Sexual Love and Western Morality,* edited by D. Verene (New York, 1972), 175.
4. laRochefoucauld, *Maxims,* translated by J. Heayd, no. 68.
5. I. Kant, *Lectures on Ethics,* translated by L. Infield (Indianapolis, 1963), 164.
6. J. Milton, *Paradise Lost* (New York, 1969), Book 8, lines 383–85.
7. F. Nietzsche, *The Antichrist,* translated by H. Kaufmann (New York, 1954), sect. 11.
8. Bernard Williams, "Morality and the Emotions," in *Problems of the Self* (Cambridge, 1973).
9. Richard Taylor, *Good and Evil* (New York, 1970), xii.
10. Barbara Herman, "The Practice of Moral Judgment," *Journal of Philosophy* 82, no. 8 (1985).
11. Bernard Gert, *The Moral Rules* (New York, 1973), 143.
12. Edward Sankowski, "Love and Moral Obligation" and "Responsibility of Persons for their Emotions" in *Canadian Journal of Philosophy* 7 (1977): 829–40.
13. G. W. F. Hegel, *Early Theological Manuscripts,* translated by T. Knox (Philadelphia, 1971), 305.
14. Amelie Rorty, "Explaining Emotions" in *Explaining Emotions* (Berkeley, 1980).
15. M. Nussbaum, "The Speech of Alcibiades," *Philosophy and Literature* 3, no. 2 (1979).
16. Ibid., and Michael Gagarin, "Socrates' Hubris and Alcibiades' Failure," *Phoenix* 31 (1977).

17.  I. Singer, *The Nature of Love*, vol. 2 (Chicago, 1986), 35–36.
18.  Ibid.
19.  Denis de Rougemont, *Love in the Western World* (New York, 1974).
20.  Singer, *Nature of Love*, 22-23.
21.  *Symposium*, 64.
22.  J. J. Rousseau, *Emile*, translated by A. Bloom (New York, 1979), 214.
23.  William Frankena, *Ethics* (Engelwood Cliffs, N.J., 1973), and in a recent newsletter to University of Michigan Philosophy Department alumni.

## CRITICAL THINKING QUESTIONS

1. How does Solomon define the combination of erös and ethics?
2. How does Solomon define romantic love? What is your definition of romantic love?
3. Write and analyze a case that incorporates romantic and sexual love within the rubric of ethics.

MICHEL FOUCAULT

## APHRODISIA

*Michel Foucault (1926–84) taught at the College de France and is the author of many books. His books are widely read in disciplines such as communication, philosophy, psychology, sociology, anthropology, and linguistics. In his excerpt from* The Use of Pleasure, *published in 1985, Foucault challenges the traditional structures defining pleasure.*

The *aphrodisia* are the acts, gestures, and contacts that produce a certain form of pleasure. When Saint Augustine in his *Confessions* recalls the friendships of his youth, the intensity of his affections, the pleasures of the days spent together, the conversations, the enthusiasms and good times, he wonders if, underneath its seeming innocence, all that did not pertain to the flesh, to that "glue" which attaches us to the flesh.[4] But when Aristotle in his *Nicomachean Ethics* wants to determine exactly which people deserve to be called "self-indulgent," his definition is cautiously restrictive: self-indulgence—*akolasia*—relates only to the pleasures of the body; and among these, the pleasures of sight, hearing, and smell must be excluded.[5] It is not self-indulgent to "delight in" *(charein)* colors, shapes, or paintings, nor in theater or music; one can, without self-indulgence, delight in the scent of fruit, roses, or incense; and, he says in the *Eudemian Ethics*,[6] anyone who would become so intensely absorbed in looking at a statue or in listening to a song as to lose his appetite or taste for lovemaking could not be reproached for self-indulgence, any more than could someone who let himself be seduced by the Sirens. For there is pleasure that is liable to *akolasia* only where there is touch and contact: contact with the mouth, the tongue, and the throat (for the pleasures of food and drink), or contact with other parts of the body (for the pleasure of sex). Moreover, Aristotle remarks that it would be unjust to suspect self-indulgence in the case of certain pleasures experienced on the surface of the body, such as the noble pleasures that are produced by massages and heat in the gymnasium: "for the

---

*One should, however, note the importance attributed by many Greek texts to the gaze and to the eyes in the genesis of desire or love; but it is not the pleasure of the gaze is self-indulgent; rather, it is thought to make an opening through which the soul is reached. In this connection, see Xenophon's *Memorabilia*.[8] As for the kiss, it was very highly valued as a physical pleasure and a communication of souls despite the danger it carried. As a matter of fact, an entire historical study could be undertaken on the "pleasure body" and its transformations.

contact characteristic of the self-indulgent man does not affect the whole body but only certain parts."[7]*

It will be one of the characteristic traits of the Christian experience of the "flesh," and later of "sexuality," that the subject is expected to exercise suspicion often, to be able to recognize from afar the manifestations of a stealthy, resourceful, and dreadful power. Reading these signs will be all the more important as this power has the ability to cloak itself in many forms other than sexual acts. There is no similar suspicion inhabiting the experience of the *aphrodisia*. To be sure, in the teaching and the exercise of moderation, it is recommended to be wary of sounds, images, and scents; but this is not because attachment to them would be only the masked form of a desire whose essence is sexual: it is because there are musical forms capable of weakening the soul with their rhythms, and because there are sights capable of affecting the soul like a venom, and because a particular scent, a particular image, is apt to call up the "memory of the thing desired."[9] And when philosophers are laughed at for claiming to love only the beautiful souls of boys, they are not suspected of harboring murky feelings of which they may not be conscious, but simply of waiting for the *tête-à-tête* in order to slip their hand under the tunic of their heart's desire.[10]

What of the form and variety of these acts? Greek natural history gives some descriptions, at least as concerns animals: Aristotle remarks that mating is not the same among all animals and does not take place in the same manner.[11] And in the part of Book VI of the *History of Animals* that deals more specifically with viviparous animals, he describes the different forms of copulation that can be observed: they vary according to the form and location of the organs, the position taken by the partners, and the duration of the act. But he also evokes the types of behavior that characterize the mating season: wild boars preparing for battle, elephants whose frenzy extends to the destruction of their keeper's house, or stallions that group their females together by tracing a big circle around them before throwing themselves against their rivals.[12] With regard to the human animal, while the description of organs and their functioning may be detailed, the subject of sexual behavior, with its possible variants, is barely touched upon. Which does not mean, however, that there was, in Greek medicine, philosophy, or ethics, a zone of strict silence around the sexual activity of humans. It is not that people were careful to avoid talking about these pleasurable acts; but when they were the subject of questioning, what was at issue was not the form they assumed, it was the activity they manifested. Their dynamics was much more important than their morphology.

This dynamics was defined by the movement that linked the *aphrodisia* to the pleasure that was associated with them and to the desire to which they gave rise. The attraction exerted by pleasure and the force of the desire that was directed toward it constituted, together with the action of the *aphrodisia* itself, a solid unity. The dissociation—or partial dissociation at least—of this ensemble would later become one of the basic features of the ethics of the flesh and the notion of sexuality. This dissociation was to be marked, on the one hand, by a certain "elision" of pleasure (a moral devaluation through the injunction given in the preaching by the Christian clergy against the pursuit of sensual pleasure as a goal of sexual practice; a theoretical devaluation shown by the extreme difficulty of finding a place for pleasure in the conception of sexuality); it would also be marked by an increasingly intense problematization of desire (in which the primordial sign of a fallen nature or the structure characteristic of the human condition would be visible). In the experience of the *aphrodisia* on the other hand, act, desire, and pleasure formed an ensemble whose elements were distinguishable certainly, but closely bound to one another. It was precisely their close linkage that constituted one of the essential characteristics of that form of activity. Nature intended (for reasons we shall consider) that the performance of the act be associated with a pleasure, and it was this pleasure that gave rise to *epithumia*, to desire, in a movement that was naturally directed toward what "gives pleasure," according to a principle that Aristotle cites: desire is always "desire for the agreeable thing" *(hē gar epithumia tou hēdeos estin)*.[13] It is true—Plato always comes back to the idea—that for the Greeks there could not be desire without privation, without the want of the thing desired and without a certain amount of suffering mixed in; but the appetite, Plato explains in the *Philebus*, can be aroused only by the representation, the image or the memory of the thing that gives pleasure; he concludes that there can be no desire except in the soul, for while the body is affected by privation, it is the soul and only the soul that can, through memory, make present the thing that is to be desired and thereby arouse the *epithumia*.[14] Thus, what seems in fact to have formed the object of moral reflection for the Greeks in matters of sexual conduct was not exactly the act itself (considered in its different modalities), or desire (viewed from the standpoint of its origin or its aim), or even pleasure (evaluated according to the different objects or practices that can cause it; it was more the dynamics that joined all three in a circular fashion (the desire that leads to the act, the act that is linked to pleasure, and the pleasure that occasions desire). The ethical question that was raised was not: which desires? which acts? which pleasures? but rather: with what force is one transported "by the pleasures and desires"? The ontology to which this ethics of sexual behavior referred was not, at least not in its general form, an ontology of deficiency and desire; it was not that of a nature setting the standard for acts; it was an ontology of a force that linked together acts, pleasures, and desires. It was this dynamic relationship that constituted what might be called the texture of the ethical experience of the *aphrodisia*.*

This dynamics is analyzed in terms of two major variables. The first is quantitative; it has to do with the degree of activity that is shown by the number and frequency of acts. What differentiates men from one another, for medicine and moral philosophy alike, is not so much the type of objects toward which they are oriented, nor the mode of sexual practice they prefer; above all, it is the intensity of that practice. The division is between lesser and greater: moderation or excess. It is rather rare, when a notable personage is depicted, for his preference for one form of sexual practice or another to be pointed up.† On the other hand, it is always important for his moral characterization to note whether he has been able to show moderation in his involvement with women or boys, like Agesilaus, who carried moderation to the point that he refused to kiss the young man that he loved; or whether he surrendered, like Alcibiades or Arcesilaus, to the appetite for the pleasures that one can enjoy with both sexes.[18] This point is supported by the famous passage of the first book of the *Laws:* it is true that Plato draws a sharp opposition in this passage between the relationship "according to nature" that joins man and woman for procreative ends, and relations "against nature" of male with male and female with female.[19] But this opposition, as marked as it is from the standpoint of naturalness, is referred by Plato to the more basic distinction between self-restraint and self-indulgence. The practices that contravene nature and the principle of procreation are not explained as the effect of an abnormal nature or of a peculiar form of desire; they are merely the result of immoderation: "a lack of self-restraint with regard to pleasure" *(akrateia hēdonēs)* is their source.[20]

---

*The frequency of expressions that link pleasures and desires very closely together should be noted. These expressions show that what is at stake in the ethical system of the *aphrodisia* is the dynamic ensemble consisting of desire and pleasure associated with the act. The *epithumiai-hēdonai* pair occurs quite commonly in Plato.[15] Frequent, too, are expressions that speak of pleasure as a force that persuades, transports, triumphs, as in Xenophon's *Memorabilia*.[16]

†It sometimes happens that a man's particular fondness for boys will be mentioned for narrative purposes. Xenophon does this in the *Anabasis,* in regard to a certain Episthenes. But when he draws a negative portrait of Menon, he does not reproach him for this kind of taste, but for misusing such pleasures: obtaining a command too young, or loving an overage boy while still being beardless himself.[17]

And when, in the *Timaeus,* Plato declares that lust should be considered as the effect, not of a bad volition of the soul, but of a sickness of the body, this disorder is described in terms of a grand pathology of excess: the sperm, instead of remaining enclosed in the marrow and its bony casing, overflows and starts to stream through the whole body, so that the latter becomes like a tree whose vegetative power exceeds all limits; the individual is thus driven to distraction for a large part of his existence by "pleasures and pains in excess."[21] This idea that immorality in the pleasures of sex is always connected with exaggeration, surplus, and excess is found again in the third book of the *Nicomachean Ethics:* Aristotle explains that for the natural desires that are common to everyone, the only offenses that one can commit are quantitative in nature: they pertain to "the more" *(to pleion);* so that natural desire only consists in satisfying needs, "to eat or drink whatever offers itself till one is surfeited is to exceed the natural amount *[tōi plēthei]*." It is true that Aristotle also makes allowance for the particular pleasures of individuals. It happens that people commit different types of offenses, either by not taking their pleasure "where they should," or by behaving "like the crowd," or again, by not taking their pleasure "as they ought." But, Aristotle adds, "self-indulgent individuals exceed *[hyperballousi]* in all these ways; they both delight in some things that they ought not to delight in, and if one ought to delight in some of the things they delight in, they do so more than one ought and than most men do." What constitutes self-indulgence in this sphere is excess, "and that is culpable."[22]* It appears, then, that the primary dividing line laid down by moral judgment in the area of sexual behavior was not prescribed by the nature of the act, with its possible variations, but by the activity and its quantitative gradations.

## CRITICAL THINKING QUESTIONS

1. According to Foucault what are the problems traditionally associated with pleasure? How does he attempt to dismiss these problems?
2. How do you interpret Aristotle's allowance for particular individual pleasures, including sexual?
3. Write and analyze a case that involves problems with traditional moral values and sexual pleasure.

---

*It should be noted, however, that Aristotle gives his attention on several occasions to the question of the "disgraceful pleasures" that some individuals tend to seek.[23]

CATHARINE MACKINNON

## Sex and Violence

*Catharine MacKinnon, a professor at the University of Michigan, is a noted feminist and legal scholar. This 1987 excerpt from* Feminism Unmodified: Discourses on Life and Law, *discusses the violent behavior toward women that is sometimes seen as acceptable by society.*

When we ask whether rape, sexual harassment, and pornography are questions of violence or questions of sexuality, it helps to ask, to whom? What is the perspective of those who are involved, whose experience it is—to rape or to have been raped, to consume pornography or to be consumed through it. As to what these things *mean* socially, it is important whether they are about sexuality to women and men or whether they are instead about "violence,"—or whether violence and sexuality can be distinguished in that way, as they are lived out.

The crime of rape—this is a legal and observed, not a subjective, individual, or feminist definition—is defined around penetration. That seems to me a very male point of view on what is means to be sexually violated. And it is exactly what heterosexuality as a social institution is fixated around, the penetration of the penis into the vagina. Rape is defined according to what men think violates women, and that is the same as what they think of as the *sine qua non* of sex. What women experience as degrading and defiling when we are raped includes as much that is distinctive to us as is our experience of sex. Someone once termed penetration a "peculiarly resented aspect" of rape—I don't know whether that meant it was peculiar that it was resented or that it was resented with heightened peculiarity. Women who have been raped often do resent having been penetrated. But that is not all there is to what was intrusive or expropriative of a woman's sexual wholeness.

I do think the crime of rape focuses more centrally on what men define as sexuality than on women's experience of our sexual being, hence its violation. A common experience of rape victims is to be unable to feel good about anything heterosexual thereafter—or anything sexual at all, or men at all. The minute they start to have sexual feelings or feel sexually touched by a man, or even woman, they start to relive the rape. I had a client who came in with her husband. She was a rape victim, a woman we had represented as a witness. Her husband sat the whole time and sobbed. They couldn't have sex anymore because every time he started to touch her, she would flash to the rape scene and see his face change into the face of the man who had raped her. That, to me, is sexual. When a woman has been raped, and it is sex that she then cannot experience without connecting it to that, it was her sexuality that was violated.

Similarly, men who are in prison for rape think it's the dumbest thing that ever happened . . . It isn't just a miscarriage of justice; they were put in jail for something very little different from what most men do most of the time and call it sex. The only difference is they got caught. That view is non-remorseful and not rehabilitative. It may also be true. It seems to me we have here a convergence between the rapist's view of what he has done and the victim's perspective on what was done to her. That is, for both, their ordinary experiences of heterosexual intercourse and the act of rape have something in common. Now this gets us into intense trouble, because that's exactly how judges and juries see it who refuse to convict men accused of rape. A rape victim has to prove that it was not intercourse. She has to show that there was force and she resisted, because if there was sex, consent is inferred. Finders of fact look for "more force than usual during the preliminaries." Rape is defined by distinction from intercourse—not nonviolence, intercourse. They ask, does this event look more like fucking or like rape? But what is their standard for sex, and is this question asked from the *woman's point of view?* The level of force is not adjudicated at her point of violation; it is adjudicated at the standard of the normal level of force. Who sets this standard?

In the criminal law, we can't put everybody in jail who does an ordinary act, right? Crime is supposed to be deviant, not normal. Women continue not to report rape, and a reason is that they believe, and they are right, that the legal system will not see it from their point of view. We get very low conviction rates for rape.[1] We also get many women who believe they have never been raped, although a lot of force was involved. They mean that they were not raped in a way that is legally provable. In other words, in all these situations, there was not *enough* violence against them to take it beyond the category of "sex"; they were not coerced enough. Maybe they were forced-fucked for years and put up with it, maybe they tried to get it over with, maybe they were coerced by something other than battery, something like economics, maybe even something like love.

What I am saying is that unless you make the point that there is much violence in intercourse, as a usual matter, none of that is changed. Also we continue to stigmatize the women who claim rape as having experienced a deviant violation and allow the rest of us to go through life feeling violated but thinking we've never been raped, when there were a great many times when we, too, have had sex and didn't want it. What this critique does that is different from the "violence, not sex" critique is ask a series of questions about normal, heterosexual intercourse and attempt to move the line between heterosexuality on the one hand—intercourse—and rape on the other, rather than allow it to stay where it is.

Having done that so extensively with rape, I can consider sexual harassment more briefly. The way the analysis of sexual harassment is sometimes expressed now (and it bothers me) is that it is an abuse of power, not sexuality. That does not allow us to pursue whether sexuality, as socially constructed in our society through gender roles, is *itself* a power structure. If you look at sexual harassment as power, not sex, what is power supposed to be? Power is employer/employee, not because courts are marxist but because this is a recognized hierarchy. Among men. Power is teacher/student, because courts recognize a hierarchy there. Power is on one side and sexuality on the other. Sexuality is ordinary affection, everyday flirtation. Only when ordinary, everyday affection and flirtation and "I was just trying to be friendly" come into the context of *another* hierarchy is it considered potentially an abuse of power. What is not considered to be a hierarchy is women and men—men on top and women on the bottom. That is not considered to be a question of power or social hierarchy, legally or politically. A feminist perspective suggests that it is.

When we have examples of coequal sexual harassment (within these other hierarchies), worker to worker on the same level, involving women and men, we have a lot of very interesting, difficult questions about sex discrimination, which is supposed to be about gender difference, but does not conceive of gender as a social hierarchy. I think that implicit in race discrimination cases for a brief moment of light was the notion that there is a social hierarchy between Blacks and whites. So that presumptively it's an exercise of power for a white person to do something egregious to a Black person or for a white institution to do something egregious systematically to many Black people. Situations of coequal power—among coworkers or students or teachers—are difficult to see as examples of sexual harassment unless you have a notion of male power. I think we lie to women when we call it not power when a woman is come onto by a man who is not her employer, not her teacher. What do we labor under, what do we feel, when a man—any man—comes and hits on us? I think we require women to feel fine about turning down male initiated sex so long as the man doesn't have some *other* form of power over us. Whenever—every and any time—a woman feels conflicted and wonders what's wrong with her that she can't decline although she has no inclination, and she feels open to male accusations, whether they come from women or men, of "why didn't you just tell him to buzz off?" we have sold her out, not named her experience. We are taught that we exist for men. We should be flattered or at least act as if we are—be careful about a man's ego because you never know what he can do to you. To flat out say to him, "You?" or "I don't want to" is not *in* most women's sex-role learning. To say it is, is bravado. And that's because he's a man, not just because you never know what he can do to you because he's your boss (that's two things—he's a man and he's the boss) or your teacher or in some other hierarchy. It seems to me that we haven't talked very much about gender as a hierarchy, as a division of power, in the way that's expressed and acted out, primarily I think sexually. And therefore we haven't expanded the definition according to women's experience of sexuality, including our own sexual intimidation, of what things are sexual in this world. So men have also defined what can be called sexual about us. They say, "I was just trying to be affectionate, flirtatious and friendly," and we were just all felt up. We criticize the idea that rape comes down to her word against his—but it really *is* her perspective against his perspective, and the law has been written from *his* perspective. If he didn't mean it to be sexual, it's not sexual. If he didn't see it as forced, it wasn't forced.[2] Which is to say, only male sexual violations, that is, only male ideas of what sexually violates us as women, are illegal. We buy into this when we say our sexual violations are abuses of power, not sex.

Just as rape is supposed to have nothing against intercourse, just as sexual harassment is supposed to have nothing against normal sexual initiation (men initiate, women consent—that's mutual?), the idea that pornography is violence against women, not sex, seems to distinguish artistic creation on the one hand from what is degrading to women on the other. It is candid and true but not enough to say of pornography, as Justice Stewart said, "I know it when I see it."[3] *He* knows what he thinks it is when he sees it—but is that what *I* know? Is that the same "it"? Is he going to know what I know when I see it? I think pretty much not, given what's on the newsstand, given what is not considered hard-core pornography. Sometimes I think what is obscene is what does *not* turn on the Supreme Court—or what revolts them more. Which is uncommon, since revulsion is eroticized. We have to admit that pornography turns men on; it is therefore erotic. It is a lie to say that pornography is not erotic. When we say it is violence, not sex, we are saying, there is this degrading to women, over here, and this erotic, over there, without saying to whom. It is overwhelmingly disproportionately men to whom pornography is erotic. It is women, on the whole, to whom it is violent, among other things. And this is not just a matter of perspective, but a matter of reality. . . .

## CRITICAL THINKING QUESTIONS

1. MacKinnon suggests that sex is inherently discriminatory to women. Do you agree or disagree? Explain.
2. Who does MacKinnon believe has defined rape? Is this definition unethical?
3. Write and analyze a case based on sexual violations against women. Within the case develop a method whereby women can be better protected.

SEAN McCOLLUM

# CAN YOU OUTLAW HATE?

*Sean McCollum is an author, particularly in the areas of gay rights and discrimination. In this 1998 article published in* Scholastic Update, *McCollum explains the importance of intimate relationships in light of hate crimes that occur with gays and lesbians. McCollum calls for a reform in current law that would protect homosexuals from those who oppose their intimacies.*

Around midnight last October 6, 21-year-old Matthew Shepard went out to the Fireside Bar in Laramie, Wyoming. The University of Wyoming student was approached by two young men—Aaron McKinney, 22, and Russell Henderson, 21. According to reports, McKinney and Henderson deceived Shepard into thinking they were gay. Shepard said he was a gay too. The three then left the bar together.

Once in McKinney's truck, the men turned on Shepard. Pulling off the road, they beat, robbed, and pistol-whipped him. Then they drove into the lonely high plains on the out-skirts of Laramie, where they tied Shepard to a buck-and-rail fence. As he begged for his life, they burned him with cigarettes, cut his face, and beat him unconscious. Then they left him to die in the cold.

Eighteen hours later, a passing mountain biker spotted the limp, nearly lifeless figure, and at first mistook him for a scarecrow. Shepard was rushed to a hospital, but never regained consciousness. He died on October 12, with his family by his side. Police say Shepard was targeted in part because he was gay.

The killing of Matthew Shepard struck a nerve. Its sheer brutality sent shudders around the world, and focused international attention on the alarming increase in hate crimes against gay people. Gay-rights groups and their anti-gay opponents, both galvanized by Shepard's death, locked horns in a fiercely emotional debate.

Thousands of mourners held candlelight vigils in cities across the U.S. Anti-gay protesters from as far away as Oklahoma and Texas traveled to Wyoming to picket Shepard's funeral, bearing signs reading "Fag Matt in Hell" and "No Tears for Queers." In Washington, President Bill Clinton urged Congress to pass the Hate Crimes Prevention Act—a bill that would increase penalties for crimes motivated by prejudice against gays, women, and the disabled. As Americans everywhere examined their own attitudes toward homosexuality, many people realized that what happened to Matt Shepard in Wyoming could happen anywhere.

In the last generation, more gays and lesbians have "come out of the closet"—openly revealed their sexuality—and moved toward the mainstream of American society. The list includes such public figures as U.S. Representative Barney Frank, actress Ellen DeGeneres, singers k.d. lang and Melissa Etheridge, and Olympic gold medalist Greg Louganis.

At the same time, a gay-rights movement has emerged to battle what supporters see as a long tradition of discrimination. "Since the 1960s, American society and schools have made a conscious effort to address problems of racism, inequality between the sexes, and the growing diversity of our population," says Rea Carey of the National Youth Advocacy Coalition (NYAC), an organization that deals with issues facing gay youth. "Anti-gay attitudes are the last frontier of discrimination."

Many conservative religious and political groups, though, consider homosexuality a sin and a threat to the traditional family. Conservative Christians cite Bible passages that condemn homosexuality. The Family Research Council, a conservative political organization, runs advertisements claiming that homosexuality can be "cured." Republican Senate Majority

Leader Trent Lott said in an interview last June, "You should try to show [homosexuals] a way to deal with [homosexuality] just like alcohol . . . or sex addiction . . . or kleptomaniacs."

The attitudes of most Americans toward gays, though, are complex. In an October Time/CNN poll, 52 percent of those questioned say that homosexual relationships are acceptable for other people, while 48 percent still believe that homosexuality is "morally wrong." While these views may be ambivalent, they reflect a dramatic increase in acceptance of homosexuality compared with 20 years ago, when 59 percent said homosexual relationships were "not acceptable at all."

Acceptance of gays and lesbians may be increasing, but "hate crimes" against gays and lesbians are still widespread. The U.S. Justice Department reports that homosexuals are "probably the most frequent victims" of crimes motivated by prejudice.

In the wake of Shepard's death, many Americans have called for the passage of hate-crime laws—laws that increase the punishment for crimes motivated by prejudice. Forty states already have some titan of these laws on the books. But 20 of them don't include crimes against gays and lesbians. Neither does the current federal law. Ten states, including Wyoming, have no hate-crime laws at all.

The Hate Crimes Prevention Act now before Congress would make anti-gay crimes a federal hate crime. Currently, federal law punishes hate crimes relating to race, religion, or ethnicity. The Hate Crimes Prevention Act would add to that list crimes against gays, women, and the disabled.

The bill's supporters argue that federal law—and federal investigators— are essential because in some places, local law enforcement is unable or unwilling to investigate. Jeffrey Montgomery of the Triangle Foundation, an organization that monitors hate crimes against gays, says that in some communities, police and the courts go easy on an offender if the victim is homosexual.

In addition, Montgomery and others value the message reinforced by hate-crime laws. "[Hate-crime legislation] indicates the will of a society and culture to say that these crimes are vicious and heinous and will not be tolerated," he says.

Opponents of the bill come from two angles. Anti-gay groups claim that hate-crime laws would give homosexuals special rights and protections not enjoyed by others. They also fear these laws are one more step in the acceptance of gays and lesbians into American society. "It would be a disaster to take something like homosexual conduct and attempt to fold it into the rubric of civil rights laws that we have," says Gary Bauer, head of Family Research Council.

Other opponents say hate-crime laws aren't needed for any group. "These laws are well-intentioned but misguided," says Kimberly Potter, a senior fellow at New York University School of Law. "We have an arsenal of laws to deal with these crimes, so new ones won't shore up any holes in our legal system." Shepard's killers, for example, already face the death penalty for murder. Potter cautions against thinking of new laws as a cure-all for society's ills. "Just because you pass a law doesn't mean that intolerance and bigotry is being solved," she says.

The political battle over hate-crime laws is just heating up. Public outrage over Shepard's murder places a great deal of pressure on lawmakers to do something, while anti-gay groups are ready, in Bauer's words, to "wage the war" against any government acceptance of homosexuality.

Whatever the outcome, the fence on which Matthew Shepard was left to die has already become a powerful symbol—of hatred and of hope. "Matt Shepard was a martyr," says Michael Bisogno, a 16-year-old gay high school student in New Jersey. "And I hope he was the last one."

## CRITICAL THINKING QUESTIONS

1. Outline the communication process necessary to work through problems of hate crimes toward gays.
2. Ethically, as well as practically, can hate crimes be made unacceptable within a society? How can this be achieved?
3. Write and analyze a case involving interpersonal communication to work through a potential hate crime situation.

# CONTEMPORARY CASE

## *Start-up Software Firm*

Four men and one woman resigned their positions with a large computer company to spinoff a small software firm. During the first year of operation they were very diligent, industrious, creative, and fortunate in developing a new and exciting product. During their second year of operation, a large firm in the East became aware of their success and was interested in a buyout. In the negotiations a male representative of the larger company was to visit the small firm. The representative was to fly in on Friday to look at the area, then on Monday the representative was to meet and consider the buyout option. Completion of this negotiation could make all of the five members of the group extremely wealthy. In order to ensure that the negotiations went well, three of the men felt that it would be wise to have the representative from the East well entertained the weekend before the meeting. They asked the female member of the group if she would volunteer to be an escort and ensure the representative had a "fun and entertaining" time.

1. What is the interpersonal problem in this case? What is being communicated by the male partners to the female partner?
2. Is it acceptable to ask a business partner to engage in sex for the sake of the company?
3. What would you do if you were the young woman?
4. What is the social construction that leads to the premise that the representative will want sexual entertainment?
5. What nonverbal communication is taking place in this case? Does this create any extra problems?

# 6

## MORALITY AND MARRIAGE

MIKE W. MARTIN

## LOVE'S CONSTANCY

*Mike W. Martin, a professor of philosophy at Chapman University, is the au-*
*thor of several books and articles on love, morality, and deception. This 1993*
*article details the importance of keeping commitments and faithfulness within*
*a marriage.*

'Marital faithfulness' refers to faithful love for a spouse or lover to whom
one is committed, rather than the narrower idea of sexual fidelity. The distinction is clearly marked in traditional wedding vows. A commitment to
love faithfully is central: 'to have and to hold from this day forward, for better for worse, for richer for poorer, in sickness and in health, to love and to
cherish, till death us do part . . . and thereto I plight [pledge] thee my troth
[faithfulness]'.[1] Sexual fidelity is promised in a subordinate clause, symbol-

---

[1] Church of England Prayer Book (1549). I will understand marriage as a moral relationship
centred *[sic]* on lifelong commitments to love and significantly involving sexual desire at some
time during the relationship, whether or not the marriage is formalized in legal or religious
ceremonies, recognizing homosexual as well as heterosexual marriages, and independently of
government intrusions. On the latter see David Palmer, 'The Consolation of the Wedded', in
*Philosophy and Sex*, 2nd edn, Robert Baker and Frederick Elliston (eds) (Buffalo, NY:
Prometheus Books, 1984), 119–129.

izing its supportive role in promoting love's constancy: 'and, forsaking all other, keep thee only unto her/him.'[2]

Martial commitments to love have been subjected to a barrage of objections. They have been criticized as unintelligible, unreasonable, inhumane, unnecessary, non-binding, and incompatible with love. I respond to these objections in Part I, seeking to uncover the partial truths as well as the confusions they embody. Then, in Part II, I explore why marital faithfulness is a virtue, that is, a morally desirable feature of spouses who make lifelong commitments, rather than simply a matter of individual preferences. Throughout, I develop a conception of 'true' (erotic) love as value-guided attitudes and relationships that constitute special ways to value persons.[3]

## COMMITMENTS TO LOVE

Consider the following conversation from Tolstoy's *Kreutzer Sonata*.

'Yes, but how is one to understand what is meant by "true love"?' said the gentleman. . . .

'Why? It's very simple,' she said, but stopped to consider. 'Love? Love is an exclusive preference for one above everybody else,' said the lady.

'Preference for how long? A month, two days, or half an hour?' said the grey-haired man and began to laugh.

'Excuse me, we are evidently not speaking of the same thing'. . . .

'Yes, I know . . . you are talking about what is supposed to be, but I am speaking of what is. Every man experiences what you call love for every pretty woman.'

---

[2] Or its *presumed* supportive role. Some couples, of course, enter into (or transform their relationship into) 'open marriages' in which they permit extramarital affairs while retaining lifetime commitments. For an early and especially interesting example, see Nigel Nicolson's portrayal of his parents in *Portrait of a Marriage* (New York: Atheneum, 1973). Two illuminating (and contrasting) discussions of the rationale for traditional links between lifetime marital commitments and sexual fidelity are: Edmund Leites, *The Puritan Conscience and Modern Sexuality* (New Haven: Yale University Press, 1986), and Roger Scruton, *Sexual Desire* (New York: Free Press, 1986).

[3] Irving Singer develops the idea of love as a special way of valuing persons in his masterful three-volume study, *The Nature of Love* (Chicago: University of Chicago Press, 1984, 1987). Whereas I understand ('true') love as permeated by the virtues, Singer separates morality and love, as a result of his constricted view of morality as demanding impartiality (by contrast with love's preference for one individual). See especially p. 11 of vol. I.

'Oh, what you say is awful! But the feeling that is called love does exist
among people, and is given not for months or years, but for a lifetime!'
'No, it does not! . . .'[4]

The cynical gentleman, who we learn later has murdered his wife, thinks
of erotic love as a feeling based on sexual desire, a feeling which comes and
goes with sexual interest. The lady initially portrays love as a paramount
preference, hinting that love is a way of valuing persons (which involves but
is not reducible to feelings). In her subsequent remarks, however, she agrees
with the gentleman that love is a feeling, and the disagreement then shifts to
how long the feeling can last. This brings us to the first objection to marital
commitments.

*Objection I: Love and Will.* Commitments to love are unintelligible, given
the nature of love. A commitment implies a resolve or pledge to engage in
actions which are under our voluntary control. But love is an emotion, not
an action. As such it happens to us; we do not choose it. The idea of committing ourselves to love is as incoherent as committing ourselves to feel
grief.

This objection assumes that commitments to love refer to love as a feeling or emotion. I suggest instead that the love referred to is primarily an attitude and a relationship. A commitment to love is a commitment to sustain
an attitude of valuing the beloved as singularly important in one's life. Thus,
spouses who say to each other 'I love you' are typically expressing a complex
and durable attitude that is revealed in patterns of conduct, rather than a
momentary feeling. In addition, a commitment to love implies taking on responsibility for a relationship. It is a commitment to activities that sustain
the relationship—activities of caring and support, of sharing resources, of
living together harmoniously.

In general, talk about 'true love' alludes to desirable attitudes and value-
guided relationships. Ideals enter into their very meaning. One traditional
ideal is to value another person above others based on a lifelong commitment. This ideal is hardly reducible to sexual desire and feelings, although it
involves sexual attraction as an important aspect of valuing the beloved (at
least throughout much of the relationship). The ideal, as well as the attitude
and relationship grounded in it, are in part constituted by the virtues of

---

[4] Leo Tolstoy, *Great Short Works of Leo Tolstoy*, trans. Louise and Aylmer Maude (New York:
Harper and Row, 1967), 361–362. Also see Paul Gilbert's discussion in *Human Relationships*
(Oxford: Blackwell, 1991), 9ff.

caring, fidelity, honesty, fairness—and faithfulness. These 'constitutive virtues' contrast with 'coping virtues', such as courage, prudence, and perseverance which enable love to flourish.

Of course, emotions are centrally involved in loving attitudes and relationships. They include strong affection, but also delight, joy, concern, hope, gratitude, jealousy, anger, pride, guilt, shame, and grief. Hence the objection can be rephrased: Commitments to love imply commitments to have emotions; those commitments are unintelligible because we cannot choose to feel emotions; therefore, commitments to love are unintelligible.

In reply, note first that the issue is not whether love can be created from scratch by a spasm of will. A strong predisposition to love's emotions is already present when the commitment to love is made, especially if we are dealing with freely chosen, rather than arranged marriages. In the early stages of love we are largely passive, as ordinary language testifies: we fall in love, get struck by lightning, are swept away by passion. We cannot voluntarily generate the deeply-felt rush of emotions that signal love (although we can willingly open or close ourselves to such experiences). Commitments to love, however, are not aimed at creating emotions from scratch; they are aimed at sustaining an already-present disposition to have them, and to enable feelings of mutual caring and delight to grow deeper.

These commitments make sense because emotions are somewhat under our control. To be sure, the idea of committing ourselves to feel exactly this or that emotion at a particular time is problematic, at least for complex emotions. We can promise to try to enjoy a party, where that means setting aside worries for a while, but complex genuine emotions are heartfelt, not mentally manufactured. Nevertheless, commitments to love are consistent with these facts. They do not imply manipulating emotions, nor turning emotions on and off like a faucet. Instead, they imply assuming responsibility for sustaining patterns of acts and thoughts that foster emotions conductive to love.[5]

Conduct influences emotions. A commitment to love implies a strong willingness to choose activities that promote love-enhancing emotions and to avoid love-threatening emotions. Couples can avoid situations which they know cause anger, jealousy, or anxiety. They can choose activities

---

[5] John Wilson, 'Can One Promise to Love Another?' *Philosophy* **64** (1989), 560. Also see Edward Sankowski, 'Responsibility of Persons for Their Emotions,' *Canadian Journal of Philosophy* **12** (1977), 829–840.

which bring mutual pleasure and evoke mutual affection and intimacy. They can set aside time together and prevent work from encroaching on their privacy. And they can learn coping skills, such as the ability and willingness to compromise, to communicate clearly, and to fight fair (in ways that minimize long-term tension and hostility).

In addition, reflection influences emotions. At the core of most emotions are beliefs, attitudes, and patterns of attention which may be more or less reasonable.[6] Assessing reasons can alter this core and thereby shape emotions. For example, couples can choose to dwell on the bright side of situations so as to encourage positive emotions, or allow themselves to dwell on the negative so as to evoke fear, anxiety, and doubt.[7] They can bring to mind a shared history of good times, and look forward to positive change in order to encourage hope, or wallow in frustrations so as to nurse despair. They can think through mitigating circumstances in order to become more forgiving of their spouses and themselves. In short, conduct and reflection can promote an already-present disposition to love's emotions within value-guided relationships.

*Objection 2: Ought Implies Can.* Lifetime commitments to love are not morally binding, given the nature of morality. Commitments imply obligations and hence 'oughts'. As Kant said, 'ought implies can': We are obligated to do only what we can do, or at least what we can reasonably be expected to do. Now, many individuals cannot sustain lifetime commitments since they involve far too many unforeseeable things beyond their control (not just emotions). In J. F. M. Hunter's words, 'a promise is binding only to the extent that its performance is reasonably within the power of the person promising. If I promise to return your book by Thursday . . . you have some right to complain of bad faith if I fail; but if I promise to enjoy a certain film, to become a millionaire, or to be your friend for twenty years, then no matter how serious you take me to be, you would not have a clear right to complain if I failed to deliver. Now, a marriage vow can be seen as a promise of the latter kind'.[8]

---

[6] Amélie Oksenberg Rorty argues that the core of some emotions is a pattern of attention rather than the more common beliefs and attitudes in 'Explaining Emotions', in *Explaining Emotions* (Berkeley: University of California Press, 1980), 103–126.

[7] Cf. Martin E. P. Seligman, *Learned Optimism* (New York: Alfred A. Knopf, 1991).

[8] J. F. M. Hunter, *Thinking about Sex and Love* (Toronto: Macmillan of Canada, 1980), 59.

To begin with, we should be careful in interpreting the slogan 'ought implies can'. While the word 'ought' is most often used to prescribe conduct, and while there is no point in prescribing that people do the impossible, 'ought' has other uses as well.[9] It is used to ascribe obligations which persons may have even after rendering themselves unable to meet them. Thus, all drivers ought to drive safely—that is their obligation, an obligation which does not disappear when they become too drunk to meet it. At the time they are drunk it may be pointless to tell them they ought not to be driving, but it is true none the less, and later (retrospectively) there may be a point in reminding them of their past failures to do what they ought to have done.

Most obligations do imply the general capacity to meet them. Morality is realistic in this sense: We are obligated to avoid stealing, to show gratitude, and to help others only in so far as we have the general capacity to do so without unreasonable sacrifice. These examples concern duties we all have, independently of our commitments, whereas the objection concerns commitments to do what turns out not to be possible. Do such commitments ever create obligations?

Consider those overly-ambitious and naive business persons who enter into contracts which they cannot meet, given their talents, other resources, and the limitations imposed by the world. Their commitments are unrealistic, but nevertheless they generate legal and moral obligations. Declaring bankruptcy may cancel the legal obligation, but an apology or more substantive expression of guilt and compensation (for wrongs done) may be appropriate where great harm is done to others. What about those lovers who commit themselves to what turns out to be impossible, a lifetime together? Well, is that what they promise? Normally they promise to do everything in their power to make a marriage work, not to do what turns out to be impossible. Hence, we need to look in each case into why the relationship did not work out. If the cause is general irresponsibility or lack of effort, then it may not have been impossible at all. If instead the cause was that one's partner abandoned one for no good reason, or that poverty and tragedy drove the couple apart, we readily excuse or forgive.

Lifetime promises may prove impossible to keep because of unforeseeable difficulties that were beyond the ability of a couple to handle, or

---

[9] Except when it inspires individuals to do more than they could have otherwise. On this, and on the entire topic of 'ought implies can', see Nicholas Rescher, *Ethical Idealism* (Berkeley: University of California Press, 1987).

beyond what is reasonable to expect them to do. It is often difficult to tell when that is, as I will emphasize later. But until those difficulties become clear, couples can intelligibly make morally-binding lifetime commitments.

I should add that marital faithfulness involves a commitment *to a person*—to love, honour and cherish one's spouse. It is faithfulness *to a promise* in a secondary, symbolic way. Why should the wedding promise be kept? The secondary answer is that the promise was made; the primary answer is to preserve, further or restore the love that led a couple to make the promise in the first place. In this way, faithfulness is primarily aimed at the substance of the wedding vow—the loving relationship itself—rather than at the one-time marital promise.[10] The longer the love continues, the wider the scope of faithfulness: Faithfulness is to the love in its full historical development, its actual past, its present achievements, and its projected future.

*Objection 3: Changing Identities.* Lifelong commitments to love are not morally binding. They lack moral import because they are unconditional and falsely presume that spouses will retain their present identities. Each of us will change dramatically over a lifetime, so much so that we can think of a person as a series of selves rather than one unified self. How can my present self morally bind a substantially different later self to do anything several decades from now? That is like trying to make a promise for another person, whereas promises are only binding on the person who makes them. Again, how can I (with moral cogency) commit myself to a partner who will be remarkably different several decades later? That is like making a blanket promise to someone I do not know.

Are marriage vows unconditional? Surely wedding vows are tacitly conditional, as Hunter argues: in the course of a marriage 'a couple may become entirely different persons, with ambitions, tastes, idiosyncrasies or emotional attachments or aversions that could not initially be foreseen, and given which it would be utterly absurd for them to marry. That being the case, it seems reasonable to treat such vows at a minimum as implicitly containing some such clause as "assuming you are substantially the person I believe you to be, and that neither of us changes, as the years go by, in ways more extreme than are common to human beings as they grow older".[11]

---

[10] Cf. P. E. Hutchings, 'Conjugal Faithfulness', *Human Values*, Godfrey Vesey (ed.) (New Jersey: Humanities Press, 1978).

[11] J. F. M. Hunter, *Thinking about Sex and Love*, 59. Cf. Derek Parfit, 'Later Selves and Moral Principles', *Philosophy and Personal Relations*, A. Montefiore (ed.) (London: Routledge and Kegan Paul, 1973).

Susan Mendus rejected this view and insisted that marital vows are unconditional. She drew a 'distinction between . . . the person who promises to love and to honour but who finds that, after a time, she has lost her commitment (perhaps on account of change in her husband's character), and . . . the person who promises to love and to honour only on condition that there be no such change in character'.[12] The latter person is not committed unconditionally, in the spirit of traditional marriage vows. The former person makes the appropriate commitment and revokes it later, something which is perfectly intelligible as a morally binding promise which, perhaps for good reason, must be broken. There is a genuine obligation, but it is not absolute; there are conditions under which it is justifiably broken. She adds that vows are unconditional when 'I cannot now envisage anything happening such as would make me give up that commitment'.[13]

Mendus's distinction is important, but her account of unconditional vows is implausible. Surely most spouses can envisage circumstances that would lead them to abandon their commitments to love each other, at least if 'envisage' means imagine. For one thing, they can imagine their spouse being transformed into a spouse-beating, child-abusing monster.[14] In making their lifelong commitments, they presuppose that will not occur, and in that sense their commitments *are* conditional.

For another thing, they can imagine their spouse leaving them; indeed, they likely fear that at one time or another, whether as a general possibility given today's fifty percent divorce rate or for reasons directly related to their partner. They would not feel obligated to sustain their marriage if their spouse abandoned them, and hence this is a second way their marital vows are conditional. At least today, wedding vows have 'escape clauses', however vague or extreme. They are implicit in the wedding ceremony in which vows are made together, conditional on their partner's reciprocal vows.

If there are always conditions, why do marriage vows fail to mention them and even seem to rule them out—'for better for worse, for richer for poorer, in sickness and in health?' And why do not enlightened couples mutter under their breath, 'unless one of us changes radically'? The answer is obvious but important. Couples have faith that their marriage will

---

[12] Susan Mendus, 'Marital Faithfulness', *Philosophy* **59** (1984), 246.

[13] P. 247.

[14] Alan Soble, *The Structure of Love* (New Haven: Yale University Press, 1990), 166–167.

endure, that they will keep their commitments, and at the very least that neither will turn into a monster. That faith can waver periodically, and it is compatible with realism about the risk that things will not work out. But marriage is an act of faith—of placing trust in, rather than merely hoping or expecting—as the unconditional tone of lifetime vows conveys. Faith is essential, not only as an expression of love, but because it tends to be self-fulfilling by providing security and trust in which relationships prosper.

*Objection 4: Motives for Loving.* Lifelong commitments to love are (ironically) incompatible with love. Commitments create obligations which threaten love by generating an onerous sense of duty to abide by a contract. As Robert Solomon once wrote, 'Love is not . . . a commitment. It is the very antithesis of a commitment. The legal tit-for-tat quasi-"social contract" thinking of commitment talk fatally confuses doing something because one *wants* to do it and doing something because one *has* to do it, whether or not one wants to at the time'.[15] 'The essence of romantic love is a decision', open-ended but by the same token perpetually insecure, open to reconsideration every moment and, of course, open to rejection by one's lover at every moment too'.[16]

Lifetime commitments do close options—decisively. They do so in order to open better options within sustained, stable, trusting relationships. There are, of course, alternative ideals of love which keep all options open. Those romantics and existentialists, not to mention libertines and Don Juans, who treasure the right to change one's mind at any moment (without culpability) do well to reject lifelong commitments. These alternate ideals, not commitments and responsibilities, are incompatible with traditional marital love.

Solomon is right about this much: relationships are in trouble once they degenerate into a quasi-legal, tit-for-tat struggle, with each partner preoccupied in asserting the rights generated by promises. But moral commitments are not reducible to contracts in the way he implies. Commitments generate responsibilities which support rather than threaten love's constancy. They do so largely by remaining in the background, perhaps surfacing in times of conflict and temptation, as reminders that help stabilize relationships. They are reinforcements, not replacements, of caring.

---

[15] Robert Solomon, *Love; Emotion, Myth and Metaphor* (Garden City, NY: Anchor Press, 1981), 224.

[16] P. 227.

It is important to distinguish between having a commitment to love and the motives for keeping the commitment.[17] The motives are primarily such things as love, caring, joy, a sense of identity and solidarity with, as well as self-interest, and only secondarily (and supportively) a sense of responsibility. The same is true of parents, for example, who have responsibilities to care for their children, but who are primarily motivated by love mixed with elements of self-interest.

*Objection 5: The Power of Love.* Lifelong commitments are unnecessary, given the power of love to conquer obstacles. Commitments and the obligations they imply are inessential, according to Solomon: 'The devotion and particularity of love are such that commitment is quite unnecessary, although it may well present itself as an expression of love'.[18] Lasting devotion does not require commitments, which generate obligations, but only a 'decision to stick with it and see it through'.[19]

So it seems—in the early stage of romance, when love seems to make everything possible, certainly its own continuance. But honeymoons end, and the world intrudes with problems about money, jobs, health, social conflicts, disagreements about furniture, and a thousand other things. Active love, understood as an ideal-guided relationship, typically requires commitments if it is to remain constant (and growing) throughout a lifetime.

Not just the world, but lovers themselves change, as an earlier objection emphasized. They grow and regress, and undergo a variety of experiences that can mute romance. Commitment generates a sense of responsibility which provides stable trust through fluctuations in temperament. Mary Midgley said in a related context, 'Campaigners against [marriage] . . . have been remarkably crass in posing the simple dilemma, "either you want to stay together or you don't—if you do, you need not promise; if you don't, you ought to part". This ignores the chances of inner conflict, and the deep human need for a continuous central life that lasts through genuine, but passing, changes of mood'.[20] Commitment is not sufficient to maintain love, but it adds an additional motive for not succumbing to, much less seeking out, temptations that threaten love.

---

[17] Cf. Lawrence A. Blum, *Friendship, Altruism and Morality* (London: Routledge and Kegan Paul, 1980).

[18] Robert Solomon, *About Love* (New York: Simon and Schuster, 1988), 40.

[19] P. 134.

[20] Mary Midgley, *Beast and Man* (New York: New American Library, 1980), 303.

*Objection 6: Creative Divorce.* Lifetime commitments are inhumane. They are essentially commitments never to divorce, and that amounts to cruelty and torture when one or both partners find a marriage unbearable. Divorce can be creative, as well as a painful necessity. Lifetime commitments are immoral because they preclude divorce.

This objection applies within societies that forbid divorce, but not to contemporary societies governed by laws that make divorce a relatively simple legal matter. Suppose that in good faith, with trust and faith that divorce will not occur, partners make lifetime commitments, and then do everything they can to make things work out. They do not succeed, and the marriage disintegrates to the point where it is no longer worthwhile. After every effort is made to repair damage, one or both partners may be fully justified in abandoning their commitment.

*Objection 7: Prudence.* Lifetime commitments are unreasonable, irrational, imprudent. They fail to show proper regard for one's long-term good. A prudent person forms a plan of life that takes into account how changing circumstances or new knowledge can radically alter one's present conception of good, as well as the means to it. Right now love brings happiness, but who knows what it will bring decades later? Lifetime commitments sacrifice far too many options, and hence it is prudent to make only short-term commitments.

Of course, lifetime commitments are unreasonable for some individuals. What is in one's interests and what serves the mutual good of couples varies too widely to generalize about. The same reason, however, should lead us to reject a universal objection to lifetime commitments. That objection omits the good-promoting features of lifetime commitments, in particular the framework they provide for ongoing mutual caring, support, joy, and fulfillment. Marriage closes some options but opens others which may be far preferable, depending on our ideals of love.

Lifetime commitments to love are not prisons; they are vehicles for helping partners deal together with changing situations, interests, and needs. Partners do commit themselves to put the relationship first, to accommodate other things to it, including careers. Other than that, however, relationships are as accommodating and flexible as partners choose to make them.

## CRITICAL THINKING QUESTIONS

1. According to Mike Martin, is marital faithfulness a virtue? Explain his reasoning. What is communicated through faithfulness?

2. Why does Martin believe it is important to take moral commitments
   seriously?
3. Write and analyze a case involving unfaithfulness in marriage that is
   not related to sexual activity.


BERTRAND RUSSELL

## MARRIAGE AND MORALS

*Bertrand Russell (1872–1970), a philosopher and logician, wrote many books
and essays on ethics, particularly social ethics. It is reported that his most important scholarly contributions were in mathematical logic. He was the recipi-
ent of the Nobel Prize for Literature in 1950. This 1929 excerpt from* Marriage
and Morals *discusses alternatives to sexual fidelity.*

. . . When we look around the world at the present day and ask ourselves
what conditions seem on the whole to make for happiness in marriage and
what for unhappiness, we are driven to a somewhat curious conclusion, that
the more civilized people become the less capable they seem of lifelong happiness with one partner. Irish peasants, although until recent times marriages were decided by the parents, were said by those who ought to know
them to be on the whole happy and virtuous in their conjugal life. In general, marriage is easiest where people are least differentiated. When a man
differs little from other men, and a woman differs little from other women,
there is no particular reason to regret not having married some one else. But
people with multifarious tastes and pursuits and interests will tend to desire
congeniality in their partners, and to feel dissatisfied when they find that
they have secured less of it than they might have obtained. The Church,
which tends to view marriage solely from the point of view of sex, sees no
reason why one partner should not do just as well as another, and can therefore uphold the indissolubility of marriage without realizing the hardship
that this often involves.

Another condition which makes for happiness in marriage is paucity of
unowned women and absence of social occasions when husbands meet
other women. If there is no possibility of sexual relations with any woman
other than one's wife, most men will make the best of the situation and, except in abnormally bad cases, will find it quite tolerable. The same thing

applies to wives, especially if they never imagine that marriage should bring much happiness. That is to say, a marriage is likely to be what is called happy if neither party ever expected to get much happiness out of it.

Fixity of social custom, for the same reason, tends to prevent what are called unhappy marriages. If the bonds of marriage are recognized as final and irrevocable, there is no stimulus to the imagination to wander outside and consider that a more ecstatic happiness might have been possible. In order to secure domestic peace where this state of mind exists, it is only necessary that neither the husband nor the wife should fall outrageously below the commonly recognized standard of decent behaviour, whatever this may be.

Among civilized people in the modern world none of these conditions for what is called happiness exist, and accordingly one finds that very few marriages after the first few years are happy. Some of the causes of unhappiness are bound up with civilization, but others would disappear if men and women were more civilized than they are. Let us begin with the latter. Of these the most important is bad sexual education, which is a far commoner thing among the well-to-do than it can ever be among peasants. Peasant children early become accustomed to what are called the facts of life, which they can observe not only among human beings but among animals. They are thus saved from both ignorance and fastidiousness. The carefully educated children of the well-to-do, on the contrary, are shielded from all practical knowledge of sexual matters, and even the most modern parents, who teach children out of books, do not give them that sense of practical familiarity which the peasant child early acquires. The triumph of Christian teaching is when a man and woman marry without either having had previous sexual experience. In nine cases out of ten where this occurs, the results are unfortunate. Sexual behaviour among human beings is not instinctive, so that the inexperienced bride and bridegroom, who are probably quite unaware of this fact, find themselves overwhelmed with shame and discomfort. It is little better when the woman alone is innocent but the man has acquired his knowledge from prostitutes. Most men do not realize that a process of wooing is necessary after marriage, and many well-brought-up women do not realize what harm they do to marriage by remaining reserved and physically aloof. All this could be put right by better sexual education, and is in fact very much better with the generation now young than it was with their parents and grandparents. There used to be a widespread belief among women that they were morally superior to men on the ground that they had less pleasure in sex. This attitude made frank companionship between husbands and wives impossible. It was, of course, in itself quite unjustifiable, since failure to enjoy sex, so far from being virtuous, is a mere physiological or psychological deficiency, like a failure to enjoy food, which also a hundred years ago was expected of elegant females.

Other modern causes of unhappiness in marriage are, however, not so easily disposed of. I think that uninhibited civilized people, whether men or women, are generally polygamous in their instincts. They may fall deeply in love and be for some years entirely absorbed in one person, but sooner or later sexual familiarity dulls the edge of passion, and then they begin to look elsewhere for a revival of the old thrill. It is, of course, possible to control this impulse in the interests of morality, but it is very difficult to prevent the impulse from existing. With the growth of women's freedom there has come a much greater opportunity for conjugal infidelity than existed in former times. The opportunity gives rise to the thought, the thought gives rise to the desire, and in the absence of religious scruples the desire gives rise to the act.

Women's emancipation has in various ways made marriage more difficult. In old days the wife had to adapt herself to the husband, but the husband did not have to adapt himself to the wife. Nowadays many wives, on grounds of woman's right to her own individuality and her own career, are unwilling to adapt themselves to their husbands beyond a point, while men who still hanker after the old tradition of masculine domination see no reason why they should do all the adapting. This trouble arises especially in connection with infidelity. In old days the husband was occasionally unfaithful, but as a rule his wife did not know of it. If she did, he confessed that he had sinned and made her believe that he was penitent. She, on the other hand, was usually virtuous. If she was not, and the fact came to her husband's knowledge, the marriage broke up. Where, as happens in many modern marriages, mutual faithfulness is not demanded, the instinct of jealousy nevertheless survives, and often proves fatal to the persistence of any deeply rooted intimacy even where no overt quarrels occur.

There is another difficulty in the way of modern marriage, which is felt especially by those who are most conscious of the value of love. Love can flourish only as long as it is free and spontaneous; it tends to be killed by the thought that it is a duty. To say that it is your duty to love so-and-so is the surest way to cause you to hate him or her. Marriage as a combination of love with legal bonds thus falls between two stools.

There can be no doubt that to close one's mind on marriage against all the approaches of love from elsewhere is to diminish receptivity and sympathy and the opportunities of valuable human contacts. It is to do violence to something which, from the most idealistic standpoint, is in itself desirable. And like every kind of restrictive morality it tends to promote what one may call a policeman's outlook upon the whole of human life—the outlook, that is to say, which is always looking for an opportunity to forbid something.

For all these reasons, many of which are bound up with things undoubtedly good, marriage has become difficult, and if it is not to be a barrier to happiness it must be conceived in a somewhat new way. One solution often suggested, and actually tried on a large scale in America, is easy divorce. I hold, of course, as every humane person must, that divorce should be granted on more grounds than are admitted in the English law, but I do not recognize in easy divorce a solution of the troubles of marriage. Where a marriage is childless, divorce may be often the right solution, even when both parties are doing their best to behave decently; but where there are children the stability of marriage is to my mind a matter of considerable importance. (This is a subject to which I shall return in connection with the family.) I think that where a marriage is fruitful and both parties to it are reasonable and decent the expectation ought to be that it will be lifelong, but not that it will exclude other sex relations. A marriage which begins with passionate love and leads to children who are desired and loved ought to produce so deep a tie between a man and woman that they will feel something infinitely precious in their companionship, even after sexual passion has decayed, and even if either or both feels sexual passion for some one else. This mellowing of marriage has been prevented by jealousy, but jealousy, though it is an instinctive emotion, is one which can be controlled if it is recognized as bad, and not supposed to be the expression of a just moral indignation. A companionship which has lasted for many years and through many deeply felt events has a richness of content which cannot belong to the first days of love, however delightful these may be. And any person who appreciates what time can do to enhance values will not lightly throw away such companionship for the sake of new love.

It is therefore possible for a civilized man and woman to be happy in marriage, although if this is to be the case a number of conditions must be fulfilled. There must be a feeling of complete equality on both sides; there must be no interference with mutual freedom; there must be the most complete physical and mental intimacy; and there must be a certain similarity in regard to standards of values. (It is fatal, for example, if one values only money while the other values only good work.) Given all these conditions, I believe marriage to be the best and most important relation that can exist between two human beings. If it has not often been realized hitherto, that is chiefly because husband and wife have regarded themselves as each other's policeman. If marriage is to achieve its possibilities, husbands and wives must learn to understand that whatever the law may say, in their private lives they must be free.

## CRITICAL THINKING QUESTIONS

1. Why does Russell believe that sexual fidelity is not important in marriage? Do you agree or disagree? Explain.
2. In a happy and harmonious marriage with children, is it acceptable to have brief, sexual affairs as long as one doesn't get caught or emotionally involved? Support your point of view.
3. Write and analyze a case involving marital sexual infidelity where neither partner confesses or gets caught. What is the role of communication within the marriage?

HELEN E. FISHER

## ANATOMY OF LOVE

*Helen E. Fisher, an anthropologist at the American Museum of Natural History, is the author of several books and articles. This 1992 excerpt from* Anatomy of Love: The History of Monogamy, Adultery and Divorce *details family and sexual practices in a variety of cultures.*

### UNFAITHFULLY YOURS IN AMERICA

. . . [A] moral code has not deterred Western men and women—or people in any other society—from cheating on their spouses. Americans are no exception. Despite our attitude that philandering is immoral, regardless of our sense of guilt when we engage in trysts, in spite of the risks to family, friends, and livelihood that adultery inevitably entails, we indulge in extramarital affairs with avid regularly. As George Burns once summed it up, "Happiness is having a large, loving, caring, close-knit family in another city."[21]

How many Americans are adulterous we will never know. In the 1920s psychiatrist Gilbert Hamilton, a pioneer in sex research, reported that 28 of 100 men and 24 of 100 women interviewed had strayed.[22] This was the talk of American dinner tables for more than a decade.

The famous Kinsey reports in the late forties and early fifties stated that a little over a third of husbands in a sample of 6,427 men were unfaithful. Because so many of these subjects were reluctant to discuss their escapades, however, Kinsey surmised that his figures were low, that probably about half of all American men were unfaithful to their wives at some point during marriage. Twenty-six percent of the 6,972 married, divorced, and widowed American women sampled, Kinsey reported, had engaged in extramarital coitus by age forty. Forty-one percent of the female adulterers had copulated with a single partner; 40 percent had made love with two to five; 19 percent had engaged more than five paramours.[23]

Almost two decades later these figures apparently had not changed significantly—despite enormous changes in American attitudes toward sex during the sixties and seventies, the pinnacle of the "sexual revolution." A survey commissioned by *Playboy* magazine and conducted by Morton Hunt in the seventies reported that 41 percent of the 691 men and about 25 percent of the 740 married white middle-class women in the sample had philandered.

Two new trends stood out, however: both sexes started their trysts earlier than in former decades, and the double standard had eroded. Whereas only 9 percent of the wives under age twenty-five in the 1950s had taken a paramour, about 25 percent of young wives in the 1970s had done so. Hunt concluded, "Woman will go outside marriage for sex as often as will man, if she and her society think that she has as much right to do so as he."[24] A poll taken by *Redbook* confirmed Hunt's data for the 1970s. Of about 100,000 women surveyed, 29 percent of those who were married had engaged in an extramarital affair—but they were cheating sooner after wedding.[25] "Why wait?" seemed to have become the motto.

Have these figures for the 1970s gone up?

Maybe—and maybe not. A survey of 106,000 readers of *Cosmopolitan* magazine in the early 1980s indicated that 54 percent of the married women had participated in at least one affair,[26] and a poll of 7,239 men reported that 72 percent of those married over two years had been adulterous.[27] These figures for both men and women were then independently verified by other researchers.[28] As the June 1, 1987, issue of *Marriage and Divorce Today* reported, "Seventy percent of all Americans engage in an affair sometimes during their marital life."[29] And adultery continues to start earlier. In a recent poll of 12,000 married individuals, about 25 percent of the men and women under twenty-five had cheated on a spouse.[30]

But who knows whether any of these figures are accurate?

Men tend to brag about sex, whereas women more regularly conceal their escapades. Perhaps married women in former decades admitted to fewer of their love affairs, whereas those of he 1980s are more honest. Maybe middle-class women today have more "opportunities," because they work outside the home. Perhaps men feel freer to philander as women become more financially independent. Undoubtedly pollsters do not reach a random sample of Americans either. And these researchers may be asking different questions or polling audiences more likely to have committed infidelities or more willing to admit their dalliances in a poll.

"Who's been sleeping in my bed?" asks Papa Bear in one of our folktales. No one knows the extent of adulterous sex in America now or in yesteryear. After all, unlike Hawthorne's Hester Prynne, adulterers do not display their trysts by wearing the letter *A*. And although adultery laws still exits in twenty-five states, our current laws concerning "no fault" divorce have shifted the emphasis of marriage to an economic partnership; sexual transgressions rarely reach the courts or census takers. So scientists who think they know the truth about American philanderers are naive.

But of one thing I am sure: despite our cultural taboo against infidelity, Americans are adulterous. Our societal mores, our religious teachings, our friends and relatives, urge us to invest all of our sexual energy on one person, a husband or a wife. But in practice a sizable percentage of both men and women actually spread their time, their vigor, and their love among multiple partners as they sneak into other bedrooms.[31]

And we are hardly extraordinary. I recently read forty-two ethnographies about different peoples past and present and found that adultery occurred in every one. Some of these peoples lived in tenements; others in row houses or thatched huts. Some raised rice; some raised money. Some were rich, some poor. Some espoused Christianity; others worshiped gods embodied in the sun, the wind, the rocks, and trees. Regardless of their traditions of marriage, despite their customs of divorce, irrespective of any of their cultural mores about sex, they all exhibited adulterous behavior—even where adultery was punished with death.

These forty-two peoples are not alone in their taste for cheating. As Kinsey concluded, "The preoccupation of the world's biography and fiction, through all ages and in all human cultures, with the non-marital sexual activities of married females and males, is evidence of the universality of human desires in these matters."[32] Adultery is a major reason for divorce and family violence in America and many other places. There exists no culture in which adultery is unknown, no cultural device or code that extinguishes philandering.

"Friendship is constant in all other things, save the office and affairs of love," Shakespeare wrote. Our human tendency toward extramarital liaisons seems to be the triumph of nature over culture. Like the stereotypic flirt, the smile, the brain physiology for infatuation, and our drive to bond with a single mate, philandering seems to be part of our ancient reproductive game.

### WHY ADULTERY?

Public whipping, branding, beating, ostracism, mutilation of genitals, chopping off of nose and ears, slashing feet, chopping at one's hips and thighs, divorce, desertion, death by stoning, burning, drowning, choking, shooting, stabbing—such cruelties are meted out by people around the world for philandering. Given these punishments, it is astonishing that human beings engage in extramarital affairs at all. Yet we do.

Why? From a Darwinian perspective, it is easy to explain why men are—by nature—interested in sexual variety. If a man has two children by one woman, he has, genetically speaking, "reproduced" himself. But if he also engages in dalliances with more women and, by chance, sires two more young, he doubles his contribution to the next generation. So, as the biological explanation goes, those men who tend to seek variety also tend to have more children. These young survive and pass to subsequent generations whatever it is in the male genetic makeup that seeks "fresh features," as Byron said of men's need for sexual novelty.[33]

But why are women adulterous? A woman cannot bear another child every time she sneaks into bed with another lover; she can get pregnant only at certain times of her menstrual cycle. Moreover, a woman takes nine months to bear the child, and then it is often several more months or years before she can conceive again. Unlike a man, a woman cannot breed every time she copulates. In fact, anthropologist Donald Symons has argued that, because the number of children a woman can bear is limited, women are biologically less motivated to seek fresh features.

Are women really less interested in sexual variety? This puzzle has several angles. So I shall take the role of devil's advocate and explore the possibility that women are just as interested in sexual variety and just as adulterous as men—albeit for different reasons. Let's begin with Symons, who has an intriguing argument for men's greater drive for sexual novelty.

Symons bases his premise that men are more interested in sexual variety than women are not only on the above genetic logic but also on the sexual habits of American homosexuals. These individuals, he believes, provide the "acid test" for gender differences in sexuality because homosexual behavior is not "masked by the compromises heterosexual relations entail and by moral injunctions."[34]

Accepting this as gospel, Symons then cites several studies in the 1960s and 1970s of gay Americans and concludes that gay men are inclined to one-night stands, to easy, anonymous, unencumbered sex, to coitus with several different, uncommitted partners, and to collecting harems and extra lovers, whereas gay women tend to seek longer relationships instead, as well as more commitment, fewer lovers, familiar partners, and sex with feeling rather than sex for sex itself.

Symons then proposes that these differences in male and female "sexual psychologies" stem from mankind's long hunting-gathering past: over countless millennia, males who liked sexual variety impregnated more females, produced more young, and bulked up their genetic lineages; hence for ancestral males philandering was adaptive.

But an ancestral woman's primary goal was to find a single protector who would ensure the survival of her children. A woman who sought sexual variety ran the risk of a jealous mate who might desert her. Moreover, female sexual escapades took time away from gathering vegetables and caring for her children. So those females who coupled with a variety of partners disproportionately died out or bred less often—passing on to modern women the propensity for fidelity.

With his Darwinian logic, his homosexual sample, and his evolutionary scenario, Symons concludes that men are, *by nature*, more interested in sexual variety than women are.

Man the natural playboy, woman the doting spouse—Americans already believed it. Because of our agrarian background and sexual double standard it became acceptable to view men as would-be Don Juans and women as the more virtuous of the genders. So when Symons presented an evolutionary explanation for men's philandering nature, many scholars bought it like a better chocolate bar. The idea that men crave sexual novelty more than women do now saturates academic books and academic minds.

### WHICH GENDER PHILANDERS MORE?

I am not convinced that homosexual behavior illustrates essential truths about male and female sexual natures however. Most experts believe that about 5 percent of all American men and fewer American women are gay.[35] Homosexual behavior does not constitute the norm in the United States or anywhere else on earth. Moreover, I cannot agree with Symons that homosexual behavior constitutes the "undiluted" nature of either sex; instead, homosexuals are probably equally affected by their environment. In the 1970s, when his sample was collected, fast, loose sex was "in" for men. Lesbians, on the other hand, may well have been constrained by the cultural belief that women should curtail their sexual escapades.

Equally important, sexuality varies with age and other factors.

Nisa summed up in a few sentences a fine adaptive explanation for female interest in sexual variety—supplementary subsistence. Extra goods and services would have provided our adulterous female forebears with more shelter and extra food, perquisites that gave them more protection and better health, ultimately enabling their young to survive disproportionately.

Second, adultery probably served ancestral females as an insurance policy. If a "husband" died or deserted home, she had another male she might be able to enlist to help with parental chores.

Third, if an ancestral woman was "married" to a poor hunter with bad eyesight and a fearful or unsupportive temperament, she stood to upgrade her genetic line by having children with another man—Mr. Good Gene.

Fourth, if a woman had offspring with an array of fathers, each child would be somewhat different, increasing the likelihood that some from among them would survive unpredictable fluctuations in the environment.

As long as prehistoric females were secretive about their extramarital affairs, they could garner extra resources, life insurance, better genes, and more varied DNA for their biological futures. Hence those who sneaked into the bushes with secret lovers lived on—unconsciously passing on through the centuries whatever it is in the female spirit that motivates modern women to philander.

Thus female philandering was probably adaptive in the past. So adaptive, in fact, that it has left its mark on female physiology. At orgasm the blood vessels of a man's genitals eject the blood back into the body cavity, the penis goes limp, and sex is over. The man must start from the beginning to achieve orgasm again. For a woman, however, sex may have just begun. Unlike her mate's, a woman's genitals have not expelled all the blood. If she knows how, she can climax again soon and again and again if she wants to. Sometimes orgasms occur in such rapid succession that one is indistinguishable from the next, a phenomenon known as continual orgasm.

This high sex drive of the human female, in conjunction with data on other primates, has led anthropologist Sarah Hrdy to a novel hypothesis about the primitive beginnings of human female adultery.[39] . . .

## CRITICAL THINKING QUESTIONS

1. Do some cultures have immoral practices because they do not resemble the American system of family?
2. Examine the concept of adultery from several cultural perspectives. According to Fisher what are the consequences (if any) for adultery?
3. Write and analyze a case involving family structure very different from your own within a distant culture. Examine interpersonal communication as part of this structure.

## NOTES

21. Burns, G. 1990. In *Newsweek Special Edition,* winter/spring, 10.
22. Lawrence, R. J. 1989. *The Poisoning of Eros: Sexual Values in Conflict.* New York: Augustine Moore Press.
23. Kinsey, A. C., W. B. Pomeroy, and C. E. Martin. 1948. *Sexual Behavior in the Human Male.* Philadelphia: W. B. Saunders. Kinsey, A. C., et al. 1953. *Sexual Behavior in the Human Female.* Philadelphia: W. B. Saunders.
24. Hunt, M. M. 1974. *Sexual Behavior in the 1970s.* Chicago: Playboy Press.
25. Tavris, C., and S. Sadd. 1977. *The Redbook Report on Female Sexuality.* New York: Delacorte Press.
26. Wolfe, L. 1981. *Women and Sex in the 80s: The Cosmo Report.* New Arbor House.
27. Hite, S. 1981. *The Hite Report on Male Sexuality.* New York: Ballantine Books.
28. Lawson, A. 1988. *Adultery: An Analysis of Love and Betrayal.* New York: Basic Books. Lampe, P. E., ed. 1987. *Adultery in the United States: Close Encounters of the Sixth (or Seventh) Kind.* Buffalo: Prometheus Books.
29. *Marriage and Divorce Today* 1987.

30.  Blumstein, P., and P. Schwartz. 1983. *American Couples: Money, Work, Sex.* New York: William Morrow.

31.  Timing and Duration of Extramarital Relationships: The duration of extramarital relationships is difficult to establish from the literature. In one study of 200 couples, husbands maintained their extramarital affairs for an average of twenty-nine months, whereas wives sustained theirs for an average of twenty-one months (Hall 1987). Kinsey (1953) noted that about 42 percent of his sample of women engaged in extramarital coitus for a year or less, 23 percent for two to three years, and 35 percent for four years or more. But he did not say how long each affair lasted, only how long these women engaged in extramarital coitus.

32.  Kinsey et al. 1953, 409.

33.  Bateman, A. J. 1948. Intra-sexual selection in drosophila. *Heredity* 2:349–68. Trivers, R. L. 1972. Parental investment and sexual selection. In *Sexual Selection and the Descent of Man, 1971–1971,* ed. B. Campbell. Chicago: Aldus. Symons, D. 1979. *The Evolution of Human Sexuality.* New York: Oxford Univ. Press.

34.  Symons 1979, v, 291.

35.  Ruse, M. 1988. *Homosexuality: A Philosophical Inquiry.* Oxford: Basil Blackwell.

36.  Kinsey, Pomeroy, and Martin 1948; Kinsey et al. 1953.

37.  Kinsey, Pomeroy, and Martin 1948.

38.  Shostak, M. (1981). *Nisa: The Life and Words of a !Kung Woman.* New York: Random House, p. 271.

39.  Hrdy, S. B. 1981. *The Woman That Never Evolved.* Cambridge: Harvard Univ. Press.

FRIEDRICH ENGELS

# THE ORIGIN OF THE FAMILY: PRIVATE PROPERTY AND THE STATE

*Friedrich Engels (1820–1895) was a social philosopher. In collaboration with Karl Marx, he drafted* The Communist Manifesto *and* The German Ideology. *In this article Engels expresses concerns about subjugation of women within a marital relationship.*

The overthrow of mother-right was the *world historical defeat of the female sex.* The man took command in the home also; the woman was degraded and reduced to servitude, she became the slave of his lust and a mere instrument for the production of children. This degraded position of the woman, especially conspicuous among the Greeks of the heroic and still more of the classical age, has gradually been palliated and glozed *[sic]* over, and sometimes clothed in a milder form; in no sense has it been abolished.

The establishment of the exclusive supremacy of the man shows its effects first in the patriarchal family, which now emerges as an intermediate form. Its essential characteristic is not polygyny, of which more later, but "the organization of a number of persons, bond and free, into a family, under paternal power, for the purpose of holding lands, and for the care of flocks and herds. . . . (In the Semitic form) the chiefs, at least, lived in polygamy. . . . Those held to servitude, and those employed as servants, lived in the marriage relation."

Its essential features are the incorporation of unfree persons, and paternal power; hence the perfect type of this form of family is the Roman. The original meaning of the word "family" (*familia*) is not that compound of sentimentality and domestic strife which forms the ideal of the present-day philistine; among the Romans it did not at first even refer to the married pair and their children, but only to the slaves. *Famulus* means domestic slave, and *familia* is the total number of slaves belonging to one man. As late as the time of Gaius, the *familia, id est patrimonium* (family, that is, the patrimony, the inheritance) was bequeathed by will. The term was invented by the Romans to denote a new social organism, whose head ruled over wife and children and a number of slaves, and was invested under Roman paternal power with rights of life and death over them all.

> This term, therefore, is no older than the iron-clad family system of the Latin tribes, which came in after field agriculture and after legalized servitude, as well as after the separation of the Greeks and Latins.

Marx adds:

> The modern family contains in germ not only slavery (*servitus*), but also serfdom, since from the beginning it is related to agricultural services. It contains *in miniature* all the contradictions which later extend throughout society and its state.

Such a form of family shows the transition of the pairing family to monogamy. In order to make certain of the wife's fidelity and therefore of the paternity of the children, she is delivered over unconditionally into the power of the husband; if he kills her, he is only exercising his rights. . . .

## The monogamous family

It develops out of the pairing family, as previously shown, in the transitional period between the upper and middle stages of barbarism; its decisive victory is one of the signs that civilization is beginning. It is based on the supremacy of the man, the express purpose being to produce children of undisputed paternity; such paternity is demanded because these children are later to come into their father's property as his natural heirs. It is distinguished from pairing marriage by the much greater strength of the marriage tie, which can no longer be dissolved at either partner's wish. As a rule, it is now only the man who can dissolve it, and put away his wife. The right of conjugal infidelity also remains secured to him, at any rate by custom (the *Code Napoléon* explicitly accords it to the husband as long as he does not bring his concubine into the house), and as social life develops he exercises his right more and more; should the wife recall the old form of sexual life and attempt to revive it, she is punished more severely than ever.

We meet this new form of the family in all its severity among the Greeks. While the position of the goddesses in their mythology, as Marx point out, brings before us an earlier period when the position of women was freer and more respected, in the heroic age we find the woman already being humiliated by the domination of the man and by competition from girl slaves. Note how Telemachus in the *Odyssey* silences his mother.* In Homer young women are booty and are handed over to the pleasure of the conquerors, the handsomest being picked by the commanders in order of rank; the entire *Iliad*, it will be remembered, turns on the quarrel of Achilles and Agamemnon over one of these slaves. If a hero is of any importance, Homer also mentions the captive girl with whom he shares his tent and his bed. These girls were also taken back to Greece and brought under the same roof as the wife, as Cassandra was brought by Agamemnon in Æschylus; the sons begotten of them received a small share of the paternal inheritance and had the full status of freemen. Teucer, for instance, is a natural son of Telamon by one of these slaves and has the right to use his father's name. The legitimate wife was expected to put up with all this, but herself to remain strictly chaste and faithful. In the heroic age a Greek woman is, indeed, more respected than in the period of civilization, but to her husband she is after all nothing but the mother of his legitimate children and heirs, his chief housekeeper and the supervisor of his female slaves, whom he can and does take as concubines if he so fancies. It is the existence of slavery side by side with monogamy, the presence of young, beautiful slaves belonging unreservedly

---

*The reference is to a passage where Telemachus, son of Odysseus and Penelope, tells his mother to get on with her weaving and leave the men to mind their own business (*Odyssey,* Bk. 21, ll. 350 ff.).—*Ed.*

to the *man,* that stamps monogamy from the very beginning with its specific character of monogamy *for the woman only,* but not for the man. And that is the character it still has today.

Coming to the later Greeks, we must distinguish between Dorians and Ionians. Among the former—Sparta is the classic example—marriage relations are in some ways still more archaic than even in Homer. The recognized form of marriage in Sparta was a pairing marriage, modified according to the Spartan conceptions of the state, in which there still survived vestiges of group marriage. Childless marriages were dissolved; King Anaxandridas (about 650 B.C.), whose first wife was childless, took a second and kept two households; about the same time, King Ariston, who had two unfruitful wives, took a third, but dismissed one of the other two. On the other hand, several brothers could have a wife in common; a friend who preferred his friend's wife could share her with him; and it was considered quite proper to place one's wife at the disposal of a sturdy "stallion," as Bismarck would say, even if he was not a citizen. A passage in Plutarch, where a Spartan woman refers an importunate wooer to her husband, seems to indicate, according to Schömann, even greater freedom. Real adultery, secret infidelity by the woman without the husband's knowledge, was therefore unheard of. On the other hand, domestic slavery was unknown in Sparta, at least during its best period; the unfree helots were segregated on the estates and the Spartans were therefore less tempted to take the helots' wives. Inevitably in these conditions women held a much more honored position in Sparta than anywhere else in Greece. The Spartan women and the élite of the Athenian *hetairai* are the only Greek women of whom the ancients speak with respect and whose words they thought it worth while to record. . . .

This is the origin of monogamy as far as we can trace it back among the most civilized and highly developed people of antiquity. It was not in any way the fruit of individual sex-love, with which it had nothing whatever to do; marriages remained as before marriages of convenience. It was the first form of the family to be based, not on natural, but on economic conditions—on the victory of private property over primitive, natural communal property. The Greeks themselves put the matter quite frankly: the sole exclusive aims of monogamous marriage were to make the man supreme in the family, and to propagate, as the future heirs to his wealth, children indisputably his own. Otherwise, marriage was a burden, a duty which had to be performed, whether one liked it or not, to gods, state, and one's ancestors. In Athens the law exacted from the man not only marriage but also the performance of a minimum of so-called conjugal duties.

Thus when monogamous marriage first makes its appearance in history, it is not as the reconciliation of man and woman, still less as the highest form of such a reconciliation. Quite the contrary. Monogamous marriage comes on the scene as the subjugation of the one sex by the other; it announces a struggle between the sexes unknown throughout the whole previous prehistoric period. In an old unpublished manuscript, written by Marx and myself in 1846, I find the words: "The first division of labor is that between man and woman for the propagation of children." And today I can add: The first class opposition that appears in history coincides with the development of the antagonism between man and woman in monogamous marriage, and the first class oppression coincides with that of the female sex by the male. Monogamous marriage was a great historical step forward; nevertheless, together with slavery and private wealth, it opens the period that has lasted until today in which every step forward is also relatively a step backward, in which prosperity and development for some is won through the misery and frustration of others. It is the cellular form of civilized society, in which the nature of the oppositions and contradictions fully active in that society can be already studied. . . .

As regards the legal equality of husband and wife in marriage, the position is no better. The legal inequality of the two partners, bequeathed to us from earlier social conditions, is not the cause but the effect of the economic oppression of the woman. In the old communistic household, which comprised many couples and their children, the task entrusted to the women of managing the household was as much a public and socially necessary industry as the procuring of food by the men. With the patriarchal family, and still more with the single monogamous family, a change came. Household management lost its public characters. It no longer concerned society. It became a *private service;* the wife became the head servant, excluded from all participation in social production. Not until the coming of modern large-scale industry was the road to social production opened to her again—and then only to the proletarian wife. But it was opened in such a manner that, if she carries out her duties in the private service of her family, she remains excluded from public production and unable to earn; and if she wants to take part in public production and earn independently, she cannot carry out family duties. And the wife's position in the factory is the position of women in all branches of business, right up to medicine and the law. The modern individual family is founded on the open or concealed domestic slavery of the wife, and modern society is a mass composed of these individual families as its molecules.

In the great majority of cases today, at least in the possessing classes, the husband is obliged to earn a living and support his family, and that in itself gives him a position of supremacy, without any need for special legal titles and privileges. Within the family he is the bourgeois and the wife represents the proletariat. In the industrial world, the specific character of the economic oppression burdening the proletariat is visible in all its sharpness only when all special legal privileges of the capitalist class have been abolished and complete legal equality of both classes established. The democratic republic does not do away with the opposition of the two classes; on the contrary, it provides the clear field on which the fight can be fought out. And in the same way, the peculiar character of the supremacy of the husband over the wife in the modern family, the necessity of creating real social equality between them, and the way to do it, will only be seen in the clear light of day when both possess legally complete equality of rights. Then it will be plain that the first condition for the liberation of the wife is to bring the whole female sex back into public industry, and that this in turn demands the abolition of the monogamous family as the economic unit of society.

We thus have three principal forms of marriage which correspond broadly to the three principal stages of human development. For the period of savagery, group marriage; for barbarism, pairing marriage; for civilization, monogamy, supplemented by adultery and prostitution. Between pairing marriage and monogamy intervenes a period in the upper stage of barbarism when men have female slaves at their command and polygamy is practiced.

As our whole presentation has shown, the progress which manifests itself in these successive forms is connected with the peculiarity that women, but not men, are increasingly deprived of the sexual freedom of group marriage. In fact, for men group marriage actually still exists even to this day. What for the woman is a crime, entailing grave legal and social consequences, is considered honorable in a man or, at the worse, a slight moral blemish which he cheerfully bears. But the more the hetaerism of the past is changed in our time by capitalist commodity production and brought into conformity with it, the more, that is to say, it is transformed into undisguised prostitution, the more demoralizing are its effects. And it demoralizes men far more than women. Among women, prostitution degrades only the unfortunate ones who become its victims, and even these by no means to the extent commonly believed. But it degrades the character of the whole male world. A long engagement, particularly, is in nine cases out of ten a regular preparatory school for conjugal infidelity.

We are now approaching a social revolution in which the economic foundations of monogamy as they have existed hitherto will disappear just as surely as those of its complement—prostitution. Monogamy arose from the concentration of considerable wealth in the hands of a single individual—a man—and from the need to bequeath this wealth to the children of that man and of no other. For this purpose, the monogamy of the woman was required, not that of the man, so this monogamy of the woman did not in any way interfere with open or concealed polygamy on the part of the man. But by transforming by far the greater portion, at any rate, of permanent, heritable wealth—the means of production—into social property, the coming social revolution will reduce to a minimum all this anxiety about bequeathing and inheriting. Having arisen from economic causes, will monogamy then disappear when these causes disappear?

One might answer, not without reason: far from disappearing, it will, on the contrary, be realized completely. For with the transformation of the means of production into social property there will disappear also wage-labor, the proletariat, and therefore the necessity for a certain—statistically calculable—number of women to surrender themselves for money. Prostitution disappears; monogamy, instead of collapsing, at last becomes a reality—also for men.

In any case, therefore, the position of men will be very much altered. But the position of women, of *all* women, also undergoes significant change. With the transfer of the means of production into common ownership, the single family ceases to be the economic unit of society. Private housekeeping is transformed into a social industry. The care and education of the children becomes a public affair; society looks after all children alike, whether they are legitimate or not. This removes all the anxiety about the "consequences," which today is the most essential social—moral as well as economic—factor that prevents a girl from giving herself completely to the man she loves. Will not that suffice to bring about the gradual growth of unconstrained sexual intercourse and with it a more tolerant public opinion in regard to a maiden's honor and a woman's shame? And, finally, have we not seen that in the modern world monogamy and prostitution are indeed contradictions, but inseparable contradictions, poles of the same state of society? Can prostitution disappear without dragging monogamy with it into the abyss?

Here a new element comes into play, an element which, at the time when monogamy was developing, existed at most in germ: individual sex-love.

Before the Middle Ages we cannot speak of individual sex-love. That personal beauty, close intimacy, similarity of tastes and so forth awakened in people of opposite sex the desire for sexual intercourse, that men and women were not totally indifferent regarding the partner with whom they entered into this most intimate relationship—that goes without saying. But it is still a very long way to our sexual love. Throughout the whole of antiquity, marriages were arranged by the parents, and the partners calmly accepted their choice. What little love there was between husband and wife in antiquity is not so much subjective inclination as objective duty, not the cause of the marriage, but its corollary. Love relationships in the modern sense only occur in antiquity outside official society. The shepherds of whose joys and sorrows in love Theocritus and Moschus sing, the Daphnis and Chloe of Longus are all slaves who have no part in the state, the free citizen's sphere of life. Except among slaves, we find love affairs only as products of the disintegration of the old world and carried on with women who also stand outside official society, with *hetairai*—that is, with foreigners or freed slaves: in Athens from the eve of its decline, in Rome under the Caesars. If there were any real love affairs between free men and free women, these occurred only in the course of adultery. And to the classical love poet of antiquity, old Anacreon, sexual love in our sense mattered so little that it did not even matter to him which sex his beloved was.

Our sexual love differs essentially from the simple sexual desire, the Eros, of the ancients. In the first place, it assumes that the person loved returns the love; to this extent the woman is on an equal footing with the man, whereas in the Eros of antiquity she was often not even asked. Secondly, our sexual love has a degree of intensity and duration which makes both lovers feel that non-possession and separation are a great, if not the greatest, calamity; to possess one another, they risk high stakes, even life itself. In the ancient world this happened only, if at all, in adultery. And, finally, there arises a new moral standard in the judgment of a sexual relationship. We do not only ask, was it within or outside marriage? but also, did it spring from love and reciprocated love or not? Of course, this new standard has fared no better in feudal or bourgeois practice than all the other standards of morality—it is ignored. But neither does it fare any worse. It is recognized just as much as they are—in theory, on paper. And for the present it cannot ask anything more.

## CRITICAL THINKING QUESTIONS

1. Why is Engels opposed to the traditional family structure?
2. Is Engels opposed to monogamy on the grounds of inequality? Explain.
3. Write and analyze a case involving equality and communal living.

KATE MILLETT

# The Sexual Revolution

*Kate Millett is a feminist activist, artist, and the author of several books on feminism, including* Sexual Politics, Prostitution Papers, Sita, The Politics of Cruelty *and* Flying. *This excerpt is from the 1969 book by the same name. Millett explores the notions of Engels and believes they still apply to marriage and women in today's society.*

## THE REVOLUTIONARY SUBSTANCE

The great value of Engels' contribution to the sexual revolution lay in his analysis of patriarchal marriage and family. Whatever his difficulties in accounting for the genesis of these institutions, the very fact of his attempt to demonstrate that they were not an eternal feature of life was in itself a radical departure. The scholars upon whose work his own is built had of course done so as well, but never with Engels' intentions. Bachofen's interest was myth; Morgan's ethnology. That Engels could subsume their theories into one of his own directed toward revolutionary social reorganization is proof of a pragmatic motivation in his study of prehistory.

If patriarchal marriage and the family, though prehistoric, have their origins in the human past, they cease to be immutable, and become subject to alteration. In treating them as historical institutions, subject to the same processes of evolution as other social phenomena, Engels had laid the sacred open to serious criticism, analysis, even to possible drastic reorganization.

Whatever the validity of his thesis that the institution of marriage (pairing and then monogamous) is the factor which ushered in the period of patriarchal rule, Engels' declaration that marriage and the family were built upon the ownership of women was a most damaging charge indeed. All the historical evidence of patriarchal law now supported Mill's charge of "domestic slavery" with a new vehemence. What Mill had thought to be a primordial evil, the inevitable consequence of man's original savagery, Engels' historical account transformed into an oppressive innovation, an innovation which brought with it innumerable other forms of oppression, each dependent upon it. Far from being the last injustice, sexual dominance became the keystone to the total structure of human injustice.

The first course of social change as Engels had charted it[140] was from consanguine group marriage, to the Punaluan consanguine group, then to maternal gens, and finally to paternal gens. And when the gens converts from maternal to paternal lineage, inherited property (and primogeniture) have already intruded as large factors in social and political life. Out of the gens or consanguine tribe who practiced democracy and held their land in common, and finally at the expense and decay of the gens, there arose with the gradual evolution of patriarchy the following institutions: slavery (the model for all later class systems and itself modeled on the ownership of persons first established over women), chiefdom, aristocracy, the social-political differentiation of economic groups into rich and poor. Finally, through the increasing importance of private property, with war serving as its catalyst, grew the state, the organ which solidified and maintained all social and economic disparities. Thus all the mechanisms of human inequality arose out of the foundations of male supremacy and the subjection of women, sexual politics serving historically as the foundation of all other social, political, and economic structures. Pairing marriages incorporated human barter, the buying and selling of women, in itself an instructive precedent for the indiscriminate human slavery which arose thereafter. Under patriarchy, the concept of property advanced from its simple origins in chattel womanhood, to private ownership of goods, land, and capital. In the subjection of female to male, Engels (and Marx as well) saw the historical

---

[140] Engels' main source here was Morgan's *Ancient Society*, an account of social organization as consanguine or gentile association, based both on the Amerindian peoples and those of the ancient Western world.

and conceptual prototype of all subsequent power systems, all invidious economic relations, and the fact of oppression itself.

The subjection of women is of course far more than an economic or even political event, but a total social and psychological phenomenon, a way of life, which Engels (whose psychology is less subtle and individualized than Mill's, and based upon collective states) frames in terms of class emotion:

> The first class antagonism appearing in history coincides with the development of the antagonism of man and wife in monogamy, and the first class oppression with that of the female by the male sex. Monogamy was a great historical progress. But by the side of slavery and private property it marks at the same time that epoch which, reaching down to our days, takes with all progress also a step backwards, relatively speaking, and develops the welfare and advancement of one by the woe and submission of the other. It is the cellular form of civilized society which enables us to study the nature of its now fully developed contrasts and contradictions.[141]

Engels distinguishes between the economic classes of his own time by pointing out that the unpropertied classes make practical use of women, while the propertied, having others to serve them, convert her into a decorative or aesthetic object with only limited uses. In asserting that "sexual love in man's relation to woman becomes and can become the rule among the oppressed classes alone, among the proletarians,"[142] Engels, in the time-honored manner of socialists, appears to romanticize the poor. His other arguments are more convincing. Patriarchy is less strongly entrenched economically among the dispossessed, for inherited property is germane to the foundation of patriarchal monogamy, and the poor are without property. The sequestration of women in the home had seriously decayed among the working class by his time through the employment of women in factories and eventually in their achieving, for the first time, a right to the profit of their labors. Then too, the legal enforcement of patriarchal law is more difficult for the poor to obtain, since law is an expensive commodity. But Engels also ignores the fact that woman is viewed, emotionally and psychologically, as chattel property by the poor as well as, and often even more than, the rich. Lacking other claims to status a working class male is still more prone to seek them in his sexual rank, often brutally asserted.

---

[141] Engels, *op.cit.*, pp. 79-80.
[142] *Ibid.*, p. 86.

Were it not sufficient to account for so much social iniquity through the two most revered forms in his culture, marriage and the family, Engels proceeded to point out that the monogamy it so publicly admired scarcely existed in fact, and that the term "monogamous marriage" was itself something of a misnomer. Primarily, it is only the female who was obliged to be monogamous, since males have traditionally reserved for themselves certain polygynous privileges through the double standard "for the simple reason that they [males], never, even to this day, had the least intention of renouncing the pleasures of group marriage."[143]

Engels is refreshingly frank about prostitution, a subject as obscured in his own time, through chivalrous tergiversation as, in ours, it is confused through a thoughtless equation of sexual freedom with sexual exploitation.[144] Prostitution is, as Engels demonstrates, the natural product of traditional monogamous marriage. This assertion is capable of proof on a number of grounds, the simplest being numerical. When chastity is prescribed and adultery severely punished in women, marriage becomes monogamous for women rather than men, yet there should not be sufficient females to satisfy masculine demand unless a sector of women, usually from among the poor, are bred or reserved for sexual exploitation. This group, who among us, are largely enlisted from the socially and economically exploited racial minorities, were in Engels' industrial England that group of poor below the working class. Smaller numbers are often set apart for additional services, such as conversation or entertainment: hetaera, geisha, courtesan, and call girl. Whatever society's official attitude may be, the demand for prostitution continues within male-supremacist culture,[145] and as Engels describes it, prostitution

> is as much a social institution as all others. It continues the old sexual freedom—for the benefit of the men. In reality not only permitted, but also assiduously practiced by the ruling class, it is denounced only nominally.

---

[143] *Ibid.*, p. 65.

[144] Reform here should mean that society should cease to punish the promiscuity in women it does not think to punish in men. This does not, and should not, mean governmental institution and regulation, which, under the deceptive rationale of greater safety for the client, creates an approved and convenient captivity for the prostitute victim. As those causes of prostitution which are not economic are psychological, it is pointless for the state to intervene either to prohibit or to regulate. Only changes in economic opportunity and social and psychological attitude can work effectively toward eliminating prostitution.

[145] Communist China is said to be the only country in the world which has no prostitution.

Still in practice, this denunciation strikes by no means the men who indulge in it, but only the women. These are ostracised and cast out of society, in order to proclaim once more the fundamental law of unconditional male supremacy over the female sex.[146]

In this last statement one might find some explanation for the persistence of prostitution even after the reforms of the first phase of the sexual revolution had helped to undermine woman's economic vulnerability and relaxed sexual mores had facilitated the practice of extramarital sexuality for both sexes. Men who might be sexually accommodated by casual pickups without expense still provide a demand for prostitution, supplied at times even by women who are not under economic compulsion. In the case of each partner to such prostitution, some need to "proclaim" or at least affirm male supremacy through the humiliation of woman seems to play a leading role. Prostitution, when unmotivated by economic need, might well be defined as a species of psychological addiction, built on self-hatred through repetitions of the act of sale by which a whore is defined. While such self-denigration is extreme, it is not inexplicable within patriarchal society which tends to hold women in contempt, a contempt which is particularly intense in association with female sexuality. There is also a sense in which the prostitute's role is an exaggeration of patriarchal economic conditions where the majority of females are driven to live through some exchange of sexuality for support. The degradation in which the prostitute is held and holds herself, the punitive attitude society adopts toward her, are but reflections of a culture whose general attitudes toward sexuality are negative and which attaches great penalties to a promiscuity in women it does not think to punish in men.

Having examined marriage, Engels turns his attention to the patriarchal family, as precious to the Victorians as it later became to conservative sociology in the period of reaction. In Engels' tart phrase, the family's "essential points are the assimilation of the unfree element and the paternal authority."[147] "It is founded on male supremacy for the pronounced purpose of breeding children of indisputable paternal lineage. The latter is required because these children shall later on inherit the fortune of their father."[148]

---

[146] Engels, *op.cit.*, p. 81.

[147] *Ibid.*, p. 70.

[148] *Ibid.*, p. 79.

Despite the decline of inherited wealth, this is still so; legitimacy is quite as important now, and thought to justify the cost and education of rearing the young in the nuclear family. . . .

There is one more cardinal point in Engels' theory of sexual revolution, bound to provoke more controversy than all the others: "With the transformation of the means of production into collective property, the monogamous family will cease to be the economic unit of society. *The care and education of children becomes a public matter.*"[156] This last point, is perhaps the most crucial of Engels' propositions, though it meets with the greatest resistance. There is something logical and even inevitable in this recommendation, for so long as every female, simply by virtue of her anatomy, is obliged, even forced, to be the sole or primary caretaker of childhood, she is prevented from being a free human being. The care of children, even from the period when their cognitive powers first emerge, is infinitely better left to the best trained practitioners of both sexes who have chosen it as a vocation, rather than to harried and all too frequently unhappy persons with little time nor taste for the work of educating minds, however young or beloved. The radical outcome of Engels' analysis is that the family, as that term is presently understood, must go. In view of the institution's history, this is a kind fate. Engels was heresy in his age. These many decades after, he is heresy still. But revolution is always heresy, perhaps sexual revolution most of all.

## CRITICAL THINKING QUESTIONS

1. Detail how Kate Millett agrees with the theories of Friedrich Engels on marriage and family. Where is communication important in the extended relationships?
2. What do you find compelling about Millett's argument? Where do you disagree with Millett's argument?
3. Write and analyze a case involving a family system that would include sexual equality.

---

[156]*Ibid.*, pp. 191-92.

C L A U D I A   C A R D

# Against Marriage and Motherhood

*Claudia Card is a professor of philosophy at the University of Wisconsin, Madison. She has written numerous books and researched extensively in the fields of ethics, women studies, feminist philosophy, environmental philosophy, and lesbian culture. This article published in* Hypatia *in 1996, explores a society in which lesbian and gay rights to legal marriage are acceptable.*

This essay argues that current advocacy of lesbian and gay rights to legal marriage and parenthood insufficiently criticizes both marriage and motherhood as they are currently practiced and structured by Northern legal institutions. Instead we would do better not to let the State define our intimate unions and parenting would be improved if the power presently concentrated in the hands of one or two guardians were diluted and distributed through an appropriately concerned community.

The title of this essay is deliberately provocative, because I fear that radical feminist perspectives on marriage and motherhood are in danger of being lost in the quest for equal rights. My concerns, however, are specific. I am skeptical of using the institution of motherhood as a source of paradigms for ethical theory. And I am skeptical of legal marriage as a way to gain a better life for lesbian and gay lovers or as a way to provide a supportive environment for lesbian and gay parents and their children. Of course, some are happy with marriage and motherhood as they now exist. My concern is with the price of that joy borne by those trapped by marriage or motherhood and deeply unlucky in the company they find there. Nevertheless, nothing that I say is intended to disparage the characters of many magnificent women who have struggled in and around these institutions to make the best of a trying set of options.

## BACKGROUNDS

My perspective on marriage is influenced not only by others' written reports and analyses but also by my own history of being raised in a lower-middle-class white village family by parents married (to each other) for more than three decades, by my firsthand experiences of urban same-sex domestic partnerships lasting from two and one half to nearly seven years (good ones and bad, some racially mixed, some white, generally mixed in class and religious backgrounds), and by my more recent experience as a lesbianfeminist whose partner of the past decade is not a domestic partner. My perspective on child rearing is influenced not by my experience as a mother, but by my experience as a daughter reared by a full-time mother-housewife, by having participated heavily in the raising of my younger siblings, and by having grown to adulthood in a community in which many of the working-class and farming families exemplified aspects of what bell hooks calls "revolutionary parenting" (hooks 1984, 133–46).

bell hooks writes, "Childrearing is a responsibility that can be shared with other childrearers, with people who do not live with children. This form of parenting is revolutionary in this society because it takes place in opposition to the idea that parents, especially mothers, should be the only childrearers. Many people raised in black communities experienced this type of community-based child care" (hooks 1984, 144). This form of child rearing may be more common than is generally acknowledged in a society in which those whose caretaking does not take place in a nuclear family are judged by those with the power to set standards as unfortunate and deprived. Although bell hooks continues to use the language of "mothering" to some extent in elaborating "revolutionary parenting," I see this revolution as offering an alternative to mothering as a social institution.

Because it appears unlikely that the legal rights of marriage and motherhood in the European American models of those institutions currently at issue in our courts will disappear or even be seriously eroded during my lifetime, my opposition to them here takes the form of skepticism primarily in the two areas mentioned above: ethical theorizing and lesbian/gay activism. I believe that women who identify as lesbian or gay should be reluctant to put our activist energy into attaining legal equity with heterosexuals in marriage and motherhood—not because the existing discrimination against us is in any way justifiable but because these institutions are so deeply flawed that they seem to be unworthy of emulation and reproduction. . . .

First, my opposition to marriage is not an opposition to intimacy, nor to long-term relationships of intimacy, nor to durable partnerships of many sorts.[1] I understand marriage as a relationship to which the State is an essential third party. Also, like the practices of footbinding and suttee, which, according to the researches of Mary Daly (1978, 113-52), originated among the powerful classes, marriage in Europe was once available only to those with substantial social power. Previously available only to members of propertied classes, the marriage relation has come to be available in modern Northern democracies to any adult heterosexual couple neither of whom is already married to someone else. This is what lesbian and gay agitation for the legal right to marry is about. This is what I find calls for extreme caution.

Second, my opposition to motherhood is neither an opposition to the guidance, education, and caretaking of children nor an opposition to the formation of many kinds of bonds between children and adults.[2] Nor am I opposed to the existence of homes, as places of long-term residence with others of a variety of ages with whom one has deeply committed relationships. When "the family" is credited with being a bulwark against a hostile world, as in the case of many families in the African and Jewish diasporas, the bulwark that is meant often consists of a variety of deeply committed personal (as opposed to legal) relationships and the stability of caring that they represent, or home as a site of these things. The bulwark is not the legitimation (often precarious or nonexistent) of such relationships through institutions of the State. The State was often one of the things that these relationships formed a bulwark against.

Marriage and motherhood in the history of modern patriarchies have been mandatory for and oppressive to women, and they have been criticized by feminists on those grounds. My concerns, however, are as much for the children as for the women that some of these children become and for the goal of avoiding the reproduction of patriarchy. Virginia Held, one optimist about the potentialities of marriage and motherhood, finds motherhood to be part of a larger conception of family, which she takes to be constructed of noncontractual relationships. She notes that although Marxists and recent communitarians might agree with her focus on noncontractual relationships, their views remain uninformed by feminist critiques of patriarchal families. The family from which she would have society and ethical theorists learn, ultimately, is a postpatriarchal family. But what is a "postpatriarchal family"? Is it a coherent concept?

"Family" is itself a family resemblance concept. Many contemporary lesbian and gay partnerships, households, and friendship networks fit no patriarchal stereotypes and are not sanctified by legal marriage, although their members still regard themselves as "family."[3] But should they? Many social institutions, such as insurance companies, do not honor such conceptions of "family." Family, as understood in contexts where material benefits tend to be at stake, is not constituted totally by noncontractual relationships. At its core is to be found one or more marriage contracts. For those who would work to enlarge the concept of family to include groupings that are currently totally noncontractual, in retaining patriarchal vocabulary there is a danger of importing patriarchal ideals and of inviting treatment as deviant or "second class" at best.

"Family," our students learn in Women's Studies 101, comes from the Latin *familia,* meaning "household," which in turn came from *famulus,* which, according to the *OED,* meant "servant." The ancient Roman *paterfamilias* was the head of a household of servants and slaves, including his wife or wives, concubines, and children. He had the power of life and death over them. The ability of contemporary male heads of households to get away with battering, incest, and murder suggests to many feminists that the family has not evolved into anything acceptable yet. Would a household of persons whose relationships with each other transcended (as those of families do) sojourns under one roof continue to be rightly called "family" if no members had significant social support for treating other members abusively? Perhaps the postpatriarchal relationships envisioned by Virginia Held and by so many lesbians and gay men should be called something else, to mark the radical departure from family history. But it is not just a matter of a word. It is difficult to imagine what such relationships would be.

In what follows, I say more about marriage than about motherhood, because it is legal marriage that sets the contexts in which and the background against which motherhood has been legitimated, and it defines contexts in which mothering easily becomes disastrous for children.

## LESBIAN (OR GAY) MARRIAGE?

A special vantage point is offered by the experience of lesbians and gay men, among whom there is currently no consensus (although much strong feeling on both sides) on whether to pursue the legal right to marry a same-sex lover (Blumenfeld; Wolfson; and Brownworth; all 1996). When heterosexual partners think about marriage, they usually consider the more limited question whether they (as individuals) should marry (each other) and if they did not marry, what the consequences would be for children they might have or raise. They consider this in the context of a State that gives them the legal option of marriage. Lesbians and gay men are currently in the position of having to consider the larger question whether the legal option of marriage is a good idea, as we do not presently have it in relation to our lovers. We have it, of course, in relation to the other sex, and many have exercised it as a cover, as insurance, for resident alien status, and so forth. If it is because we already have rights to marry heterosexually that right-wing attackers of lesbian or gay rights complain of our wanting "special rights," we should reply that, of course, any legalization of same-sex marriage should extend that "privilege" to heterosexuals as well.

The question whether lesbians and gay men should pursue the right to marry is not the same as the question whether the law is wrong in its refusal to honor same-sex marriages. Richard Mohr (1994, 31–53) defends gay marriage from that point of view as well as I have seen it done. Evan Wolfson develops powerfully an analogy between the denial of marriage to same-sex couples and the antimiscegenation laws that were overturned in the United States just little more than a quarter century ago (Wolfson 1996). What I have to say should apply to relationships between lovers (or parents) of different races as well as to those of same-sex lovers (or parents). The ways we have been treated are abominable. But it does not follow that we should seek legal marriage.

It is one thing to argue that others are wrong to deny us something and another to argue that what they would deny us is something we should fight for the right to have. I do not deny that others are wrong to exclude same-sex lovers and lovers of different races from the rights of marriage. I question only whether we should fight for those rights, even if we do not intend to exercise them. Suppose that slave-owning in some mythical society were denied to otherwise free women, on the ground that such women as slave-owners would pervert the institution of slavery. Women (both free and un-free) could (unfortunately) document empirically the falsity of beliefs underlying such grounds. It would not follow that women should fight for the right to own slaves, or even for the rights of other women to own slaves. Likewise, if marriage is a deeply flawed institution, even though it is a special injustice to exclude lesbians and gay men arbitrarily from participating in it, it would not necessarily advance the cause of justice on the whole to remove the special injustice of discrimination.

About same-sex marriage I feel something like the way I feel about prostitution. Let us, by all means, *decriminalize* sodomy and so forth. Although marriage rights would be *sufficient* to enable lovers to have sex legally, such rights should not be *necessary* for that purpose. Where they *are* legally necessary and also available for protection against the social oppression of same-sex lovers, as for lovers of different races, there will be enormous pressure to marry. Let us not pretend their marriage is basically a good thing on the ground that durable intimate relationships are. Let us not be eager to have the State regulate our unions. Let us work to remove barriers to our enjoying some of the privileges presently available only to heterosexual married couples. But in doing so, we should also be careful not to support discrimination against those who choose not to marry and not to support continued state definition of the legitimacy of intimate relationships. I would rather see the state *de*regulate heterosexual marriage than see it begin to regulate same-sex marriage.

As the child of parents married to each other for thirty-two years, I once thought I knew what marriage meant, even though laws vary from one jurisdiction to another and the dictionary, as Mohr notes, sends us around in a circle, referring us to "husband" and "wife," in turn defined by "marriage." Mohr argues convincingly that "marriage" need not presuppose the gendered concepts of "husband" and "wife" (1994, 31–53). I will not rehearse that ground here. History seems to support him. After reading cover to cover and with great interest John Boswell's *Same-Sex Unions in Premodern Europe* (1994), however, I no longer feel so confident that I know when a "union" counts as a "marriage." Boswell, who discusses many kinds of unions, refrains from using the term "marriage" to describe the same-sex unions he researched, even though they were sanctified by religious ceremonies. Some understandings of such unions, apparently, did not presuppose that the partners were not at the same time married to someone of the other sex. . . .

Central to the idea of marriage, historically, has been intimate access to the persons, belongings, activities, even histories of one another. More important than sexual access, marriage gives spouses physical access to each other's residences and belongings, and it gives access to information about each other, including financial status, that other friends and certainly the neighbors do not ordinarily have. For all that has been said about the privacy that marriage protects, what astonishes me is how much privacy one gives up in marrying. . . .

Among the trappings of marriage that have received attention and become controversial, ceremonies and rituals are much discussed. I have no firm opinions about ceremonies or rituals. A far more important issue seems to me to be the marriage *license,* which receives hardly any attention at all. Ceremonies affirming a relationship can take place at any point in the relationship. But a license is what one needs to initiate a legal marriage. To marry legally, one applies to the state for a license, and marriage, once entered into, licenses spouses to certain kinds of access to each other's persons and lives. It is a mistake to think of a license as simply enhancing everyone's freedom. One person's license, in this case, can be another's prison. Prerequisites for marriage licenses are astonishingly lax. Anyone of a certain age, not presently married to someone else, and free of certain communicable diseases automatically qualifies. A criminal record for violent crimes is, to my knowledge, no bar. Compare this with other licenses, such as a driver's license. In Wisconsin, to retain a driver's license, we submit periodically to eye exams. Some states have more stringent requirements. To obtain a driver's license, all drivers have to pass a written and a behind-the-wheel test to demonstrate knowledge and skill. In Madison, Wisconsin, even to adopt a cat from the humane society, we have to fill out a form demonstrating knowledge of relevant ordinances for pet-guardians. Yet to marry, applicants need demonstrate no knowledge of the laws pertaining to marriage nor any relationship skills nor even the modicum of self-control required to respect another human being. And once the marriage exists, the burden of proof is always on those who would dissolve it, never on those who would continue it in perpetuity.

Further disanalogies between drivers' and marriage licenses confirm that in our society there is greater concern for victims of bad driving than for those of bad marriages. You cannot legally drive without a license, whereas it is now in many jurisdictions not illegal for unmarried adults of whatever sex to cohabit. One can acquire the status of spousehood simply by cohabiting heterosexually for several years, whereas one does not acquire a driver's license simply by driving for years without one. Driving without the requisite skills and scruples is recognized as a great danger to others and treated accordingly. No comparable recognition is given the dangers of legally sanctioning the access of one person to the person and life of another without evidence of the relevant knowledge and scruples of those so licensed. The consequence is that married victims of partner battering and rape have less protection than anyone except children. What is at stake are permanently disabling and life-threatening injuries, for those who survive. I do not, at present, see how this vulnerability can be acceptably removed from the institution of legal marriage. Measures could be taken to render its disastrous consequences less likely than they are presently but at the cost of considerable state intrusion into our lives.

The right of cohabitation seems to be central to the question whether legal marriage can be made an acceptable institution, especially to the question whether marriage can be envisaged in such a way that its partners could protect themselves, or be protected, adequately against spousal rape and battery. Although many states now recognize on paper the crimes of marital rape and stalking and are better educated than before about marital battering, the progress has been mostly on paper. Wives continue to die daily at a dizzying rate.

Thus I conclude that legalizing lesbian and gay marriage, turning a personal commitment into a license regulable and enforceable by the state, is probably a very bad idea and that lesbians and gay men are probably better off, all things considered, without the "option" (and its consequent pressures) to obtain and act on such a license, despite some of the immediate material and spiritual gains to some of being able to do so. Had we any chance of success, we might do better to agitate for the abolition of legal marriage altogether.

Nevertheless, many will object that marriage provides an important environment for the rearing of children. An appreciation of the conduciveness of marriage to murder and mayhem challenges that assumption. Historically, marriage and motherhood have gone hand in hand— ideologically, although often enough not in fact. That marriage can provide a valuable context for motherhood—even if it is unlikely to do so—as an argument in favor of marriage seems to presuppose that motherhood is a good thing. So let us consider next whether that is so.

## WHY MOTHERHOOD?

The term "mother" is ambiguous between a woman who gives birth and a female who parents, that is, rears a child—often but not necessarily the same woman. The term "motherhood" is ambiguous between the experience of mothers (in either sense, usually the second) and a social practice the rules of which structure child rearing. It is the latter that interests me here. Just as some today would stretch the concept of "family" to cover any committed partnership, household, or close and enduring network of friends, others would stretch the concept of "motherhood" to cover any mode of child rearing. That is not how I understand "motherhood." Just as not every durable intimate partnership is a marriage, not every mode of child rearing exemplifies motherhood. Historically, motherhood has been a core element of patriarchy. Within the institution of motherhood, mother's primary commitments have been to father and only secondarily to his children. Unmarried women have been held responsible by the State for the primary care of children they birth, unless a man wished to claim them. In fact, of course, children are raised by grandparents, single parents (heterosexual, lesbian, gay, asexual, and so on), and extended families, all in the midst of patriarchies. But these have been regarded as deviant parentings, with nothing like the prestige or social and legal support available to patriarchal mothers, as evidenced in the description of the relevant "families" in many cases as providing at best "broken homes."

Apart from the institution of marriage and historical ideals of the family, it is uncertain what characteristics mother-child relationships would have, for many alternatives are possible. In the good ones, mother-child relationships would not be as characterized as they have been by involuntary uncompensated caretaking. Even today, an ever-increasing amount of caretaking is being done contractually in day-care centers, with the result that a legitimate mother's relationship to her child is often much less a caretaking relationship than her mother's relationship to her was. Nor are paid day-care workers "mothers" (even though they may engage briefly in some "mothering activities"), because they are free to walk away from their jobs. Their relationships with a child may be no more permanent or special to the child than those of a babysitter. Boswell's history *The Kindness of Strangers* (1988) describes centuries of children being taken in by those at whose doorsteps babies were deposited, often anonymously. Not all such children had anyone to call "Mother." Children have been raised in convents, orphanages, or boarding schools rather than in households. Many raised in households are cared for by hired help, rather than by anyone they call "Mother." Many children today commute between separated or divorced parents, spending less time in a single household than many children of lesbian parents, some of whom, like Lesléa Newman's Heather, have two people to call "Mother" (Newman 1989). Many children are raised by older siblings, even in households in which someone else is called "Mother." . . .

Because mothers in a society that generally refuses to take collective responsibility for reproduction are often the best or even the only protection that children have, in the short run it is worth fighting for the right to adopt and raise children within lesbian and gay households. This is emergency care for young people, many of whom are already here and desperately in need of care. There is little that heterosexual couples can do to rebel as individual couples in a society in which their relationship is turned into a common law relationship after some years by the State and in which they are given the responsibilities and rights of parents over any children they may raise. Communal action is what is required to implement new models of parenting. In the long run, it seems best to keep open the option of mak-

CARD: AGAINST MARRIAGE AND MOTHERHOOD

ing parenting more "revolutionary" along the lines of communal practices such as those described by bell hooks. Instead of encouraging such a revolution, legal marriage interferes with it in a state that glorifies marriage and takes the marriage relationship to be the only truly healthy context in which to raise children. Lesbian and gay unions have great potentiality to further the revolution, in part because we *cannot* marry.

If motherhood is transcended, the importance of attending to the experiences and environments of children remains. The "children" if not the "mothers" in society are all of us. Not each of us will choose motherhood under present conditions. But each of us has been a child, and each future human survivor will have childhood to survive. Among the most engaging aspects of a major feminist treatise on the institution of motherhood, Adrienne Rich's *Of Woman Born* (1976), are that it is written from the perspective of a daughter who was mothered and that it is addressed to daughters as well as to mothers. This work, like that of Annette Baier, Virginia Held, bell hooks, Patricia Hill Collins, and Sara Ruddick, has the potential to focus our attention not entirely or even especially on mothers but on those who have been (or have not been) mother*ed*, ultimately, on the experience of children in general. Instead of finding that the mother-child relationship provides a valuable paradigm for moral theorizing, even one who has mothered might find, reflecting on both her experience as a mother and her experience of having been mothered, that mothering should not be necessary, or that it should be less necessary than has been thought, and that it has more potential to do harm than good. The power of mothers over children may have been historically far more detrimental to daughters than to sons, at least in societies where daughters have been more controlled, more excluded from well-rewarded careers, and more compelled to engage in family service than sons. Such a finding would be in keeping with the project of drawing on the usually unacknowledged historically characteristic experiences of women.

In suggesting that the experience of being mothered has great potential for harm to children, I do not have in mind the kinds of concerns recently expressed by political conservatives about mothers who abuse drugs or are sexually promiscuous. Even these mothers are often the best protection their children have. I have in mind the environments provided by mothers who in fact do live up to contemporary norms of ideal motherhood or even exceed the demands of such norms in the degree of attention and concern they manifest for their children in providing a child-centered home as fully constructed as their resources allow.

Everyone would benefit from a society that was more attentive to the experiences of children, to the relationships of children with adults and with each other, and to the conditions under which children make the transition to adulthood. Moral philosophy might also be transformed by greater attention to the fact that adult experience and its potentialities are significantly conditioned by the childhoods of adults and of those children's relationship to (yet earlier) adults. Whether or not one agrees with the idea that motherhood offers a valuable paradigm for moral theorizing, in getting us to take seriously the significance of the child's experience of childhood and to take up the standpoint of the "child" in all of us, philosophical work exploring the significance of mother-child relationships is doing feminism and moral philosophy a great service.

## CRITICAL THINKING QUESTIONS

1. What is Card's major argument against marriage and motherhood? Do you agree with her? Why or why not?
2. What are the long-term consequences and benefits of Card's plan? How does communication benefit the process?
3. Write and analyze a case that would implement Card's plan to abolish marriage and motherhood.

## NOTES

Thanks to Harry Brighouse, Vicky Davion, Virginia Held, Sara Ruddick, anonymous reviewers for *Hypatia,* and especially to Lynne Tirrell for helpful comments and suggestions and to audiences who heard ancestors of this essay at the Pacific and Central Divisions of the American Philosophical Association in 1995.

1.   Betty Berzon claims that her book *Permanent Partners* is about "reinventing our gay and lesbian relationships" and "learning to imbue them with all the *solemnity* of marriage without necessarily imitating the heterosexual model" (1988, 7), and yet by the end of the book it is difficult to think of anything in legal ideals of the heterosexual nuclear family that she had not urged us to imitate.

2.   Thus I am not an advocate of the equal legal rights for children movement as that movement is presented and criticized by Purdy (1992), namely, as a movement advocating that children have exactly the same legal rights as adults, including the legal right not to attend school.

3.  See, for example, Weston (1991), Burke (1993), and Slater (1995). In contrast, Berzon (1988) uses the language of partnership, reserving "family" for social structures based on heterosexual unions, as in chap. 12, subtitled "Integrating Your Families into Your Life as a Couple."

4.  An outstanding anthology on the many varieties of lesbian parenting is Arnup (1995). Also interesting is the anthropological study of lesbian mothers by Lewin (1993). Both are rich in references to many resources on both lesbian and gay parenting.

5.  Lewin (1993) finds, for example, that lesbian mothers tend to assume all care-taking responsibilities themselves, or in some cases share them with a partner, turning to their families of origin, rather than to a friendship network of peers, for additionally needed support.

## REFERENCES

Arnup, Katherine, ed. 1995. *Lesbian parenting: Living with pride and prejudice.* Charlottetown, P.E.I.: Gynergy Books.

Baier, Annette C. 1994. *Moral prejudices: Essays on ethics.* Cambridge: Harvard University Press.

Berzon, Betty. 1988. *Permanent partnerships: Building lesbian and gay relationships that last.* New York: Penguin.

Blumenfeld, Warren J. 1996. Same-sex marriage: Introducing the discussion. *Journal of Gay, Lesbian, and Bisexual Identity* 1(1): 77.

Boswell, John. 1988. *The kindness of strangers: The abandonment of children in Western Europe from late antiquity to the Renaissance.* New York: Pantheon.

———. 1994. *Same-sex unions in premodern Europe.* New York: Villard.

Brownworth, Victoria A. 1996. Tying the knot or the hangman's noose: The case against marriage. *Journal of Gay, Lesbian, and Bisexual Identity* 1(1): 91–98.

Burke, Phyllis. 1993. *Family values: Two moms and their son.* New York: Random House.

Card, Claudia. 1988. Gratitude and obligation. *American Philosophical Quarterly* 25 92): 115–27.

———. 1990. Gender and moral luck. In *Identity, character, and morality: Essays in moral psychology,* ed. Owen Flanagan and Amelie Oksenberg Rorty. Cambridge: MIT Press.

———. 1995. *Lesbian choices.* New York: Columbia University Press.

Collins, Patricia Hill. 1991. *Black feminist thought: Knowledge, consciousness, and the politics of empowerment.* New York: Routledge.

Daly, Mary. 1978. *Gyn/Ecology: The metaethics of radical feminism.* Boston: Beacon.

Faulkner, Sandra, with Judy Nelson. 1993. *Love match: Nelson vs. Navratilova.* New York: Birch Lane Press.

Friedman, Marilyn. 1993. *What are friends for? Feminist perspectives on personal relationships and moral theory.* Ithaca: Cornell University Press.

Gilman, Charlotte Perkins. 1966. *Women and economics: The economic factor between men and women as a factor in social evolution,* ed. Carl Degler. New York: Harper.

————. 1992. Herland. In *Herland and selected stories by Charlotte Perkins Gilman*, ed. Barbara H. Solomon. New York: Signet.

Goldman, Emma. 1969. Marriage and love. In *Anarchism and other essays*. New York: Dover.

Hall, Radclyffe. 1950. *The well of loneliness*. New York: Pocket Books. (Many editions; first published 1928).

Held, Virginia. 1993. *Feminist morality: Transforming culture, society, and politics*. Chicago: University of Chicago Press.

Hoagland, Sarah Lucia. 1988. *Lesbian ethics: Toward new value*. Palo Alto, CA: Institute of Lesbian Studies.

hooks, bell. 1984. *Feminist theory from margin to center*. Boston: South End Press.

Island, David, and Patrick Letellier. 1991. *Men who beat the men who love them: Battered gay men and domestic violence*. New York: Harrington Park Press.

Lewin, Ellen. 1993. *Lesbian mothers*. Ithaca: Cornell University Press.

Lobel, Kerry, ed. 1986. *Naming the violence: Speaking out about lesbian battering*. Seattle: Seal Press.

Lorde, Audre. 1984. *Sister outsider: Essays and speeches*. Trumansburg: Crossing Press.

Mahmoody, Betty, with William Hoffer. 1987. *Not without my daughter*. New York: St. Martin's.

Mohr, Richard D. 1994. *A more perfect union: Why straight America must stand up for gay rights*. Boston: Beacon.

Newman, Leslea. 1989. *Heather has two mommies*. Northampton, MA: In Other Words Publishing.

Noddings, Nel. 1984. *Caring: A feminine approach to ethics and moral education*. Berkeley: University of California Press.

Pierce, Christine. 1995. Gay marriage. *Journal of Social Philosophy* 28 (2): 5–16.

Purdy, Laura M. 1992. *In their best interest? The case against equal rights for children*. Ithaca: Cornell University Press.

Renzetti, Clair M. 1992. *Violent betrayal: Partner abuse in lesbian relationships*. Newbury Park, CA: Sage Publications.

Rich, Adrienne. 1976. *Of woman born: Motherhood as experience and as institution*. New York: Norton.

Ruddick, Sara. 1989. *Maternal thinking: Toward a politics of peace*. Boston: Beacon.

Slater, Suzanne. 1995. *The lesbian family life cycle*. New York: Free Press.

Trebilcot, Joyce, ed. 1983. *Mothering: Essays in feminist theory*. Totowa, N.J.: Rowman and Allanheld.

Weston, Kath. 1991. *Families we choose*. New York: Columbia University Press.

Wolfson, Evan. 1996. Why we should fight for the freedom to marry: The challenges and opportunities that will follow a win in Hawaii. *Journal of Lesbian, Gay, and Bisexual Identity* 1(1): 79–89.

# CONTEMPORARY CASE

## *Extramarital Affairs: The Traveler*

Sam is employed by a beverage company who pays him high commissions for his sales and marketing. He is often in the company of his boss, who enjoys being in the company of attractive women. Sam is married, but Sam's boss is not. When Sam travels with his boss, he double dates with his boss. Often Sam and his evening date will enjoy sexual intercourse.

Sam has not mentioned his dating and sexual activities to his wife under the assumption that what she doesn't know won't hurt her.

After noticing shooting muscle pain and fever, Sam checks in with is physician. His physician informs him that he has genital herpes. He states that soon he will have blisters that could become extremely painful sores. The physician asks Sam if his wife also has genital herpes. Sam say he doesn't think so. The physician then asks Sam from whom he contracted the virus. Sam says he doesn't know, indicating it could be from one of eight women he has seen in the past six months. The physician says this is a serious situation, and that Sam should be tested for AIDS. He also tells him he would like Sam's wife to come in for an examination. He states most likely Sam's wife will also now have genital herpes and that it is a lifetime condition.

1. Explain the ethical consequences of Sam's sexual activities with other women.
2. Should Sam have confessed earlier to his wife of his sexual activities?
3. Are these complications that Bertrand Russell should have discussed in his essay? Why or why not?
4. Is sexual faithfulness important in marriage? Defend your answer with the theory of one of the authors in this chapter.
5. Should Sam accuse his wife of infidelity before confessing he has genital herpes?

# 7

## ETHICS AND CONCEPTS OF FAMILY IN INTERPERSONAL RELATIONSHIPS

PLATO

## A PROPOSAL TO ABOLISH THE PRIVATE FAMILY

*Plato (427–347 B.C.E.) was the top student of and scribe for Socrates. He founded the Academy in Athens, a school or society devoted to the scholarly and social education of boys. In this excerpt, Plato argues that women and children should be the common property of a society.*

"It is plain then, that we shall make marriages as sacred as ever we can; and sacred would mean the most useful."

"By all means."

"Then how will they be most useful? Tell me that, Glaucon. For I see in your house hunting dogs and numbers of pedigree game birds. Pray, have you paid any attention to their matings and breedings?"

"What sort of attention?" he asked.

"First of all, in this admittedly pedigree stock there are some, aren't there, which turn out to be the best?"

"There are."

"Then do you breed from all alike, or do you take the greatest care to choose the best?"

"I choose the best."

"What of their age—do you take the youngest or the oldest, or as far as possible those in their prime?"

"Those in their prime."

"And if the breeding should not be done in this way, you consider the stock will be much worse both in bird and dog?"

"I do," said he.

"What of horses," said I, "and other animals? Is it different in them?"

"That would be odd indeed," he said.

"Bless my soul!" said I. "My friend, what simply tiptop rulers we need to have, if the same is true of mankind!"

"Well, it is," he said, "but why do you say that, pray?"

"Because," said I, "they will have to use all those drugs. We thought even an inferior physician was enough, I take it, for bodies willingly subjected to a proper diet and needing no drugs; but when drugs must be used, we know that the physician must be braver."

"True: but what has that to do with it?"

"This," I said. "Often the rulers will have really to use falsehood and deceit for the benefit of the ruled; and we said all such things were useful as a kind of drugs."

"Yes, and that was right," he said.

"In their weddings and child-gettings, then, it seems this right will be rightest."

"How so?"

"It follows from what we agreed that the best men must mingle most often with the best women, but the opposite, the worst with the worst, least often; and the children of the best must be brought up but not the others, if the flock is to be tiptop. And none must know this to be going on except the rulers alone, if the herd of guardians is also to be as free as possible from quarrels."

"Quite right," he said.

"Then holidays must be provided by law, when we shall bring together the brides and bridegrooms, and there must be festivals, and hymns must be made by our poets suitable to the weddings which come about. But the number of weddings we will leave the rulers to decide, so that they may keep the number of the men as far as possible the same, taking into account war and disease and so forth, in order to keep the city from becoming either too large or too small as far as possible."

"That is right," he said.

"And there must be some clever kind of lots devised, I think, so that your worthless creature will blame his bad luck on any conjunction, not his rulers."

"Just so," he said.

"And I suppose, when young men prove themselves good and true in war or anywhere else, honours must be given them, and prizes, and particularly more generous freedom of intercourse with women; at the same time, this will be a good excuse for letting as many children as possible be begotten of such men."

"That is right."

"Then the officials who are set over these will receive the children as they are born; they may be men or women or both, for offices are common, of course, to both women and men."

"Yes."

"The children of the good, then, they will take, I think, into the fold, and hand them over to certain nurses who will live in some place apart in the city; those of the inferior sort, and any one of the others who may be born defective, they will put away as is proper in some mysterious, unknown place."

"Yes," he said, "if the breed of the guardians is to be pure."

"Those officials, then, will have charge of their nurture; they will bring into the fold the mothers when they are in milk, taking every precaution that no mother shall recognise her own; if these are not able, they shall provide others who have milk. They shall be careful that these mothers do not suckle too long; sleepless nights and other troubles will be left for nurses and nannies."

"What an easy job you make it," he said, "for the guardians' wives to have children!"

"As it should be," I said. "But now let us go on with the next part of our scheme. We said, you remember, that the offspring ought to be born from parents in their prime."

"True."

"Do you think, as I do, that the prime of life might fairly be counted as lasting twenty years for a woman, and thirty for a man?"

"Which years would you choose?" he asked.

"The woman," I said, "shall bear for the state from the age of twenty to forty; the man shall beget for the state from the time when 'his quickest racing speed is past'[1] to the age of five and fifty."

---

[1] A poetic quotation, which probably referred to a horse.

"At all events," he said, "that is the prime of both in body and mind."

"Then if a man either older or younger than these shall meddle in begetting for the state, we shall say this offence is neither lawful nor right. He has planted a child in the city, which will be born, if the secret is kept, not as one conceived in the grace of sanctity; no holy rite and prayers will be heard over it, such as priestesses and priests will intone for each wedding while the whole city prays that the children born may be better children of good parents, and more useful children of useful parents, from generation to generation; instead it was begotten in darkness with incontinence to the common danger."

"You are right," said he.

"The same law will hold," said I, "if one still within the creative age touch a woman within her age without a ruler's pairing; bastard and unaccredited and unsanctified we shall call that child which he dumps upon the city."

"Quite rightly so," he said.

"But I think, as soon as the women and the men pass the age of begetting, we shall leave the men free to consort with any they will, except with daughter or mother, and daughters' children, and those of an earlier generation than the mother; and the women again free except for son or father or those above and below as before. However, with all this allowance, we must warn them to be as careful as possible not to bring any of such conceptions into the light, not even one; but if a child is born, if one forces its way through, they must dispose of it on the understanding that there is no food or nurture for such a one."

"Yes," he said, "that is quite reasonable too; but how will they recognise each others' fathers and daughters and other relations you spoke of just now?"

"They will not," said I. "But whenever one of them becomes a bridegroom, he will call all the male children sons and all the female children daughters, who are born in the tenth month, or indeed the seventh month, counting from the day of his marriage; and they will call him father; and likewise he will call their offspring grandchildren, and they again will call these grandfathers and grandmothers. And those born in that particular time when their mothers and fathers were begetting they will call sisters and brothers. So these will not touch each other in the way we spoke of; but brothers and sisters the law will allow to live together, if the lot falls that way and if the Pythian oracle sanctions."

"Quite right," he said.

"So you see, Glaucon, what is meant by having women and children in common among the city's guardians. Now we must establish by the argument that this fits in with our general constitution and is by far the best. Or what shall we do next?"

"Surely this," he said.

"Surely, then, the beginning of our agreement is to ask ourselves what we can name as the greatest good for furnishing a city which the lawgiver should aim at in laying down the laws; and what is the greatest evil. Then we must enquire whether what we have just described fits the footstep of the good and does not suit that of the bad."

"Most of all," he said.

"Then can we name any greater evil for a city than that which tears it asunder and makes it many instead of one? Or a greater good than what binds it together and makes it one?"

"We cannot."

"Surely community in pleasure and pain binds it together. That is when, as far as possible, all the citizens alike are glad or sorry, on the same occasions of births and successes or deaths and disasters?"

"Certainly," he said.

"But if each has his own feelings apart about such happenings the bonds are cut, if some are very happy and some very much pained while the same things happen to the city and those who are in the city."

"Of course."

"And does not this come because the people do not utter in unison the words 'mine' and 'not mine,' or likewise the word 'another's'?"

"Exactly so."

"So that city is best managed in which the greatest number say 'mine' and 'not mine' with the same meaning about the same thing?"

"Much the best."

"That is when the city is nearest the single man. For example, what happens when your finger is hurt? The whole community, arranged throughout the body, stretching to the soul as one orderly whole under that which rules in it, feels the pain, and the community has pain all together as a whole when the part is in trouble: so we say the man has pain in the finger, and the same is said of any other of the parts of the man, about pain when a part is in trouble and about pleasure when a part gets better."

"Just the same," he said, "and as you put it, the best governed city comes nearest to such a man."

"Then," I said, "if something either good or bad happens to any one of the citizens, such a city will be most likely to say that the sufferer is part of the city, and it will be happy or unhappy as a whole."

"There is necessity in that," he said, "for the well-managed city."

## CRITICAL THINKING QUESTIONS

1. What were Plato's major goals in abolishing the private family. In what ways could this create a more moral society? In what ways is this more harmful?
2. What is Plato communicating about the role of women and children in society? How would you modify Plato's proposal to give better equality?
3. Write and analyze a case involving your ideal for the private family.

## ARISTOTLE

# ON PLATO'S PROPOSAL

*Aristotle (384–322 B.C.E.) was born in northern Greece. He studied with Plato for 18 years and set up his own school in Athens. In this excerpt from* Politics *Book II, Aristotle explains that women and children should not be common property of the state. He believes that common property is not taken care of properly.*

## BOOK II

. . . We will begin with the natural beginning of the subject. Three alternatives are conceivable: The members of a State must either have (1) all things or (2) nothing in common, or (3) some things in common and some not. That they should have nothing in common is clearly impossible, for the State is a community, and must at any rate have a common place—one city will be in one place, and the citizens are those who share in that one city. But should a well-ordered State have all things, as far as may be, in common, or some only and not others? For the citizens might conceivably have wives and children and property in common, as Socrates proposes in the "Republic" of Plato. Which is better, our present condition, or the proposed new order of society?

There are many difficulties in the community of women. And the principle on which Socrates rests the necessity of such an institution does not appear to be established by his arguments. The end which he ascribes to the State, taken literally, is impossible, and how we are to interpret it is nowhere precisely stated. I am speaking of the premise from which the argument of Socrates proceeds, "that the greater the unity of the State the better." Is it not obvious that a State may at length attain such a degree of unity as to be no longer a State?—since the nature of a State is to be a plurality, and in tending to greater unity, from being a State, it becomes a family, and from being a family, an individual; for the family may be said to be more one than the State, and the individual than the family. So that we ought not to attain this greatest unity even if we could, for it would be the destruction of the State. Again, a State is not made up only of so many men, but of different kinds of men; for similars do not constitute a State. It is not like a military alliance, of which the usefulness depends upon its quantity even where there is no difference in quality. For in that mutual protection is the end aimed at; and the question is the same as about the scales of a balance: which is the heavier? ..

But, even supposing that it were best for the community to have the greatest degree of unity, this unity is by no means proved to follow from the fact "of all men saying 'mine' and 'not mine' at the same instant of time," which, according to Socrates,[h] is the sign of perfect unity in a State. For the word "all" is ambiguous. If the meaning be that every individual says "mine" and "not mine" at the same time, than perhaps the result at which Socrates aims may be in some degree accomplished; each man will call the same person his own son and his own wife, and so of his property and of all that belongs to him. This, however, is not the way in which people would speak who had their wives and children in common; they would say "all" but not

---

h Pl. rep. v. 462 c.

"each." In like manner their property would be described as belonging to them, not severally but collectively. There is an obvious fallacy in the term "all": like some other words, "both," "odd," "even," it is ambiguous, and in argument becomes a source of logical puzzles. That all persons call the same thing mine in the sense in which each does so may be a fine thing, but it is impracticable; or if the words are taken in the other sense [*i.e.* the sense which distinguishes "all" from "each"], such a unity in no way conduces to harmony. And there is another objection to the proposal. For that which is common to the greatest number has the least care bestowed upon it. Everyone thinks chiefly of his own, hardly at all of the common interest; and only when he is himself concerned as an individual. For besides other considerations, everybody is more inclined to neglect the duty which he expects another to fulfil; as in families many attendants are often less useful than a few. Each citizen will have a thousand sons who will not be his sons individually, but anybody will be equally the son of anybody, and will therefore be neglected by all alike. Further, upon this principle, everyone will call another "mine" or "not mine" according as he is prosperous or the reverse;— however small a fraction he may be of the whole number, he will say of every individual of the thousand, or whatever by the number of the city, "such a one is mine," "such a one his"; and even about this he will not be positive; for it is impossible to know who chanced to have a child, or whether, if one came into existence, it has survived. But which is better—to be able to say "mine" about every one of the two thousand or the ten thousand citizens, or to use the word "mine" in the ordinary and more restricted sense? For usually the same person is called by one man his son whom another calls his brother or cousin or kinsman or blood-relation or connection by marriage either of himself or of some relation of his, and these relationships he distinguishes from the tie which binds him to his tribe or ward; and how much better is it to be the real cousin of somebody than to be a son after Plato's fashion! Nor is there any way of preventing brothers and children and fathers and mothers from sometimes recognizing one another; for children are born like their parents, and they will necessarily be finding indications of their relationship to one another. Geographers declare such to be the fact; they say that in Upper Libya, where the women are common, nevertheless the children who are born are assigned to their respective fathers on the ground of their likeness.[i] And some women, like the

---

i Cp. Herod. iv. 180.

females of other animals—for example, mares and cows—have a strong tendency to produce offspring resembling their parents, as was the case with the Pharsalian mare called Dicaea (the Just)[j]

Other evils, against which it is not easy for the authors of such a community to guard, will be assaults and homicides, voluntary as well as involuntary, quarrels and slanders, all which are most unholy acts when committed against fathers and mothers and near relations, but not equally unholy when there is no relationship. Moreover, they are much more likely to occur if the relationship is unknown, and, when they have occurred, the customary expiations of them cannot be made. Again, how strange it is that Socrates, after having made the children common, should hinder lovers from carnal intercourse only, but should permit familiarities between father and son or between brother and brother, than which nothing can be more unseemly, since even without them, love of this sort is improper. How strange, too, to forbid intercourse for no other reason than the violence of the pleasure, as though the relationship of father and son or of brothers with one another made no difference.

This community of wives and children seems better suited to the husbandmen than to the guardians, for if they have wives and children in common, they will be bound to one another by weaker ties, as a subject class should be, and they will remain obedient and not rebel. In a word, the result of such a law would be just the opposite of that which good laws ought to have, and the intention of Socrates in making these regulations about women and children would defeat itself. For friendship we believe to be the greatest good of States[k] and the preservative of them against revolutions; neither is there anything which Socrates so greatly lauds as the unity of the State which he and all the world declare to be created by friendship. But the unity which he commends would be like that of the lovers in the "Symposium,"[l] who, as Aristophanes says, desire to grow together in the excess of their affection, and from being two to become one, in which case one or both would certainly perish. Whereas [the very opposite will really happen] in a State having women and children common, love will be watery; and the father will certainly not say "my son," or the son "my father." As a little sweet wine mingled with a great deal of water is imperceptible in the mixture, so, in this sort of community, the idea of relationship which is based upon these names will

---

[j] Cp. Hist. Anim. vii. 6, p. 586 a. 13.

[k] Cp. N. Eth., viii. I, § 4.

[l] Symp. 189-193.

be lost; there is no reason why the so-called father should care about the son, or the son about the father, or brothers about one another. Of the two qualities which chiefly inspire regard and affection—that a thing is your own and that you love it—neither can exist in such a state as this.

Again, the transfer of children as soon as they are born from the rank of husbandmen or of artisans to that of guardians, and from the rank of guardians into a lower rank,<sup>m</sup> will be very difficult to arrange; the givers or transferrers cannot but know whom they are giving and transferring, and to whom. And the previously mentioned evils, such as assaults, unlawful loves, homicides, will happens more often amongst those who are transferred to the lower classes, or who have a place assigned to them among the guardians; for they will no longer call the members of any other class brothers, and children, and fathers, and mothers, and will not, therefore, be afraid of committing any crimes by reason of consanguinity. Touching the community of wives and children, let this be our conclusion.

## CRITICAL THINKING QUESTIONS

1. Why does Aristotle openly disagree with Plato on concepts of the private family?
2. Does Aristotle's theory seem more equitable? Could it be implemented? What virtue(s) is Aristotle's theory based on?
3. Write and analyze a case involving an interpersonal communication strategy that could ethically strengthen the position of women and children within the Greek city state.

JOHN  SIMMONS

# RIGHTS AND THE FAMILY

*John Simmons is a professor of philosophy at the University of Virginia. In this excerpt from* The Lockean Theory of Rights *published in 1992, Simmons explicates Locke's arguments on individual rights.*

---

*m* Rep. iii. 415.

Conjugal society, Locke writes, "is made by a voluntary compact between man and woman" (II, 78). The rights of the husband (and the wife) are "founded on contract" (I, 98; II, 82–83), and are thus what I have called (in 2.3) consensual special rights. Locke is clearly speaking here of marriage as a *moral,* not a legal, relationship (II, 83; I, 123), and one whose terms are thus not to be thought of as constrained by any particular legal (or other) rules or conventions (II, 83). Husband and wife may promise to love, honor, cherish, and obey one another, or they may bind themselves by different and more specific agreements. The contract must be consistent with the ends of conjugal society, or else it cannot count as a *marriage* contract; but all else can "be varied and regulated by that contract which unites man and wife" (II, 83). There is thus a wide range of possible contracts between a woman and a man, ranging from purely economic (nonmarital) contracts, through "standard" marriage contracts, to quite individual and unconventional marriage contracts. For Locke, of course, the end or point of conjugal society is procreation and the care of the "common offspring" (II, 78–83); so any marriage contract necessarily must be understood to include an agreement to care for and educate any children resulting from the union, and to "support and assist" one another during the time that the rearing of children takes place (II, 78, 83). For those of us who may disagree with this (or any other essentialist) account of marriage, however, Locke's contractualist view of marriage can still be accepted, with marriage contracts only exhibiting certain "family resemblances" to one another.[15]

Locke is, I think, correct in supposing that the rights (and duties) of spouses (or of any other persons involved in long-term, monogamous relationships) are primarily determined by consent, as the appropriate source of bonds between equals.[16] While there need not be anything so formal as a contract, voluntary agreements or understandings may distribute the rights and duties within the relationship as the partners please. That is the fundamental moral component of marriage. Religious and legal recognition of certain unions, the profound emotional ties that usually accompany them, and the function such unions play in social interaction do not alter this fundamental component, nor do other moral aspects of marriage that may add

---

[15] Kant, for instance, claims that while the *natural* end of marriage is producing and educating children, this is not *essential* to marriage, since people may have other ends *(Metaphysics of Morals,* part 1, section 24).

[16] Again, see Kant, *Metaphysics of Morals,* part 1, section 24.

to it.[17] That marriage aims, in a sense, at overcoming the partners' preoccupation with their moral rights and duties with respect to one another, in no way suggests that they lack these rights and duties or that they are not based in a voluntary undertaking.[18] A more troubling problem, however, is that the "contractual" undertaking between wife and husband may be uninformed, seriously underspecified, or amorphous, leaving it uncertain just how the rights and duties within a marriage ought to be distributed. In such cases the natural solution is to favor equality between the parties; but it is in this context that Locke's least liberal (and most sexist) views on marriage are expressed.[19]

While a husband has no *absolute* power (right, authority) over his wife,[20] Locke argues (I, 48; II, 82–83), he does have a certain "priority" over her (she "owes" him a limited "subjection" [I, 48]). Every husband has the right "to order the things of private concernment in his family, as proprietor of the goods and land there, and to have his will take place before that of his wife in all things of their common concernment" (I, 48). In disagreements between husband and wife, the man has the right of "last determination" in "things of their common interest and property" (II, 82). Why this priority of the man's will? Aside from references to God's punishment of women for Eve's transgressions (I, 47) (which, I argue below, Locke does *not* intend as

---

[17] See the discussion of reciprocity between spouses in Becker, *Reciprocity,* 186–95. I do not think that considerations of reciprocity can *override* the genuinely voluntary undertakings of spouses.

[18] Contrary to what Hegel seems to have thought *(Philosophy of Right,* section 163).

[19] Locke must receive mixed reviews on his liberality with regard to equality of the sexes. The passages I consider below (and Locke's views on paternal control of property) make it easy to simply dismiss his views as thoroughly permeated with the deep and casual sexism of his age. (See, e.g., Clark; "Women and John Locke," 721–24; Seliger, *Liberal Politics,* 211–12.) But while Dunn is certainly right that Locke's sexual egalitarianism fought a losing battle with his acceptance of the radically inegalitarian conventions of his age *(Political Thought,* 121–22n), there was at least a battle. Locke's insistence on equal parental authority and his very liberal views on the free determination of nonconventional marriage contracts deserve some notice. And, as I argue below, other aspects of Locke's views on the rights of women deserve more charitable readings than they usually receive. See Yolton, *Locke,* 58.

[20] Locke's proof of this claim seems seriously confused (again involving a blurring of moral with physical "powers"). He argues that if the husband *did* have absolute power over his wife, "there could be no matrimony in any of those countries where the husband is allowed no such absolute authority" (II, 83). This seems to amount to the quite silly claim that if the state denies you exercise of a right to X, you cannot have a moral right to X (a claim, of course, which Locke emphatically and correctly rejects throughout the body of his work).

a source of man's authority over woman), Locke says only this: when husband and wife disagree, it "being necessary that the last determination, i.e., the rule, should be placed somewhere, it naturally falls to the man's share, as the abler and stronger" (II, 82).

Even supposing (falsely) that men (individually or as a group) are "abler and stronger" than women, it is hard to see why Locke should have thought this fact a ground for unequal rights between husband and wife.[21] After all, other natural inequalities in strength or ability (those between adult males, for instance) do not seem to justify inequalities in *their* rights, on Locke's view (as we saw in 2.2). This apparent inconsistency seems easy to explain if we simply ascribe to Locke a firm commitment to the natural superiority and dominion of men over women, a prephilosophical commitment that his general philosophical principles cannot budge (even at the price of inconsistency). We could then argue that for Locke the "natural dominion of one sex over the other" is so obvious that it "does not even have to be justified."[22] Locke may *say* conjugal society is consensual; but given Locke's view of women's weakness and inequality, any contract of marriage would border on unconscionability.[23] In the end, the argument goes, Locke's real view is that men enjoy a *natural* (not contractual) dominion over women, both in and out of marriage. He should not be credited with having espoused a more "liberal attitude toward marriage and the relation of the sexes."[24]

This reading of Locke, I think, is unfair to him, for he quite specifically denies that man has any natural dominion over woman. God never gave him any such dominion: He never gave "any authority to Adam over Eve, or to men over their wives."[25] Women are not naturally subject to their husbands, although, Locke "grants," there is "a foundation in nature for it" (I,

---

[21] I will concentrate here on the husband's right to decide in conflicts over their common concerns; wives' property rights—which they can acquire by "labor or compact" (II, 183)—I discuss separately in 4.4.

[22] "Women and John Locke," 702–4, 708. See also Pateman, *Problem of Political Obligation,* 75.

[23] Clark, "Women and John Locke," 709–11. On unconscionable contracts, see my "Consent, Free Choice," section 5.

[24] Ibid., 721. See also Pateman, "Women and Consent," 152. While Locke never indicates any interest in considering, for instance, female citizenship, these assessments of his views still seem unduly harsh (for reasons specified below).

[25] The biblical text at issue merely "foretells what should be woman's lot" (I, 47); it does not *prescribe* it. Locke uses this same style of biblical interpretation on other occasions in the *First Treatise* (e.g., I, 118).

47). What is this natural "foundation" for an artificial authority? It is quite clearly meant to be man's superior strength and ability—not as the source of his authority, but as a natural fact to which man's achievement of conventional authority is connected. What, then, is the relevance of this natural superiority? First, of course, it is natural (not *obligatory*) to defer in certain ways to those who are abler, stronger, wiser, older, or more virtuous (as Locke says elsewhere—e.g., II, 54). As a result, it is natural (and, subsequently, conventional) for women to *give* men greater authority than they reserve for themselves in their free marriage contracts. This is natural and conventional, not *necessary*—for Locke mentions instances in which women have elected *not* to give their husbands this authority (e.g., I, 47; II, 65). And *because* it is natural (and thus inevitably conventional), Locke assumes, if the marriage contract does not specify alternative arrangements, we may understand it to give greater authority to the husband. But Locke has, I think, a second reason for his belief that husbands typically have (limited) authority over their wives. In voluntary unions between persons that do not involve a precise specification of the methods for settling disputes, the right to determine the body's actions must be understood to lie with the greatest "force" in the body. This is an important principle for Locke, for it underlies his defense of majority rule as the understood rule of resolution for *political* unions: "it being necessary to that which is one body to move one way; it is necessary the body should move that way whither the greater force carries it, which is the consent of the majority: or else it is impossible it should act or continue one body" (II, 96). Locke's reasoning about the husband's right of "last determination" in a marriage proceeds similarly: this right must "be placed somewhere," so it "naturally falls to the man's share, as the abler and stronger" (II, 82).

Locke's argument is in neither case very convincing.[26] But the important point to note here is that he is in neither case arguing for a natural authority (of majorities or husbands). In both cases he is trying to give reasons for

---

[26] In the case of majority rule, of course, there is nothing straightforwardly more authoritative or fair about this procedure than many alternatives (e.g., lotteries, votes weighted by intensity of preference, etc.). Even the physical analogy (right must follow force) will not help here, since an intense minority might be a "greater force" than an apathetic majority. In the case of marriage contracts, even if greater ability *were* a ground for greater authority, a right of "last determination" is far from the only way to implement this authority. And again, the "greater force" in a dispute need not fall on the side of the party possessing the greater physical strength.

interpreting an inexplicit contract in a certain way, for understanding where the artificial authority to make decisions for a body must be taken to lie, when it has not been explicitly stated in the contract. And in both cases he allows that if there *has* been an explicit agreement on some alternative arrangement for decision-making, this agreement overrides the reasoning he has advanced. Thus, political bodies may "expressly agree" to require more than a simple majority for binding decisions (II, 99); and, presumably, this means they may opt for different procedures altogether (e.g., lottery, weighted lottery, plural voting for the more able, etc.). Similarly, *every* aspect of the marriage contract (except the responsibility to provide for offspring) may be varied by express agreement (II, 83). Wives may have the right of "last determination" themselves, if this is agreed on, or the mates may decide conflicts by lottery or by taking turns, and so on. The authority of husbands is neither natural nor necessary.

Where, then, does this leave a Lockean contractual account of "marital morality"? If we deprive the account of its false factual assumptions (about man's superior strength and ability), it seems not at all unreasonable or illiberal. Marriage contracts may distribute rights and duties between the partners as they specify. In the absence of explicit specification by or understanding of the partners, we should take the contract to have the conventional form.[27] In Locke's day, this meant a superior position for the husband; but the voluntariness and fairness of marriage contracts in Locke's day were typically undermined by the vastly inferior bargaining position of the woman (based on her economic dependency and social limitations).[28] Fairness, then, would have dictated that we interpret inexplicit contracts more equitably than the conventions of Locke's day would have suggested. Today, when conventions are more egalitarian and women's dependency on male approval less profound, the problem of unfair contracts is less dramatic. Women can, if they wish, accept a traditional or limited role in family decision-making; or they can insist on equal (or greater than equal) rights in this area as a condition of the marriage contract. Only unfairness and duress (etc.) involved in entry into a marriage will require us to question the terms of an explicit contract or interpret an inexplicit one in other than conventional terms.[29] . . .

---

[27] Sidgwick. *Methods of Ethics,* 256.

[28] Locke accepts the idea that unfair bargaining position can void an apparent contract (see, e.g., I, 42).

[29] I leave untouched myriad difficulties concerning degrees of voluntariness, social conditioning, "false consciousness," and so on, as well as questions about the terms of the marriage

Parents are said at various times by Locke to have natural rights to respect, gratitude, assistance, honor, support, obedience, defense, reverence, and acknowledgment. Children have (under appropriate conditions) correlative natural duties or obligations to satisfy these claims. But the (noninstitutional) rights of parents (and filial duties) can in fact be divided neatly into two main classes: what Locke calls the "right of tuition" and the "right of honor" (II, 67). And these two (classes of) rights arise from very different sources. It is on this subject that Locke's remarks on familial morality are at their most plausible, and many contemporary writers have followed the Lockean line as a result. It will try here to summarize Locke's views and to motivate certain natural extensions of them, in order to defend a Lockean position on natural parental rights and filial duties.

Parental rights are for Locke, first, rights held by *both* parents. While he occasionally uses the more traditional term "paternal power" in place of "parental power" (e.g., II, 69, 170, 173),[36] Locke's view that these rights are shared is clearly stated in both *Treatises* (e.g., I, 6, 55, 61, 62; II, 52). This group is shared parental rights is divided by Locke (following Aquinas, and as suggested above) into two distinct rights (or better, subgroups of rights), each of which seems as well to have two parts, and each of which has a distinct ground.

What Locke calls the "right of tuition" is "a sort of rule and jurisdiction" (II, 55) or "temporary government" (II, 67) that parents have over their children, a right to rear them and control them in ways which will ultimately result in the children's healthy independence and moral agency. It is a right to rule "paternalistically" (i.e., for the good of the one ruled[37]) over one's children, to help them through "the weakness and imperfection of their

---

contract (may they be renegotiated when one or both of the partners changes or grows in ways that make the initial specification unrewarding or inappropriate?).

[36] Schochet briefly discusses Locke's waffling in "Family," 85. Locke's emphasis on fathers' rights throughout his discussion is due (at least in part) to his polemical task, for he needs to refute Filmer's various claims about the nature and extent of paternal authority. Filmer, obviously, made no claims to refute concerning *maternal* authority.

[37] Locke does not seem to have in mind that parents must *maximize* the benefits they provide for their children. They must only refrain from harming their children and provide them with the necessary means to self-government (which includes, as I argue below, both satisfying their basic needs and providing reasonable comforts, where possible). Parental rule is limited at least to that authority which is consistent with the performance of these parental duties. The *Education* makes it clear that parental education and discipline must be aimed at making children capable of liberty—that is, rational, virtuous, and free.

nonage" (II, 65) by informing their minds and governing their actions (II, 58). Locke should be understood here to have two kinds of rights in mind under the heading of the right of tuition. On the one hand, parents have a right to rear their children as they see fit (within the limits set by the *point* of that right—i.e., the good of the children), a right that is held against the world at large. This is a right not to have the job of parenting stolen or usurped by others. Natural parents have the right of "first try" in rearing their offspring. While Locke nowhere explicitly discusses this aspect of the right of tuition, it is clearly presumed (since Locke even denies the power of the state to overturn natural parental rights [e.g., I, 64]). The second aspect or part of the right of tuition is a right held not against society, but against one's children. Parents have a right to obedience from their children during their minority (at least when they are parenting properly). "The power of commanding and chastising" (II, 67) falls to parents, as those who are in charge of governing for their children's good, until the children "come to the use of reason" and are able to govern themselves (II, 170). The right of tuition, in both its parts, cannot be taken from a natural parent without cause. But it can be forfeited by parental incompetence, abuse, or neglect (whether from inability or from deliberate breach of duty); it can be alienated by the parents' decision to "put the tuition of [their child] in other hands" (II, 69); and it is naturally dissolved when children reach the "age of discretion."[38] It is thus a right that is far indeed from *absolute* dominion of parents over children (I, 51–53; II, 53, 64, 69, 74).

The second parental right is the "right of honor," a right held by parents against their children and one that must also be understood to have two parts. Its first part concerns the *nonmaterial* support and responses to which parents have a right from their children—that "honor" that is due parents "by the Fifth Commandment" (I, 64). Parents have a right to be respected and revered by their children (II, 67), to be shown gratitude and receive acknowledgment for the benefits they have bestowed upon their children. Deference to and compliance with parental wishes are appropriate even after children have matured and are self-supporting (II, 69). Second, the right of honor is also a right to *material* support from one's children, where this is needed and the children are able to supply it (*after* one's children provide

---

[38] Locke's specifications of the ways in which parental power can (and cannot) change hands are, of course, important to his case against Filmer, since for Filmer political authority was an instance of paternal authority that had "changed hands" all down through the ages.

for their *own* children, if any). Parents are entitled to "support and subsistence" (a "return of goods") from their children, and even have a claim to inherit from their children if there are no grandchildren with prior claims (I, 90). Like the right of tuition, the right of honor is imprescriptible.[39] Locke describes the right as "perpetual" (e.g., II, 67), but he clearly intends that it may be forfeited by parental neglect, at least in large measure.[40] Unlike the right of tuition, however, the right of honor cannot be alienated (transferred voluntarily).[41]

As should be plain by now, the right of tuition is a right parents have over children (primarily) in their minority, while the right of honor largely refers to the claims of parents against their grown children (although, of course, even young children should honor their parents in ways appropriate to their ages). As a result, the correlative duties or obligations of children are similarly divided by age, with the duties being "stronger on grown than younger children" (II, 68). Young children, then, have a duty of obedience to their parents' commands, correlating with (part of) the right of tuition (II, 65, 67). Even grown children may owe some obedience, although this seems to be thought by Locke to be part of the duty of honor (correlating with parents' right of honor), rather than being a simple extension of the young child's duty of obedience (II, 68). The duty of honor, then, is owed by grown children to their parents, and is a "perpetual obligation . . . containing in it an inward esteem and reverence to be shown by all outward expressions" (II, 66). It is a duty to "honor and support" one's parents (II, 68) in the ways just specified.[42]

---

[39] To call a right "imprescriptible" is to say that it may not be simply taken away from the rightholder by some other party. See my "Inalienable Rights," 178–79.

[40] In I,100, Locke first says this right can be forfeited "to some degrees" and later that "much" of the right can be forfeited. In II, 65, Locke suggests the stronger view that forfeiture of parental power can be total.

[41] Again, Locke is unclear about how *much* of the right of honor may be alienated. In I, 65, he doubts that the father "can alien *wholly* the right of honor that is due" (my emphasis); in I,100, however, the father can "transfer none of it," making the right of honor in principle inalienable. I criticize this argument for inalienability in "Inalienable Rights," 186–87.

[42] There is one peculiar suggestion in Locke that these filial debts are paid (in large part) "by taking care and providing for [one's] own children" (I,90). The idea that a debt owed by A (the child) to B (the parent) could be paid by rendering services to C (the grandchild) makes no sense at all, unless there is a clear understanding or agreement between A and B that this shall be an appropriate manner of paying the debt. Nonetheless, this odd suggestion is repeated by Olafson in "Rights and Duties." Olafson's claims are criticized in Melden, "Olafson," and in Schrag. "Children: Their Rights and Needs."

What, then, are the grounds (source) of these parental rights and filial duties? By examining Locke's arguments for his claims, we will be led, I think, to make certain changes in the contents (scope) of the rights and duties just described. At times, of course, it appears that Locke wants to ground parental rights simply in the biological relation of parents to children (blood, as they say, is thicker than water). He refers to the ground of these rights as "nature" (e.g., II, 173) and calls their basis "the right of generation" (II, 52) or the "right of fatherhood" (I, 64); and the *First Treatise* is filled with apparent agreements with Filmer that mere "begetting" is sufficient to ground parental rights (e.g., I, 63, 74, 98, 101, 111). It is tempting here to compare the rights of parents over their children to the self-evident "right of creation" enjoyed by God over His creatures (discussed above in 1.2), and Locke did occasionally suggest this comparison.[43] But, of course, parents do not *own* their children in the way God owns His creatures (as Locke argued at length against Filmer's, and, e.g., Aristotle's, contrary claims[44]), and in the strict sense they do not *create* their children at all (and so cannot have a "right of creation" over them). Parents lack the knowledge and skills necessary for the creation of so remarkable and mysterious a creature as a child. Only God possesses these, and only God can be credited as the maker or creator of children (I, 52–54). Parents are only "the occasions of life to their children" (II, 66; I, 54). They are *pro*creators, not creators, only deputies and trustees for a higher authority. Their rights must thus be explained differently from God's (supposing that God's are even capable of explanation).

Locke's considered opinion seems to be this. Parental rights (at least for the most part) do not derive from mere begetting or biological relation at all (II, 65). They must be earned by the provision of care and support to the child. The one kind of right that mere begetting does in part ground is that portion of the right of tuition that I called earlier the right of "first try." Natural parents have first claim on rearing their own children, a claim held against the world as a whole. Other parental rights belong only to those who actually pursue parenting (i.e., those who do not abandon, give away, or abuse their children). The distinction between the two basic (classes of) parental rights with regard to their grounds is simple: the right of tuition derives from parents' duty to care for their children (II, 58, 67) and the correlative rights to care that these children possess (II, 63, 67, 78; I, 89–90); the

---

[43] See Colman, *Moral Philosophy*, 45–46.

[44] For a contemporary version of the parental ownership thesis, see Rothbard, *The Ethics of Liberty*, 99.

right of honor, by contrast, is grounded in the provision of benefits by parents to children, and is a right to a return that is proportionate to the extent of these benefits (II, 65, 67, 70; I, 100).

## CRITICAL THINKING QUESTIONS

1. How does Locke define the family, and what rights does Locke believe are fundamental for the family?
2. Where do you disagree with Locke's proposal on family rights?
3. Write and analyze a case involving the obtaining of important rights within a society.

### DAVID POPENOE

# WHAT IS FAMILY DECLINE?

*David Popenoe is a professor of sociology at Rutgers, The State University of New Jersey. A Fulbright scholar, Popenoe is a specialist in comparative sociology of communities. He has authored and edited six books and numerous articles. In this 1988 work,* Disturbing the Nest: Family Change and Decline in Modern Societies, *Popenoe discusses different theories on the decline of the "nuclear" or traditional family.*

"Few popular ideas are more widespread than the belief that the importance of the family in human affairs has been weakening, that the family as an institution is under great strain. . . ."[1] So said sociologist Alex Inkeles, echoing a familiar and probably accurate perception. This postulation of a decline in the institution of the family is buttressed by compelling evidence that the family in advanced societies has undergone greater change, and at a faster rate, in the past several decades than in any previous period of similar length in human history, except after some major catastrophes.

A belief in the reality of family decline, however, is by no means widespread among sociologists of the family, the experts who presumably have the facts. Inkeles goes on to state, for example, that "one cannot make a convincing case that in modern society the family has suffered a substantial decline in its human importance relative to the other institutions and relations in which individuals invest their emotions, their loyalties, and their time."[2] Many sociologists have put this no-family-decline view in stronger terms. Glen Elder referred to the idea of family decline as "a fictional image of family change that had managed to survive from the 1920's."[3] In a recent pathbreaking family textbook Randall Collins concludes that "although it lives with strains, nevertheless the family seems to be in better shape than ever."[4] Theodore Caplow, discussing family change in "Middletown, U.S.A.," asserted in a chapter entitled "The Myth of the Declining Family": "Insofar as changes in the institution can be measured, they seem to reflect a strengthening of the institutional form."[5]

Labeling the idea a myth has become one of the most common devices adopted by sociologists who appear to be vigorously engaged in a battle against the idea of family decline. Thus a widely read book on the family decries the fact that "the myth of the decaying American family is often publicly used to bolster arguments for legislative action."[6] A book of marriage and the family readings for undergraduates has sections on "the marriage-breakdown myth" and "the family-breakdown myth."[7]

The sociological thesis that the family is not in decline is of relatively recent origin, and has been put forth with intensity only in the last few decades. Family decline is one of the oldest ideas in the social sciences, having been promulgated in one form or another by many of the prominent sociologists of the past. Contradictions between the views of today's sociologists and those of the past, and between sociological and popular opinion, give rise to some interesting questions. . . . What has happened to modify the perspective of sociologists? Has newly uncovered evidence shown the sociologists of the past, as well as the general public, to have been wrong in their views? Have recent family events required a reshaping of sociological opinion?

A central problem in discussing family decline is confusion over the meaning of the idea. Few in the current debate ever take the trouble to define exactly what they mean by either family or decline. It is important, therefore, to begin with an attempt to develop conceptual clarification in this area. I admit to some trepidation at starting a book with sociological definitions, and running the risk of providing more grounds for the common criticism of sociology that "it tells us in bad English things we already know." My fears are overridden, however, by the knowledge that definitions are fundamental in giving clarity and significance to ideas; and by the realization that for a topic such as the family, which is so embedded in our personal experiences, extra efforts must be made to refine meanings if we are to rise above those experiences into the realm of objective analysis.

"Family" and "decline" have multiple meanings, and trying to define "the family" has long posed a difficult task; scholars have never been able to agree on a single definition. My goal, however, is not to provide a scholarly arbitration of definitional problems. It is, rather, to explore the common sociological meanings of "family" by examining the components of definitions, and to put forth the definitions of family and decline that guide the analysis of family change in this book.

## DEFINING THE FAMILY

The term "family", simple and straightforward though it may seem, refers to a complex social reality. In the dictionary I use, 15 definitions are listed. Certain meanings of the family are better suited for some purposes than for others, and the definition one selects has serious implications for scholarly analysis. Take, for example, the definition of the family used by The U.S. Bureau of the Census: "two or more persons living together and related by blood, marriage or adoption." This is useful for the collection and aggregation of census data, but it presents problems for the type of analysis of the family presented here. Among other things, it seems to rule out all families in which the adults are "cohabiting outside of marriage." Moreover, it includes two or more adult brothers or sisters living together, a group not normally thought of as a family. Another definition of family, one gaining currency, is "anyone living in a household." By this definition the family manifestly has not declined, for there are more households per capita today than ever before.

As is the case with other complex concepts, no single set of features can define all families at all times in all places. There is one approach that helps in developing a definition of the family suitable for sociological analysis. A prototype set of features that is recognized widely as making up a "true" family is put forth. The more of these features that are taken away, the less likely it is that one is talking about a family. At some point, when enough features are taken away, a unit may no longer be considered a family.

But the point at which something ceases to be a family is a matter of controversy. So, too, is the original prototype. The prototype family most commonly used today is "a married couple who live together with their children." With this prototype, much of the debate about defining the family revolves around the question of whether one still has a family if (to cite some examples) one half of the couple is taken away, the couple is not married, the children are removed, or some members do not live together. Because so many actual families today are not married couples who live together with their children, a number of social scientists no longer consider this prototype to be very useful.

Another prototypical family used in scholarly analyses, one more suitable for our purposes, is as follows: The family is a relatively small domestic group consisting of at least one adult and one person dependent on that adult. Thus the family is defined, first, as a domestic group (a group of people who live together and perform domestic activities), to distinguish it from other groups that may carry out some of the family's traditional functions. Second, the family is a group that includes dependent persons, usually children, to distinguish it from merely an "intimate relationship" between two adults (whether married or not).

The family as a domestic group must also be differentiated (although there is often great overlap) from the broader kinship group that is typically concerned not with domestic activities, but with the structuring of kinship relations. A problem here is that the English term "family" is typically used to refer both to the domestic and to the kin group. In a common definition that combines the ideas of kinship and domestic group, the family is "a group of kin (or people in a kinlike relationship) who live together and function as a cooperative unit."

Note that such terms as "domestic activities" and "function as a cooperative unit" refer to what a family does, not what it is. This, too, is a necessary part of a family definition for purposes of scholarly analysis. To look at a family with regard to what it does is to see it as a social institution. In sociological terms, a social institution is a relatively stable cluster of social structures (roles and norms) organized to meet some basic needs of a society. Such a meaning denotes a cultural frame of reference (roles and norms) and emphasizes that lynchpin of functionalism—a society's "basic needs."[8]

Social scientists generally agree that the basic needs the family as an institution is intended to meet (functions or activities of the family) are as follows: the procreation (reproduction) and socialization of children; the provision to its members of care, affection, and companionship; sexual regulation (so that sexual activity in a society is not completely permissive and people are made responsible for the consequences of their sexuality); and economic cooperation (the sharing of economic resources, especially shelter, food, and clothing). Other minor activities could be added, but these are the main social functions performed by families for advanced societies. These functions, then, should constitute another important part of a definition of the family.

Combining these definitional pieces, one comes up with a general, albeit cumbersome, definition of the prototypical family: a relatively small domestic group of kin (or people in a kinlike relationship) consisting of at least one adult and one dependent person, the adult (or adults) being charged by society with carrying out (although not necessarily exclusively) the social functions of procreation and socialization of children; provision of care, affection, and companionship; sexual regulation; and economic cooperation. A "domestic group" is one in which people typically live together in a household and function as a cooperative unit in the pursuit of domestic activities, particularly by sharing economic resources. The term "socialization" is intended to include the upbringing, economic support, and regulation of the conduct of dependent children. Finally, "kin" refers to people "related" through blood, marriage, adoption, or their equivalents (including informal pledges and vows). This definition signifies the family not just as a type of social group but as a social institution. To speak of the social institution of the family, or more simply the family, is to refer collectively to all such domestic groups in a society and the functions they are intended to perform.

This meaning of family still poses many problems, but I am not going to bore you with a long definition when I have already done so with a shorter one. As a prototype, this definition cannot cover all family situations. There will be those who object to the inclusion of dependents, wishing the term "family" to have a wider application. For academic studies like this one, however, it is important to distinguish mere "intimate relationships between adults," no matter how permanent, from the group that results when children are present. Both psychologically and institutionally the group with children is significantly different.[9] Others may point out that the definition makes no reference to the fact that a family does not dissolve merely because the children grow up and leave home, usually setting up their own families. This life-course shift is typically dealt with by distinguishing between the family of orientation (or origin), and the family of procreation (or marriage).

Still others may object that the definition focuses on a discrete domestic group. They may argue that parents need not be living together (coresiding) to form a family unit. For example, divorce and separation need not mean family dissolution, but merely marital dissolution; the family remains, though geographically split into several households. Furthermore, a family split by divorce may be no different from the family, for example, of a traveling salesperson who is frequently away from home.

In addition, the definition is tied to particular conditions in modern societies; it has aspects that make it less useful or cross-cultural anthropological studies. It focuses on the separate household, for example, which is not appropriate for families in highly extended family systems where households may be large, complex, and comprised of many different kin groupings. Also, the idea that the nuclear family's basic function is to provide its members with affection and companionship is foreign to most nonmodern societies; even in advanced societies it is a relatively recent historical development.

Our definition, however, does not mean by family merely the traditional nuclear family, as do some other definitions. It allows for considerable structural variation and flexibility, with only the basic social functions and the presence in a domestic group of at least one adult and one child (or other dependent) necessarily held constant.

## THE MEANING OF FAMILY DECLINE

For purposes of social analysis one cannot be very happy with the term "decline." Like "family," it is an imprecise and ambiguous word with multiple meanings. This becomes clear immediately when one poses an antonym to "decline." In my analysis "decline" is used with the common meaning of "getting weaker"; its opposite is "getting stronger." Thus if the family is not declining, it is either getting stronger or remaining unchanged. Others consider the opposite of "decline" to be "advance" or "progress."[10] With this meaning, family decline involves not just weakening but the much more general "regress." This meaning is to be avoided in social scientific analysis, in my judgment, because weakening is a measurable concept while regress (and progress) are to a much larger degree complex value judgments.

As noted above, it has become faddish for sociologists to attack the belief (using the words of one family sociology text) "that the family is 'breaking down,' 'falling apart,' 'declining,' 'disintegrating,' 'disappearing,' 'besieged,' or . . . 'in trouble,'" as if all of these words meant approximately the same thing.[11] Yet the difference between "decline" and "disappear" is enormous. The issue that is the proper focus of attention is one of tendencies, not of extremes. Declining or weakening, or what Victor Fuchs has called "fading,"[12] does not necessarily mean "falling apart" or "disappearing." To be sure, one *result* of something declining or weakening could be eventual breakup or disappearance; but other possibilities are stabilization at the weaker level and eventual reorganization with renewed strength.

Using "decline" to mean "weakening" and defining the family as indicated above, the concept of family decline in this book refers to the weakening of domestic groups in a society—the groups of kin who live together and function as cooperative units in the performance of their functions. This perspective, I believe, is little different from that held by the great majority of people when they discuss family trends. The principal focus is: what is happening to and within the home, why is it happening, and with what effects? Because the family is a social institution, one can also speak of the "deinstitutionalization" of the family, and that rather unpleasant term will be used occasionally as a synonym for family decline.

## FAMILY DECLINE IN ADVANCED SOCIETIES: AN OVERVIEW

How does the concept of family decline apply to contemporary family change? The institution of the family in advanced societies is weakening, as I document in this book, in five main ways.

1. Family groups are becoming internally deinstitutionalized, that is, their individual members are more autonomous and less bound by the group and the domestic group as a whole is less cohesive. In a highly institutionalized group or organization there is a strong coordination of internal relationships and the directing of group activities toward collective goals.[13] Families, I shall argue, are becoming less institutionalized in this sense. Examples of this are the decline of economic interdependence between husband and wife and the weakening of parental authority over children.

2. The family is weakening in carrying out many of its traditional social functions. With a birthrate that is below the replacement level, this is demonstrably true for the function of procreation. It seems true as well, given the amount of premarital and extramarital sexuality, for the control of sexual behavior. I shall maintain, in addition, that the family is weakening in its functions of socializing children and providing care for its members.

3. The family as an institution is losing power to other institutional groups in society. Examples of this are the decline of nepotism in political and economic life, the rise of mandatory public schooling, and conflicts between the family and the state, in which the state increasingly wins.

4. The family is weakening in the sense that individual family groups are decreasing in size and becoming more unstable, with a shorter life span, and people are members of such groups for a smaller percentage of their life course.

5. Finally, family decline is occurring in the sense that familism as a cultural value is weakening in favor of such values as self-fulfillment and egalitarianism.

Each of these dimensions of family decline or family deinstitutionaliza-tion, I shall suggest, is clearly expressed through the trend in advanced soci-eties for people to invest a decreasing amount of their time, money, and en-ergy in family life and to turn more and more to other groups and activities.

It is important at the outset to put forth some caveats about what I shall not be asserting. I shall not assert that family decline is necessarily "bad." It may well be that many aspects of family decline are "good," for the individ-ual, for society, or for both. To think of family decline only in the negative makes no more sense than to think only negatively about the decline of feu-dalism, hereditary monarchies, or dictatorships.

Perhaps societies today need the family less than they once did. Perhaps other institutions are now more capable than the family of performing tra-ditional family functions. The fact that an institution has declined or weak-ened does not necessarily imply that its traditional functions are no longer being performed or are being performed in an inadequate manner. (Nor does it mean, of course, that *all* individual institutional units are weaken-ing in carrying out their functions.) Rather, it may be that these traditional functions are being performed by other institutions to which, at least in part, they have been transferred (the sociological issue of "functional alter-natives"). Thus child care may be provided more adequately today, even though it is conducted less by the family than in previous generations. The questions of transfer and adequacy must remain open in any discussion of institutional decline and be subject to close empirical scrutiny.

I shall also not assert that the general life conditions of individuals liv-ing in (or outside) declining family groups are necessarily getting worse. Despite family decline, so many things have improved in life, such as health and economic security, than most people living today in advanced societies may indeed be happier or more satisfied than ever before (at least this is what people tell survey researchers). Children, even if parents could be shown to be increasingly "neglectful," might still be "better off" because of improved schools, day-care centers, therapists, and medical care. Life is a series of tradeoffs, and it could well be that any negative effects of family decline on individuals are more than offset by positive effects. Such issues need to be explored theoretically and empirically, not taken for granted.

Despite these caveats, I take issues with those contemporary sociologists and other social scientists who find little in modern family trends about which to be concerned. Family decline, in my view, is not only real, but also has an impact, especially on children and thereby on future generations, that should be of concern to the citizens of every modern nation. Yet if the moral and social judgments of sociologists can lay claim to any special legitimacy, it can only emanate from a refined knowledge of empirical reality.

## NOTES

[1]Alex Inkeles (1980), "Modernization and Family Patterns: A Test of Convergence Theory," pp. 31–63 in Dwight W. Hoover and John T. A. Koumoulides (eds.), *Conspectus of History I-IV: Family History:* 48–49.

[2]Ibid.

[3]Glen H. Elder, Jr. (1978), "Approaches to Social Change and the Family," pp. 1–38 in John Demos and Sarane S. Boocock (eds.), *Turning Points: Historical and Sociological Essays on the Family:* 9.

[4]Randall Collins (1985), *Sociology of Marriage and the Family:* 475.

[5]Theodore Caplow, Howard M. Bahr, Bruce A. Chadwick, Reuben Hill, and Margaret Holmes Williamson (1983), *Middletown Families:* 327.

[6]Mary Jo Bane (1976), *Here to Stay: American Families in the Twentieth Century:* 69.

[7]John F Crosby (1985), *Reply to Myth: Perspectives on Intimacy.*

[8]It might be noted here that using a functionalist definition is not the same as using a functional analysis.

[9]There have long been attempts by sociologists and others to confuse the family and marriage by maintaining that they are essentially the same thing, or to reduce the one to the other. See Christopher Lasch (1977), *Haven in a Heartless World:* Chapter 2 and pp. 137–39. Recently, we can see this confusion in the heading "Family and Intimate Lifestyles" to cover family books in sociology's leading book-review journal *Contemporary Sociology* (the heading was introduced in the 1970s and lasted until March 1984) and in books that discuss under the heading "alternatives to the family" such "alternative life-styles" as homosexuality and remaining single. These, of course, are alternatives not to the family, but to marriage.

[10] For example, Bane (1976), *Here to Stay:* 3.

[11]Arlene S. Skolnick and Jerome H. Skolnick (1986), *Family in Transition:* 2–3.

[12]Victor R. Fuchs (1983), *How We Live.*

[13]Marvin E. Olsen (1968), *The Process of Social Organization:* 82.

## CRITICAL THINKING QUESTIONS

1. How does Popenoe defend his position on family decline? Do you agree with his theory on decline?

2. Examine how failures in communication, particularly interpersonal communication, have brought about family decline in America. Give an example from your own experience.

3. Write and analyze a case involving a specific area of family decline. Suggest whether the decline is appropriate or if it should be corrected.

SUSAN MOLLER OKIN

# Marriage and the Unjust Treatment of Women

*Susan Moller Okin is a professor of political science at Stanford University. She has written extensively on political theory, feminist theory-history, and philosophy. In this excerpt from the 1989 work,* Justice Gender and the Family, *Okin discusses the notion of marriage protecting or allowing the mistreatment of women.*

## CONCLUSION: TOWARD A HUMANIST JUSTICE

. . . Marriage has become an increasingly peculiar contract, a complex and ambiguous combination of anachronism and present-day reality. There is no longer the kind of agreement that once prevailed about what is expected of the parties to a marriage. Clearly, at least in the United States, it is no longer reasonable to assume that marriage will last a lifetime, since only half of current marriages are expected to. And yet, in spite of the increasing legal equality of men and women and the highly publicized figures about married women's increased participation in the labor force, many couples continue to adhere to more or less traditional patterns of role differentiation. As a recent article put it, women are "out of the house but not out of the kitchen."[2] Consequently, often working part-time or taking time out from wage work to care for family members, especially children, most wives are in a very different position from their husbands in their ability to be economically self-supporting. This is reflected, as we have seen, in power differentials between the sexes within the family. It means also, in the increasingly common event of divorce, usually by mutual agreement, that it is the mother who in 90 percent of cases will have physical custody of the children. But whereas the greater need for money goes one way, the bulk of the earning power almost always goes the other. This is one of the most important causes of the feminization of poverty, which is affecting the life chances of ever larger numbers of children as well as their mothers. The division of labor within families has always adversely affected women, by making them economically dependent on men. Because of the increasing instability of marriage, its effects on children have now reached crisis proportions.

Some who are critical of the present structure and practices of marriage have suggested that men and women simply be made free to make their own agreements about family life, contracting with each other, much as business contracts are made.[3] But this takes insufficient account of the history of gender in our culture and our own psychologies, of the present substantive inequalities between the sexes, and, most important, of the well-being of the children who result from the relationship. As has long been recognized in the realm of labor relations, justice is by no means always enhanced by the maximization of freedom of contract, if the individuals involved are in unequal positions to start with. Some have even suggested that it is consistent with justice to leave spouses to work out their own divorce settlement.[4] By this time, however, the two people ending a marriage are likely to be far *more* unequal. Such a practice would be even more catastrophic for most women and children than is the present system. Wives in any but the rare cases in which they as individuals have remained their husbands' socioeconomic equals could hardly be expected to reach a just solution if left "free" to "bargain" the terms of financial support or child custody. What would they have to bargain *with*?

There are many directions that public policy can and should take in order to make relations between men and women more just. In discussing these, I shall look back to some of the contemporary ways of thinking about justice that I find most convincing. I draw particularly on Rawls's idea of the original position and Walzer's conception of the complex equality found in separate spheres of justice, between which I find no inconsistency. I also keep in mind critical legal theorists' critique of contract, and the related idea, suggested earlier, that rights to privacy that are to be valuable to all of us can be enjoyed only insofar as the sphere of life in which we enjoy them ensures the equality of its adult members and protects children. Let us begin by asking what kind of arrangements persons in a Rawlsian original position would agree to regarding marriage, parental and other domestic responsibilities, and divorce. What kinds of policies would they agree to for other aspects of social life, such as the workplace and schools, that affect men, women, and children and relations among them? And let us consider whether these arrangements would satisfy Walzer's separate spheres test—that inequalities in one sphere of life not be allowed to overflow into another. Will they foster equality within the sphere of family

life? For the protection of the privacy of a domestic sphere in which inequality exists is the protection of the right of the strong to exploit and
abuse the weak.

Let us first try to imagine ourselves, as far as possible, in the original position, knowing neither what our sex nor any other of our personal characteristics will be once the veil of ignorance is lifted.* Neither do we know our
place in society or our particular conception of the good life. Particularly
relevant in this context, of course, is our lack of knowledge of our beliefs
about the characteristics of men and women and our related convictions
about the appropriate division of labor between the sexes. Thus the positions we represent must include a wide variety of beliefs on these matters.
We may, once the veil of ignorance is lifted, find ourselves feminist men or
feminist women whose conception of the good life includes the minimiza-
tion of social differentiation between the sexes. Or we may find ourselves
traditionalist men or women, whose conception of the good life, for religious or other reasons, is bound up in an adherence to the conventional division of labor between the sexes. The challenge is to arrive at and apply
principles of justice having to do with the family and the division of labor
between the sexes that can satisfy these vastly disparate points of view and
the many that fall between.

There are some traditionalist positions so extreme that they ought not be
admitted for consideration, since they violate such fundamentals as equal
basic liberty and self-respect. We need not, and should not, that is to say, admit for consideration views based on the notion that women are inherently
inferior beings whose function is to fulfill the needs of men. Such a view is
no more admissible in the construction of just institutions for a modern
pluralist society than is the view, however deeply held, that some are naturally slaves and others naturally and justifiably their masters. We need not,
therefore, consider approaches to marriage that view it as an inherently and
desirably hierarchical structure of dominance and subordination. Even if it
were conceivable that a person who did not know whether he or she would
turn out to be a man or a woman in the society being planned would sub-

---

*I say "so far as possible" because of the difficulties already pointed out in chapter 5. Given the
deep effects of gender on our psychologies, it is probably more difficult for us, having grown
up in a gender-structured society, to imagine not knowing our sex than anything else about
ourselves. Nevertheless, this should not prevent us from trying.

scribe to such views, they are not admissible. Even if there were no other reasons to refuse to admit such views, they must be excluded for the sake of children, for everyone in the original position has a high personal stake in the quality of childhood. Marriages of dominance and submission are bad for children as well as for their mothers, and the socioeconomic outcome of divorce after such a marriage is very likely to damage their lives and seriously restrict their opportunities.

With this proviso, what social structures and public policies regarding relations between the sexes, and the family in particular, could we agree on in the original position? I think we would arrive at a basic model that would absolutely minimize gender. I shall first give an account of some of what this would consist in. We would also, however, build in carefully protective institutions for those who wished to follow gender-structured modes of life. These too I shall try to spell out in some detail.

## NOTES

1. See chap. 3, pp. 67–68.
2. "Women: Out of the House But Not Out of the Kitchen," *New York Times,* February 24, 1984, pp, A1, C10.
3. See, for example, Marjorie Maguire Schultz, "Contractual Ordering of Marriage: A New Mood for State Policy," *California Law Review* 70, no. 2 (1982); Lenore Weitzman, *The Marriage Contract Spouses, Lovers, and the Law* (New York: The Free Press, 1981), parts 3–4.
4. See, for example, David L. Kirp, Mark G. Yudof, and Marlene Strong Franks, *Gender Justice* (Chicago: University of Chicago Press, 1986), pp. 183-85. Robert H. Mnookin takes an only slightly less laissez-faire approach, in "Divorce Bargaining: The Limits on Private Ordering," *University of Michigan Journal of Law Reform* 18, no. 4 (1985).

## CRITICAL THINKING QUESTIONS

1. Do you agree or disagree with Okin that women are mistreated in society because of marriage? Explain.
2. What are some of the traditional roots of unjust treatment of women? How does interpersonal communication play a role in this?
3. Write and analyze a case defending a system of equality for the entire family.

SHULAMITH FIRESTONE

# The Ultimate Revolution

*Shulamith Firestone is a founder of Redstockings, a radical feminist group in New York. In addition to* The Dialectic of Sex, *she is the author of other numerous writings. In this excerpt from the 1970 work,* The Dialectic of Sex, *Firestone explains the variety of unethical treatments that occur in the name of love or love relationships.*

Many social scientists are now proposing as a solution to the population problem the encouragement of "deviant life styles" that by definition imply nonfertility. Richard Meier suggests that glamorous single professions previously assigned only to men should now be opened to women as well, for example, "astronaut." He notes that where these occupations exist for women, e.g., stewardess, they are based on the sex appeal of a young woman, and thus can be only limited way stations on the way to a better job or marriage. And, he adds, "so many limitations are imposed [on women's work outside the home] . . . that one suspects the existence of a culture-wide conspiracy which makes the occupational role sufficiently unpleasant that 90 percent or more would choose homemaking as a superior alternative." With the extension of whatever single roles still exist in our culture to include women, the creation of more such roles, and a program of incentives to make these professions rewarding, we could, painlessly, reduce the number of people interested in parenthood at all.

*"Living Together."* Practiced at first only in Bohemian or intellectual circles and now increasingly in the population at large—especially by metropolitan youth—"living together" is becoming a common social practice. "Living together" is the loose social form in which two or more partners, of whatever sex, enter a nonlegal sex/companionate arrangement the duration of which varies with the internal dynamics of the relationship. Their contract is only with each other; society has no interest, since neither reproduction nor production—dependencies of one party on the other—is involved. This flexible non-form could be expanded to become the standard unit in which most people would live for most of their lives.

At first, in the transitional period, sexual relationships would probably be monogamous (single standard, female-style, this time around), even if the couple chose to live with others. We might even see the continuation of strictly nonsexual group living arrangements ("roommates"). However, after several generations of nonfamily living, our psychosexual structures may become altered so radically that the monogamous couple, or the "aim-inhibited" relationship, would become obsolescent. We can only guess what might replace it—perhaps true "group marriages," transexual group marriages which also involved older children? We don't know.

The two options we have suggested so far—single professions and "living together"—already exist, but only outside the mainstream of our society, or for brief periods in the life of the normal individual. We want to *broaden* these options to include many more people for longer periods of their lives, to transfer here instead all the cultural incentives now supporting marriage—making these alternatives, finally, as common and acceptable as marriage is today.

But what about children? Doesn't everyone want children sometime in their lives? There is no denying that people now feel a genuine desire to have children. But we don't know how much of this is the product of an authentic liking for children, and how much is a displacement of other needs. We have seen that parental satisfaction is obtainable only through crippling the child: The attempted extension of ego through one's children—in the case of the man, the "immortalizing" of name, property, class, and ethnic identification, and in the case of the woman, motherhood as the justification of her existence, the resulting attempt to live through the child, child-as-project—in the end damages or destroys either the child or the parent, or both when neither wins, as the case may be. Perhaps when we strip parenthood of these other functions, we will find a real instinct for parenthood even on the part of men, a simple physical desire to associate with the young. But then we have lost nothing, for a basic demand of our alternative system is some form of intimate interaction with children. If a parenthood instinct does in fact exist, it will be allowed to operate even more freely, having shed the practical burdens of parenthood that now make it such an anguished hell.

But what, on the other hand, if we find that there is no parenthood instinct after all? Perhaps all this time society has persuaded the individual to have children only by imposing on parenthood ego concerns that had no proper outlet. This may have been unavoidable in the past—but perhaps it's now time to start more directly satisfying those ego needs. As long as natural reproduction is still necessary, we can devise less destructive cultural inducements. But it is likely that, once the ego investments in parenthood are removed, artificial reproduction will be developed and widely accepted.

*Households.* I shall now outline a system that I believe will satisfy any remaining needs for children after ego concerns are no longer part of our motivations. Suppose a person or a couple at some point in their lives desires to live around children in a family-size unit. While we will no longer have reproduction as the life goal of the normal individual—we have seen how single and group nonreproductive life styles could be enlarged to become satisfactory for many people for their whole lifetimes and for others, for good portions of their lifetime—certain people may still prefer community-style group living permanently, and other people may want to experience it at some time in their lives, especially during early childhood.

Thus at any given time a proportion of the population will want to live in reproductive social structures. Correspondingly, the society in general will still need reproduction, though reduced, if only to create a new generation.

The proportion of the population will be automatically a select group with a predictably higher rate of stability, because they will have had a freedom of choice now generally unavailable. Today those who do not marry and have children by a certain age are penalized: they find themselves alone, excluded, and miserable, on the margins of a society in which everyone else is compartmentalized into lifetime generational families, chauvinism and exclusiveness their chief characteristic. (Only in Manhattan is single living even tolerable, and that can be debated.) Most people are still forced into marriage by family pressure, the "shotgun," economic considerations, and other reasons that have nothing to do with choice of life style. In our new reproductive unit, however, with the limited contract (see below), childrearing so diffused as to be practically eliminated, economic considerations nonexistent, and all participating members having entered only on the basis of personal preference, "unstable" reproductive social structures will have disappeared.

This unit I shall call a *household* rather than an extended family. The distinction is important: The word *family* implies biological reproduction and some degree of division of labor by sex, and thus the traditional dependencies and resulting power relations, extended over generations; though the size of the family—in this case, the larger numbers of the "extended" family—may affect the strength of this hierarchy, it does not change its structural definition. "Household," however, connotes only a large grouping of people living together for an unspecified time, and with no specified set of interpersonal relations. How would a "household" operate?

*Limited Contract.* If the household replaced marriage perhaps we would at first legalize it in the same way—if this is necessary at all. A group of ten or so consenting adults of varying ages* could apply for a license as a group in much the same way as a young couple today applies for a marriage license, perhaps even undergoing some form of ritual ceremony, and then might proceed in the same way to set up house. The household license would, however, apply only for a given period, perhaps seven to ten years, or whatever was decided on as the minimal time in which children needed a stable structure in which to grow up—but probably a much shorter period than we now imagine. If at the end of this period the group decided to stay together, it could always get a renewal. However, no single individual would be contracted to stay after this period, and perhaps some members of the unit might transfer out, or new members come in. Or, the unit could disband altogether.

There are many advantages to short-term households, stable compositional units lasting for only ten-year periods: the end of family chauvinism, built up over generations, of prejudices passed down from one generation to the next, the inclusion of people of all ages in the childrearing process, the integration of many age groups into one social unit, the breadth of personality that comes from exposure to many rather than to (the idiosyncrasies of) a few, and so on.

*Children.* A regulated percentage of each household—say one-third—would be children. But whether, at first, genetic children created by couples within the household, or at some future time—after a few generations of household living had severed the special connection of adults with "their" children—children were produced artificially, or adopted, would not matter: (minimal) responsibility for the early physical dependence of children would be evenly diffused among all members of the household.

But though it would still be structurally sound, we must be aware that as long as we use natural childbirth methods, the "household" could never be a totally liberating social form. A mother who undergoes a nine-month pregnancy is likely to feel that the product of all that pain and discomfort "belongs" to her ("To think of what I went through to have you!"). But we want to destroy this possessiveness along with its cultural reinforcements so that no one child will be *a priori* favored over another, so that children will be loved for their own sake. . . .

---

*An added advantage of the household is that it allows older people past their fertile years to share fully in parenthood when they so desire.

*Legal Rights and Transfers.* With the weakening and severance of the blood ties, the power hierarchy of the family would break down. The legal structure—as long as it is still necessary—would reflect this democracy at the roots of our society. Women would be identical under the law with men. Children would no longer be "minors," under the patronage of "parents"— they would have full rights. Remaining physical inequalities could be legally compensated for: for example, if a child were beaten, perhaps he could report it to a special simplified "household" court where he would be granted instant legal redress.

Another special right of children would be the right of immediate transfer: if the child for any reason did not like the household into which he had been born so arbitrarily he would be helped to transfer out. An adult on the other hand—one who had lived one span in a household (seven to ten years)—might have to present his case to the court, which would then decide, as do divorce courts today whether he had adequate grounds for breaking his contract. A certain number of transfers within the seven-year period might be necessary for the smooth functioning of the household, and would not be injurious to its stability as a unit so long as a core remained. (In fact, new people now and then might be a refreshing change.) However, the unit, for its own best economy, might have to place a ceiling on the number of transfers in or out, to avoid depletion, excessive growth, and/or friction.

## CRITICAL THINKING QUESTIONS

1. According to Firestone love is used to oppress and subjugate women. Do you agree or disagree? Explain.
2. Do you agree that some women are better off not marrying because of the social constructions that define women? What benefits are there for women who decide not to marry? What might a woman lose by deciding not to get married? Consider legal, financial, health, and interpersonal perspectives.
3. Write and analyze a case in which love was used to oppress and silence women.

# CONTEMPORARY CASE

## *What Constitutes a Family? The Nanny's Dilemma*

While under the employ of a couple with two small children, a young lady, working as the couple's nanny, happened to overhear a conversation of the husband. It was very clear from the conversation that the husband was having an affair with another woman. The nanny held strong beliefs in the sanctity of marriage and was now facing a dilemma.

1. Are there any moral absolutes involved in this dilemma?
2. What are the long-term consequences involved? What is the "greatest good for the greatest number"?
3. Is the conscience of the nanny important in this case? Explain her options and suggested course of behavior.
4. What communication might be helpful in the interpersonal relationships?
5. Explain problems with nonverbal communication in this case.

# BIBLIOGRAPHY

Anderson, J., & Englehardt, E. (2001). *The organizational self and ethical conduct: sunlit virtue and shadowed resistance* (thoughts from Chapter 4). Los Angeles: Harcourt Brace.

Angelou, M. (1969). Mama and the dentist. In *I know why the caged bird sings* (pp. 180–189) New York: Random House.

Baier, A. (1986). Trust and antitrust. *Ethics 96,* 231–260.

Bayles, M. D. (1975). Marriage, love and procreation. In R. Baker & F. Elliston (Eds.), *Philosophy and sex* (pp. 195–204, Notes: 204–206). Buffalo, NY: Prometheus.

Card, C. (1996). Against marriage and motherhood. *Hypatia II,* 3, 95–100, 103–109.

de Beauvoir, S. (1989). Myth and reality. In *The second sex* (pp. 153–157). New York: Vintage Books.

Dixon, M., & Duck, S. (1993). Understanding relationship processes: uncovering the human search for meaning. In S. Duck (Ed.), *Individuals in relationships* (pp. 175-181). Newbury Park, CA: Sage Publications.

Donagan, A. (1977). First order precepts. In *A theory of morality* (pp. 101–104). Chicago: University of Chicago Press.

Engels, F. (1975). *The origin of the family, private property and the state* (pp. 50, 54–57, 65–68). New York: International.

Epicurus (1926). Friendship. In *Epicurus, The extant remains* (Cyril Bailey, Trans). (pp. 114–117) Oxford, Clarendon Press.

Firestone, S. (1970). The ultimate revolution. In *The dialectic of sex* (pp. 258–265). New York: William Morrow and Company.

Fisher, H. (1992). Anatomy of love. In *Anatomy of love: the natural history of monogamy, adultery and divorce* (pp. 33–39). New York: Norton and Company.

Foucault, M. (1985). Aphrodisia. In *The use of pleasure* (Vol. 2) (pp. 40–45). *The history of sexuality.* (R. Hurley, Trans). New York: Vintage Books.

Fromm, E. (1947). Selfishness, self-love and self-interest. In *Man for himself: an inquiry into the psychology of ethics* (pp. 124–144). Greenwich, CN: Fawcett Publications.

Gergen, K. (1994). Moral action from a constructionist standpoint. In *Realities and relationships: soundings in social construction* (pp. 103–108). Cambridge, MA: Harvard University Press.

Gilligan, C. (1982). Images of relationship. In *In a different voice* (pp. 7–10, 16–19, 24–32). Cambridge, MA: Harvard University Press.

Herman, B. (1993). *The practice of moral judgment* (pp. 189–198). Cambridge, MA: Harvard University Press.

Jowett, B. (1937). A proposal to abolish the private family. In *Dialogues of Plato* (pp. 22–27). New York: Random House.

King, M. L., Jr. (1981). On being a good neighbor. In *Strength to love* (pp. 16–24). Minneapolis, MN: Augsburg Fortress.

MacKinnon, C. A. (1987). Sex and Violence. In *Feminism unmodified: discourses on life and law* (pp. 85–92). Boston: Harvard University Press.

Martin, M. (1993). Love's Constancy, *Philosophy 68,* 63–71.

McCollum, S. (1998). Can You Outlaw Hate? *Scholastic Update 131,* December 14, 1998, i7, 15.

McKeon, R. (1941). Answer to Plato. In *Aristotle's politics* (pp. 251–263). New York: Random House. Book II, Chap. 1,3.

Mill, J. S. (1897). Of individuality as one of the elements of well-being. In *Utilitarianism* (pp. 260–267). London: Longmans Green.

Millett, K. (1969). The sexual revolution. In *Sexual politics* (pp. 169–179). New York: Ballantine Books.

Noddings N. (1984). An ethics of care. In *Caring: A feminine approach to ethics and moral education* (pp. 81–85, 96–99, Notes: pp. 206–207). Berkeley: University of California Press.

Okin, S. M. (1989). Marriage and the unjust treatment of women. In *Justice gender and the family* (pp. 72–75). New York: Basic Books.

Popenoe, D. (1988). What is family decline? In *Disturbing the family nest, family change and decline in modern societies* (pp. 3–10). New York: Aldine de Gruyter.

Rawlins, W. K. (1992). Adult friendships. In *Friendship matters communication, dialectics and the life course* (pp. 157–167). New York: Aldine De Gruyter.

Russell, B. (1929). *Marriage and morals* (pp. 135–144). Garden City, NY: Horace Liveright, Inc.

Simmons, J. (1992). Rights and the family. In *The Lockean theory of rights* (pp. 170–175, 177–181). Princeton, NJ: Princeton University Press.

Solomon, R. C. (1988). The Virtue of (Erotic) Love. *Midwest studies in philosophy XIII: Ethical theory: Character and virtue* (pp. 12–16, 21, 26–28, 31). Edited by Peter A. French, Theodore E. Uehling, and Howard K. Wittstein. Notre Dame, IN: University of Notre Dame Press.

Tracy, L. (1991). Intimacy and judgment among sisters and friends. In *The secret between us: Competition among women* (pp. 220–231). Boston: Little, Brown and Company.

# ADDITIONAL SOURCES

Althusser, L. (1971). Ideology and the ideological state apparatuses (notes toward an investigation). In L. Althusser (Ed.), *Lenin and philosophy and other essays*. New York: Monthly Review Press.

Altman, I. (1981). *The environment and social behavior: Privacy, personal space, territory and crowding*. New York: Irvington.

Alvesson, M. (1993). The play of metaphors. In J. Hassard & M. Parker (Eds.), *Postmodernism and organizations* (pp. 114–131). Thousand Oaks, CA: Sage.

Alvesson, M. (1996). *Communication, power, and organization*. New York: de Gruyter.

Alvesson, M., & Deetz, S. (1996). Critical theory and postmodernism approaches to organizational studies. In S. R. Clegg, C. Hardy, & W. Nord (Eds.), *Handbook of organization studies* (pp. 191–217). London: Sage.

Anderson, J. A. (1996). *Communication theory: Epistemological foundations*. New York: Guilford.

Anderson, J. A., & Meyer, T. P. (1988). *Mediated communication: A social action perspective*. Newbury Park, CA: Sage.

Anderson, R. (1997). Women, welfare, and United States media. In C. G. Christians (Ed.), *Communications ethics and universal values* (pp. 300–326). Thousand Oaks, CA: Sage.

Apel, K-O. (1980). *Toward a transformation of philosophy* (G. Adley & D. Frisby, Trans.). London: Routledge & Kegan Paul.

Baier, A. (1985). *Postures of the mind*. Minneapolis: University of Minnesota Press.

Bakhtin, M. M. (1981). *The dialogic imagination*. M. Holquist (Ed.). C. Emerson & Holquist (Trans.). Austin: University of Texas Press.

Bakhtin, M. M. (1986). *Speech genres & other late essays*. C. Emerson & M. Holquist (Eds.). V. W. McGee (Trans.). Austin: University of Texas Press.

Bakhtin, M. M. (1990). *Art and answerability*. M. Holquist & B. Liapunov (Eds.). V. Liapunov (Trans.). Austin: University of Texas Press.

Banta, M. (1993). *Taylored lives*. Chicago: University of Chicago Press.

Bateson, G. (1958). *Naven*. Stanford, CA: Stanford University Press.

Bateson, G. (1972). *Steps to an ecology of mind*. New York: Ballantine Books.

Bateson, G. (1979). *Mind and nature: A necessary unity*. Toronto: Bantam Books.

Bellah, R. N., Madsen, R., Sullivan, W. M., Swindler, A., & Tipton, S. M. (1996). *Habits of the heart: Individualism and commitment in American life*. Berkeley: University of California Press.

Bender, J. W. (1989). Coherence, justification and knowledge: The current debate. In J. W. Bender (Ed.), *The current state of the coherence theory* (pp. 1–15). Dordrecht, The Netherlands: Kluwer Academic Publishers.

Benhabib, S. (1992). *Situating the self: Gender, community and postmodernism in contemporary ethics.* New York: Routledge.

Berger, P. L., & Luckmann, T. (1966). *The social construction of reality: the treatise in the sociology of knowledge.* New York: Doubleday.

Berman, A. (1994). *Preface to modernism.* Urbana: University of Illinois Press.

Bogue, R. (1989). *Deleuze and Guattari.* London: Routledge.

Bohm, D. (1994). *Thought as a system.* London: Routledge.

Bormann, E. G. (1982). Symbolic convergence: Organizational communication and culture. In L. L. Putnam & M. E. Pacanowsky (Eds.), *Communication and organizations: An interpretive approach* (pp. 99–122). Beverly Hills, CA: Sage.

Bourdieu, P. (1984). *Language and symbolic power.* Cambridge, MA: Harvard University Press.

Bridge, K., & Baxter, L. A. (1992). Blended Friendships: Friends and work associates. *Western Journal of Communication, 56,* 200–225.

Brockelman, P. (1985). *Time and self: Phenomenological explorations.* NY: Crossroad Publishing.

Brown, B. B., Altman, I., & Werner, C. (1992). Close Relationships in the Physical and Social World. *Communication Yearbook, 15,* 508–521.

Burleson, B. R. (1997). A different voice on different cultures. *Personal Relationships, 4,* 229–241.

Butler, J. (1993). *Bodies that matter: On the discursive limits of "sex."* New York: Routledge.

Butler, J. (1997). *The psychic life of power.* Stanford, CA: Stanford University Press.

Calas, M., & Smircich, L. (1996). From "the woman's" point of view: Feminist approaches to organization studies. In S. R. Clegg, C. Hardy, & W. Nord (Eds.), *Handbook of organization studies* (pp. 218–257). London: Sage.

Canary, D. J., Stafford, L. (1994). *Communication and relational maintenance.* New York: Academic Press.

Caputo, J. D. (1993). *Against ethics.* Bloomington, IN: Indiana University Press.

Castañeda, H-N. (1989). The multiple faces of knowing: The hierarchies of epistemic species. In J. W. Bender (Ed.), *The current state of the coherence theory* (pp. 231–241). Dordrecht, The Netherlands: Kluwer Academic Publishers.

Chafe, W. (1994). *Discourse, consciousness and time: The flow and displacement of conscious experience in speaking and writing.* Chicago: University of Chicago Press.

Chisholm, R. M. (1982). *The foundations of knowledge.* Minneapolis: University of Minnesota Press.

Christians, C. G. (1997). The ethics of being in a communications context. In C. G. Christians (Ed.), *Communication ethics and universal values* (pp. 3–23). Thousand Oaks, CA: Sage.

Clark, K., & Holquist, M. (1984). *Mikhail Bakhtin.* Cambridge, MA: Harvard University Press.

Clark, M. (1990). *Nietzsche on truth and philosophy.* Cambridge: Cambridge University Press.

Clegg, S. R. (1975). *Power, rule and domination.* London: Routledge & Kegan Paul.

Clegg, S. R. (1987). The power of language, the language of power. *Organization Studies, 8,* 60–70.

Clegg, S. R., & Dunkerley, D. (1980). *Organization, class and control.* London: Routledge & Kegan Paul.

Conquergood, D. (1992). Life in big red: Struggles and accommodations in a Chicago polyethnic tenement. In L. Lamphere, (Ed.). *Structuring diversity: Ethnographic perspectives on the new immigration* (pp. 95–144). Chicago: University of Chicago Press.

Coupland, N., Coupland, J., & Giles, H. (1991). *Language, society and the elderly: Discourse, identity and ageing.* Oxford, UK: Blackwell.

Crespi, F. (1994). Hermeneutics and the theory of social action. In P. Sztompka (Ed.), *Agency and structure: Reorienting social theory* (pp. 125–142). Yverdon, Switzerland: Gordon and Breach.

Csordias, T. J. (1994). *Embodiment and experience: The existential ground of culture and self.* Cambridge, UK: Cambridge University Press.

Cupach, W. E., Spitzberg, B. H. (1994). *The dark side of interpersonal communication.* Hillsdale, NJ: Lawrence Erlbaum.

Daly, J., & Wiemann, J. (1994). *Strategic Interpersonal Communication.* Hillsdale, NJ: Lawrence Erlbaum.

Deaux, K., & Major, B. (1987). Putting gender into context: An interactive model of gender-related behavior. *Psychological Review, 94,* 369–389.

De Certeau, M. (1984). *The practice of everyday life.* Berkeley, CA: University of California Press.

DeMarco, J. P. (1996). *Moral theory: A contemporary overview.* Boston: Jones & Bartlett.

Duck, S. (1993). *Individuals in relationships.* Newbury Park, CA: Sage.

Duck, S. (1986). *Close relationships: Development, dynamics, and deterioration.* Beverly Hills, CA: Sage.

Duck, S. (1986). *The emerging field of personal relationships.* Hillsdale, NJ: Lawrence Erlbaum.

Duck, S. (1993). *Learning about relationships.* Newbury Park, CA: Sage.

Duck, S. (1988). *Handbook of personal relationships.* New York: Wiley.

Dunne, J. (1996). Beyond sovereignty and deconstruction: The storied self. In R. Kearney (Ed.), *Paul Ricoeur: The hermeneutics of action* (pp. 137–158). Thousand Oaks, CA: Sage.

Eagleton, T. (1996). *Literary theory* (2nd ed.). Minneapolis: University of Minnesota Press.

Edwards, D., & Potter, J. (1992). *Discursive psychology.* London: Sage.

Elliott, D. (1997). Universal values and moral development theories. In C. G. Christians (Ed.), *Communicaiton ethics and universal values* (pp. 68–83). Thousand Oaks, CA: Sage.

Emmott, C. (1997). *Narrative comprehension: A discourse perspective.* Oxford: UK: Clarendon Press.

Fairchild, H. H. (1985). Black, Negro, or Afro-American? The differences are crucial! *Journal of Black Studies, 16,* 47–55.

Finnis, J. (1983). *Fundamentals of ethics.* Oxford, UK: Clarendon Press.

Fischer, J. M., & Ravizza, (S. J.) M. (1998). *Responsibility and control: A theory of moral responsibility.* Cambridge, UK: Cambridge University Press.

Foot, P. (1978). *Virtues and Vices and Other Essays in Moral Philosophy.* Berkeley: University of California Press.

Foster, D. A. (1987). *Confession and complicity in narrative.* Cambridge, UK: Cambridge University Press.

Foucault, M. (1977). *Discipline and punish: The birth of the prison.* Harmondsworth: Penguin.

Foucault, M. (1980). *Power/knowledge: Selected interviews and other writings, 1972–1977.* (C. Gordon, Ed.; C. Gordon, L. Marshall, J. Mepham, & K. Soper, Trans.). New York: Pantheon Books.

Foucault, M. (1986). *The care of the self: The history of sexuality,* vol. 3. New York: Pantheon Books.

Foucault, M. (1994). *Ethics: Subjectivity and truth* (Vol. 1; Ed. P. Rabinow; Trans. R. Hurley). New York: The New Press.

Frederick, W. C. (1995). *Values, nature, and culture in the American corporation.* New York: Oxford University Press Inc.

Gergen, K. (1991). *The saturated self.* NY: Basic Books.

Gergen, K. (1994). *Realities and relationships: Soundings in social construction.* Cambridge, MA: Harvard University Press.

Gert, B. (1988). *Morality: A new justification of the moral rules.* New York: Oxford University Press.

Giddens, A. (1979). *Central problems in social theory.* Berkeley: University of California Press.

Giddens, A. (1984). *The constitution of society: Outline of the theory of structuration.* Berkeley: University of California Press.

Giddens, A. (1990). *The consequences of modernity.* Stanford, CA: Stanford University Press.

Giddens, A. (1991). *Modernity and self-identity.* Stanford, CA: Stanford University Press.

Gilbert, M. (1996). *Living together: Rationality, sociality, and obligation.* Lanham, MA: Rowman & Littlefield Publishers Inc.

Goffman, E. (1959). *The presentation of self in everyday life*. New York: Doubleday Anchor.

Goldman, A. (1988). *Moral knowledge*. London: Routledge.

Habermas, J. (1990). *Moral consciousness and communicative action* (Trans. C. Lenhardt & S. Weber Nicholsen). Cambridge, MA: MIT Press.

Hare, R. M. (1995). Foundationalism and coherentism in ethics. In W. Sinnott-Armstrong & M. Timmons (Eds.), *Moral knowledge? New readings in moral epistemology* (pp. 190–199). New York: Oxford University Press.

Harman, G. (1977). *The nature of morality: An introduction to ethics*. New York: Oxford University Press.

Harman, G. (1995). Moral relativism defended. In S. C. Cahn & J. G. Haber (Eds.), *20th-Century ethical theory* (pp. 519–530). Englewood Cliffs, NJ: Prentice-Hall, Inc.

Harman, G., & Thomson, J. J. (1996). *Moral relativism and moral objectivity*. Cambridge, MA: Blackwell.

Harré, R. (1986). An outline of the social constructionist viewpoint. In R. Harré (Ed.), *The social construction of emotion*. London: Blackwell.

Harré, R. (1991). The discursive production of selves. *Theory and psychology, 50*, 51–63.

Harré, R. (1992). Introduction: The second cognitive revolution. *American Behavioral Scientist, 36*, 5–7.

Harré, R. (1995). Agentive discourse. In R. Harré and P. Stearns (Eds.). *Discursive psychology in practice* (pp. 120-136). London: Sage.

Harrison, B. (1991). *Inconvenient fictions: Literature and the limits of theory*. New Haven, CT: Yale University Press.

Hatfield, E., Rapson, R. L. (1993). *Love, Sex and Intimacy: Their psychology, biology, and history*. New York: Harper Collins College Publishers.

Hegelsen, S. (1990). *The female advantage: Woman's ways of leadership*. New York: Doubleday.

Heidegger, M. (1996). *Being and Time: A translation of Sien and Zeit* (J. Stambaugh, Trans.). Albany, NY: State University of New York Press.

Hobbes, T. (1921/1651). *Leviathan*. New York: Everyman's Library.

Jackall, R. (1988). *Moral mazes: The world of corporate managers*. New York: Oxford University Press.

Jacobs, J. (1995). *Practical realism and moral psychology*. Washington, D.C.: Georgetown University Press.

Jacques, R. (1996). *Manufacturing the employee*. London: Sage.

Jaggar, A. (1989). Feminist Ethics: Some Issues for the Nineties. *Journal of Social Philosophy*. Vol. 20, numbers 1, 2, Spring/Fall.

James, G. G. (1988). *Stolen legacy*. San Francisco: Julian Richardson Associates.

James, W. (1890). *The principles of psychology*. New York: Henry Holt.

Johnson, M. (1987). *The body in the mind: The bodily basis of meaning, imagination, and reason.* Chicago: University of Chicago Press.

Kagan, S. (1998). *Normative ethics.* Boulder, CO: Westview Press.

Kamm, F. M. (1988). Ethics, applied ethics, and applying applied ethics. In D. M. Rosenthal & F. Shehadi (Eds.), *Applied ethics and ethical theory* (pp. 162–187). Salt Lake City: University of Utah Press.

Kant, I. (1785/1988). *Fundamental principles of the metaphysic of morals* (T. K. Abbott, Trans.). Buffalo, NY: Prometheus Books.

Katz, J. H. (1978). Racism as a white problem: Theoretical perspectives and overview. In J. H. Katz (Ed.), *White awareness.* Norman, OK: University of Oklahoma Press.

Knapp, M., Hall, J. (1992). *Nonverbal communication in human interaction,* 3rd ed. New York: Holt, Rinehart and Winston.

Knapp, M., Miller, G. (1994). *Handbook of interpersonal communication.* Thousand Oaks, CA: Sage.

Knapp, M., Vangelisti, A. (1992). *Interpersonal communication and human relationships,* 2nd ed. Boston: Allyn and Bacon.

Knights, D., & Vurdubakis, T. (1994). Foucault, power, resistance and all that. In J. Jermier, D. Knights and W. Nord (Eds.), *Resistance and power in organizations* (pp. 167–198). London: Routledge.

Knights, D., & Willmott, H. (1985). Power and identity in theory and practice. *The Sociological Review, 33,* 22–46.

Knights, D., & Willmott, H. (1989). Power and subjectivity at work. *Sociology, 23,* 4, 535–558.

Kuhn, T. (1970). *The structure of scientific revolutions* (2nd ed.). Chicago: University of Chicago Press.

Kymlicka, W. (1989). *Liberalism, community and culture.* Oxford, UK: Clarendon Press.

Lacan, J. (1977). *Ecrits: A selection.* (A. Sheridan, Trans.). New York: Norton.

Laclau, E. (1990). *New reflections on the revolution of our time.* London: Verso.

Lakoff, G., & Johnson, M. (1988). *Metaphors we live by.* Chicago: University of Chicago Press.

Laing, R. D. (1971). *The politics of the family and other essays.* New York: Vintage Books.

Laing, R. D. (1982). *The divided self.* New York: Pantheon Books.

Lanigan, R. L. (1990). Is Erving Goffman a phenomenologist? In S. H. Riggins (Ed.), *Beyond Goffman: Studies on communications, institution, and social interaction* (pp. 99–112). New York: Mouton de Gruyter.

Latour, B. (1987). *Science in action.* Cambridge: Harvard University Press.

Levin, G. (1992). *Constructions of the self.* New Brunswick, NJ: Rutgers University Press.

Luhmann, N. (1990). *Essays on self-reference.* New York: Cambridge University Press.

MacIntyre, A. (1981). *After virtue.* London, 1981.

MacIntyre, A. (1988). *Whose justice? Which rationality?* Notre Dame, IN: University of Notre Dame Press.

Martin, L. H., Gutman, H., & Hutton, P. H. (1988). *Technologies of the self: A seminar with Michel Foucault.* Amherst: University of Massachusetts Press.

Martin, R. (1977). *The sociology of power.* London: Routledge & Kegan Paul.

Maturana, H. R., & Varela, F. J. (1980). *Autopoiesis and cognition: The realization of the living.* Dordrecht, The Netherlands: D. Reidel Publishing Company.

Maturana, H. R., & Varela, F. J. (1992). *The tree of knowledge: The biological roots of understanding.* Boston: Shambala.

Mayo, E. (1945). *The social problems of industrial civilization.* Cambridge, MA: Harvard University Press.

McNamee, S. (1997). Research as relationally situated activity: Ethical implications, *Journal of Feminist Family Therapy.*

Mieth, D. (1997). The basic norm of truthfulness: Its ethical justification and universality. In C. G. Christians (Ed.), *Communication ethics and universal values* (pp. 87–104). Thousand Oaks, CA: Sage.

Mill, J. S. (1897). *Utilitarianism.* London: Longmans Green.

Mills, A. J. (1993). Organizational discourse and the gendering of identity. In J. Hassard & M. Parker (Eds.), *Postmodernism and organizations* (pp. 132–148). Thousand Oaks, CA: Sage.

Mintzberg, H. (1973). *The nature of managerial work.* New York: Harper & Row.

More, T. (1516/1964). *Utopia.* New Haven, CT: Yale University Press.

Morgan, G. (1997). *Images of organizations.* Thousand Oaks, CA: Sage.

Nietzsche, F. (1967). *The will to power.* (W. Kaufmann & R. J. Hollingdale, Trans.). New York: Random House.

Nietzsche, F. (1969). *On the genealogy of morals.* (W. Kaufmann & R. J. Hollingdale, Trans.). New York: Random House.

Nöth, W. (1990). *Handbook of semiotics.* Bloomington: Indiana University Press.

Pearce, W. B., & Cronen, V. E. (1980). *Communication, action and meaning: The creation of social realities.* New York: Praeger.

Perrow, C. (1986). *Complex organizations: A critical essay.* New York: Random House.

Potter, J., & Wetherell, M. (1987). *Discourse and social psychology: Beyond attitudes and behavior.* London: Routledge.

Rachels, J. (1993). *The elements of moral philosophy* (2nd ed.). New York: McGraw-Hill, Inc.

Railton, P. (1996). Moral realism: Prospects and problems. In W. Sinnott-Armstrong & M. Timmons (Eds.), *Moral knowledge?* (pp. 49–81). New York: Oxford University Press.

Rainwater, M. (1996). Refiguring Ricoeur: Narrative force and communicative ethics. In R. Kearney (Ed.), *Paul Ricoeur: The hermeneutics of action* (pp. 99–110). Thousand Oaks, CA: Sage.

Rasch, W. (1995). Immanent systems, transcendental temptations, and the limits of ethics. *Culture Critique, 30,* 193–221.

Rasmussen, D. (1996). Rethinking subjectivity: narrative identity and the self. In R. Kearney (Ed.), *Paul Ricoeur: The hermeneutics of action* (pp. 158–172). Thousand Oaks, CA: Sage.

Rawlins, W. K. (1987). Gregory Bateson and the composition of human communication. *Research on Language and Social Interaction, 20,* 53–77.

Rawlins, W. K. (1992). *Friendship matters: Communication, dialectics, and the life course.* New York: Aldine de Gruyter.

Rawls, J. (1954/1995). Two concepts of rules. In S. M. Cahn & J. G. Haber (Eds.), *20th-century ethical theory* (pp. 273–290). Englewood Clifts, NJ: Prentice-Hall Inc.

Ricoeur, P. (1991). *From text to action: Essays in hermeneutics, II.* Evanston, IL: Northwestern University Press.

Ricoeur, P. (1992). *Oneself as another* (K. Blamey, Trans). Chicago: University of Chicago Press.

Ross, P. J. (1994). *De-privatizing morality.* Brookfield, VT: Ashgate Publishing Co.

Sackmann, S. J. (1991). *Cultural knowledge in organizations: Exploring the collective mind.* Newbury Park, CA: Sage.

Sartre, J-P. (1956). *Being and nothingness.* New York: Philosophical Library, Inc.

Sayre-McCord, G. (1996). Coherentist epistemology and moral theory. In W. Sinnott-Armstrong & M. Timmons (Eds.), *Moral knowledge? New readings in moral epistemology* (pp. 137–189). New York: Oxford University Press, Inc.

Scott, C. E. (1990). *The question of ethics: Nietzsche, Foucault, Heidegger.* Bloomington: Indiana University Press.

Scott, J. C. (1990). *Domination and the arts of resistance.* New Haven, CT: Yale University Press.

Scott, W. G., & Hart, D. K. (1989). *Organizational values in America.* New Brunswick, NJ: Transaction Publishers.

Searle, J. R. (1969). *Speech acts, an essay in the philosophy of language.* New York: Cambridge University Press.

Searle, J. R. (1995). *The social construction of reality.* New York: The Free Press.

Sheets-Johnstone, M. (1994). *The roots of power: Animate form and gendered bodies.* Chicago: Open Court.

Shotter, J. (1993a). *Conversational realities.* London: Sage.

Shotter, J. (1993b). Becoming someone: Identity and belonging. In N. Coupland & J. F. Nussbaum, (Eds.), *Discourse and lifespan identity* (pp. 5–28). Newbury Park, CA: Sage.

Sigman, S. J. (1987). *A perspective on social communication.* Lexington, MA: Lexington Books.

Spivak, G. C. (1988). *In other worlds: Essays in cultural politics.* New York: Routledge.

Sterba, J. P. (1995). Reconciling conceptions of justice. In J. P. Sterba et al. (Eds.), *Morality and social justice: Point/counterpoint* (pp. 1-38). Lanham, MD: Rowman & Littlefield Publishers, Inc.

Sternberg, R. K., Barnes, M. L. (1988). *The psychology of love.* New Haven, CT: Yale University Press.

Taylor, C. (1982). Rationality. In M. Hollis & S. Lukes (Eds.), *Rationality and relativism* (pp. 87–105). Oxford, UK: Basil Blackwell.

Taylor, C. (1989). *Sources of the self: The making of the modern identity.* Cambridge, MA: Harvard University Press.

Taylor, M. C. (1980). *Journeys to selfhood: Hegel & Kierkegaard.* Berkeley: University of California Press.

Thoreau, H. D. (1849/1960). *Walden: Or life in the woods.* Garden City, NY: Dolphin Books.

Toulmin, S. (1950). *The place of reason in ethics.* New York: Cambridge University Press.

Traber, M. (1997). Conclusion: An ethics of communication worthy of human beings. In C. G. Christians (Ed.), *Communication ethics and universal values* (pp. 327-343). Thousand Oaks, CA: Sage.

Tracy, K. (1991). *Understanding face to face interaction.* Hillsdale, NJ: Lawrence Erlbaum.

Vangelisti, A. L., & Daly, J. A. (1997). Gender differences in standards for romantic relationships. *Personal Relationships, 4,* 203–219.

Varela, F. J., Thompson, E., & Rosch, E. (1991). *The embodied mind: Cognitive science and human experience.* Cambridge, MA: MIT Press.

Volosinov, V. N. (1973). *Marxism and the philosophy of language.* New York: Seminar Press.

Volosinov, V. N. (1976). *Freudianism: A Marxist critique.* New York: Academic Press.

Vygotsky, L. S. (1978). *Mind in society: The development of higher psychological processes.* Cambridge, MA: Harvard University Press.

Wade, J. (1996). *Changes of mind: A holonomioc theory of the evolution of consciousness.* Albany: State University of New York Press.

Walker, R. C. S. (1989). *The coherence theory of truth.* London: Routledge.

Werhane, P., & Doering J. (1995). Conflicts of interest and conflicts of commitment. *Professional Ethics, 4,* 47–81.

West, C. (1982). *Prophesy deliverance! An Afro-American revolutionary Christianity.* Philadelphia: Westminster.

Wilber, K. (1993). *The spectrum of consciousness.* Wheaton, IL: Quest Books.

Wilson, J. Q. (1993). *The moral sense.* New York: Free Press.

Wood, J., (1997). Clarifying the issues. *Personal Relationships, 4,* 221–228.

Wood, J. T. (1994). *Gendered lives: Communication, gender and culture.* Belmont, CA: Wadsworth.

Wood, J. T. (1995). *Relational communication.* New York: Wadsworth.

Wong, D. (1984). *Moral relativity.* Berkeley: University of California Press.

Wrong, D. (1979). *Power: Its forms, bases and uses.* Oxford, UK: Basil Blackwell.

Zimmerman, M. J. (1996). *The concept of moral obligation.* Melbourne: Oxford University Press.

## INTERNET RESOURCES

http://www.acusd.edu/ethics/diversity.html (ethical theory on gender and diversity)
http://www.coe.missouri.edu/~mesched/cpe/ethics.html (ethics, diversity and gender)

# INDEX

# CREDITS